I0803129

IMAGES
of America

METROPOLIS

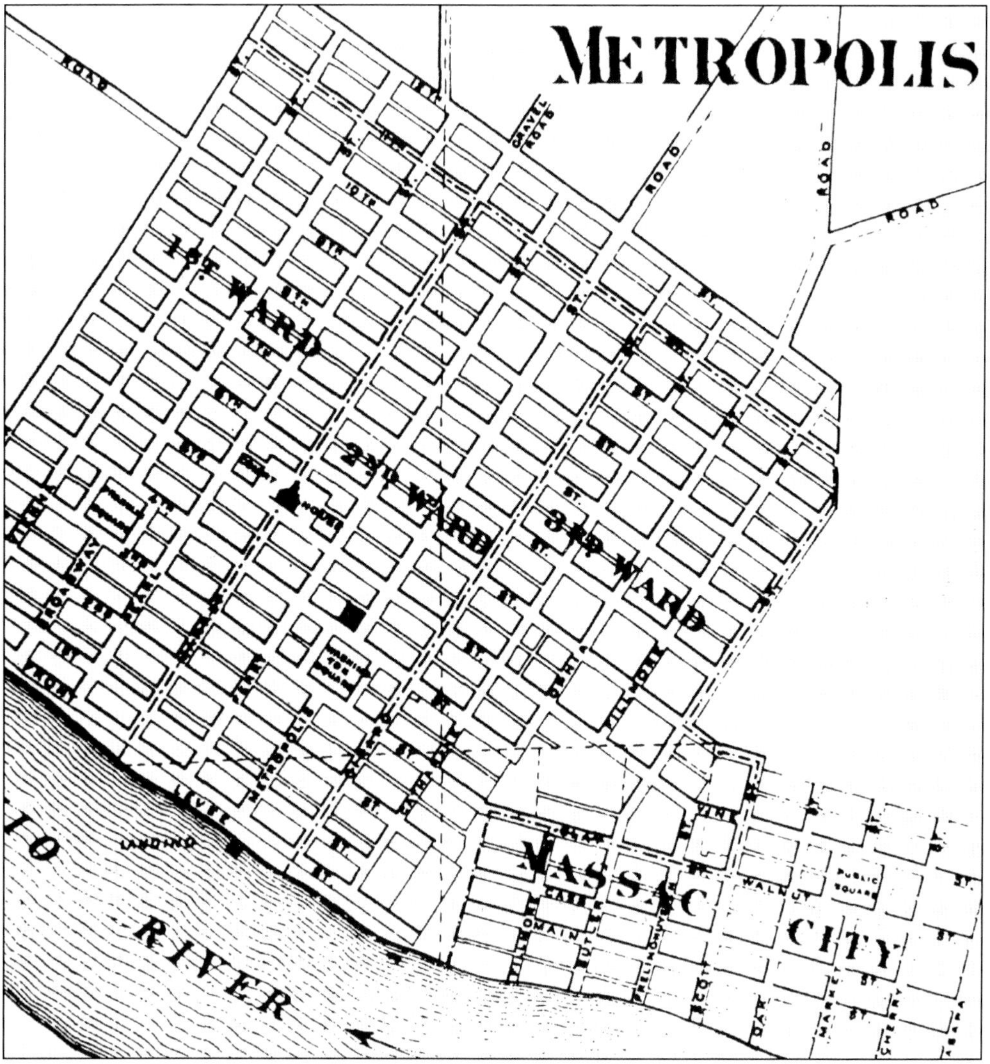

This map of Metropolis shows the adjacent, smaller community of Massac City, also founded in 1839, just a few months before Metropolis. Home to many of the lumber, woodworking, and shipbuilding companies in the area during the 19th century, it would become fully annexed by Metropolis by 1890 and is frequently referred to today as East Metropolis. (Courtesy Massac County Historical Society.)

On the Cover: The *George Cowling* was the second of two steamboats Edward Cowling named to honor his father, whose riverboat business he had inherited. Between father and son, the line ran for about 40 years between Metropolis and Brookport, Illinois, and Paducah, Kentucky. Built in 1904 at a shipyard near Fort Massac, the boat was sunk in 1921, then raised and renamed the *Alton*. (Courtesy Metropolis Public Library.)

IMAGES
of America

METROPOLIS

Michael E. Bragg and Jon M. Bragg

ARCADIA
PUBLISHING

ISBN 978-0-7385-9359-3

Published by Arcadia Publishing
Charleston, South Carolina

Printed in the United States of America

Library of Congress Control Number: 2011937154

For all general information, please contact Arcadia Publishing:
Telephone 843-853-2070
Fax 843-853-0044
E-mail sales@arcadiapublishing.com
For customer service and orders:
Toll-Free 1-888-313-2665

Visit us on the Internet at www.arcadiapublishing.com

This book is dedicated to the intrepid souls who founded and settled Metropolis in its earliest days, as well as to their descendants and those who arrived later who fought the occasional flood and weathered the shifting economic tides to make this a great town in which to live.

Also, to my grandchildren (Jon's nephew and nieces) Nicolas, Lily, and Emma, who seem to love history—here's hoping this small book will help to make that feeling grow stronger.

Contents

ACKNOWLEDGMENTS

We must, before all the others, thank Brenda Mizell. Brenda is the president of the Massac County Historical Society and, at the time of our beginning trials with this endeavor, was the genealogical librarian for the Metropolis Public Library. She greeted us as if we were not strangers and helped us greatly from day one. Simply put, this book would not have been possible without her involvement.

We also want to thank Paul Fellows, secretary of the Massac County Historical Society. Paul gave his time to help us with labeling and provided us generous access to the historical society's archive, kept at the society's headquarters at the Elijah P. Curtis Home.

In addition, we thank all the members of the Massac County Historical Society; Areia Hathcock and Michele Longworth of the *Metropolis Planet*; the always helpful staff of the Metropolis Public Library; and everyone we met in Metropolis and from Metropolis who shared their memories, suggestions, and photographs readily.

A thanks goes to Robert Swenson, associate professor of architecture at Southern Illinois University, for sharing his insights into the steamboat-building industry in Metropolis. He is, with the assistance of local historian Ann Laird, compiling his research on the subject into a forthcoming book.

A special thanks goes to our family and friends, whose support, encouragement, and tolerance were essential to carrying out this project—in particular Richard and Rita Cannon and Phyllis Hearn. They were always quick to give us somewhere to work, eat, and, when necessary, sleep; and they loaned us their computers when ours crashed, their expertise when we needed it, and their love when all else failed.

Attention could not have been given to this project without the assistance of Judy Underwood and Kathy Michalak, friend and neighbor, respectively, whose cat sitting always allowed the many necessary trips to Metropolis at a moment's notice.

And finally, thanks to all the Metropolis photographers of yesterday, professional and otherwise, whose documentation of their surroundings made it possible for us to shed a little light on their bygone world.

Unless otherwise noted, all images appear courtesy of the Massac County Historical Society.

INTRODUCTION

In 1839, William McBane, a young merchant from Pittsburgh with a flatboat loaded with building materials, arrived at a spot on the northern bank of the Ohio River near the site of the former Fort Massac. The area impressed him as a natural spot for the location of a great city, with ground he deemed high enough to avoid all but the worst flooding, ideally situated along the great waterway between the mighty industrial centers of the East and the burgeoning expanses of the new West. He found a partner in local landowner and ferryboat operator James Hendricks Gains Wilcox, whose family had lived in the area a number of years. Together, they envisioned a city that would attract the expanding commerce of river and rail. On April 18, 1839, they founded Metropolis City, later to become the city of Metropolis, choosing a name—from the Greek for "mother city"—befitting the grandeur of their vision for its future. They platted the city with an eye toward expansion, with wide, accommodating streets and land set aside for public use, fully intending that those streets would one day be bustling with commercial activity from the railroad crossing they knew would be ideal for the area, as well as the expected river traffic. Much of what they predicted would come to pass, though not to the extent necessary to match their Eastern models of urbanity.

The year 1938, virtually 100 years after the founding of Metropolis, would see the first publication of the brainchild of another young visionary, the fruits of whose labors would end up vastly exceeding anything even he could have imagined. In *Action Comics No. 1*, the world was introduced to the adventures of Superman, perhaps the first genuinely mythic character in American fiction since Paul Bunyan. Though Jerry Siegel, an introverted science fiction fan desperately trying to eke out a living in the comic book field of the pre–World War II era, could be seen in some ways as the polar opposite of McBane, an entrepreneurial man-of-action of the early Industrial Age, they did share some things in common besides an eye toward the future. Both men needed partners to allow them to bring their visions to fruition, which Siegel found in his boyhood friend, artist Joe Schuster. As Wilcox gave McBane access to the raw materials necessary to flesh out their ambitious venture, Schuster put the flesh on the bones of Siegel's brainchild. Both Siegel and McBane also gave the cities of their imaginations a name that was more often a purely descriptive term used for great urban centers. Though Siegel's choice for Superman's home base was likely a fictionalized stand-in for New York City, he too chose the name *Metropolis*. In time, the respective creations of the two pairs of men would be linked in other ways.

In the intervening near-100 years between the founding of McBane and Wilcox's Metropolis and the "founding" of Superman's hometown, the former went a long way toward meeting the expectations of its founders. In an age when locomotive travel was in its infancy and river traffic was vital to American industry and commerce, Metropolis was indeed well placed to benefit from that traffic. Located between the confluence of the Ohio and Tennessee Rivers at Paducah, Kentucky, and the convergence of the Ohio and Mississippi Rivers at Cairo, Illinois, Metropolis was right in the middle of everything. Besides providing a route from Pittsburgh to New Orleans or Kansas City to Knoxville, the various major and minor tributaries of the Ohio and Mississippi Rivers gave access to every town and city along a navigable part of the Mississippi basin, and all manner of travelers and traders wishing to go between the established industrial centers of the East and the expanding territories of the West went through that stretch of the Ohio River. The river acted as the superhighway of its day, with boats of all types cruising up and down it constantly—some local ferries and packet boats, passing goods and passengers between Paducah, Cairo, and Metropolis, and some on through trips to St. Louis, Cincinnati, or New Orleans. Factories and mills lined much of the waterfront, and dozens of boats at a time could be found along the Metropolis shoreline, unloading logs from along the Wabash, Cumberland, Tennessee, and Ohio Rivers and reloading them as finished wood products, from cut lumber and railroad ties to boxes and barrels, plow handles and wagon parts. Before long, steamboat parts—requiring highly skilled craftsmen—were being produced and shipped to St. Louis or Paducah to be formed into finished boats. Then, entire boats were built in Metropolis by several companies, including that of Alfred Cutting, who had come to the area during the Civil War to supervise the building of hulls for several ironclad warships being made in St. Louis. By 1869, his shipyard had become the firm of Cutting & Woods.

Once the era of the steamboat started to wane, these skilled wood craftsmen were still in demand by businesses like the Metropolis Bending Company, who made bentwood items requiring specialized equipment, including parts for buggies and carriages (and later, automobiles). The railroad bridge envisioned by the city founders was finally completed in 1917—one of the most ambitious projects of its type at the time—allowing passenger and freight trains to cross the Ohio River without the aid of the rail ferryboats previously required. With those ferries, as well as the transportation of railroad ties all over the country, the steamboat could be said to have contributed to its own extinction, as the locomotive increasingly took its place as the primary transporter of people and goods. Metropolis was still a center of production during this period, continuing to supply wood products, as well as stoves, cigars, and, eventually, gloves.

Times changed again, however, and so did Metropolis. The automobile started to eclipse the train as a mode of travel, and passenger rail service to Metropolis ceased in 1941. Interstate trucking gradually became the preferred method of transporting goods. Eventually, most of the larger factories in town closed down. By the 1970s, things were looking grim for Metropolitans, until Robert Westerfield, a recent transplant from Owensboro, Kentucky, with members of the Metropolis Chamber of Commerce, had an idea, apparently inspired by the Metropolis Post Office having received mail from children addressed to Superman for years. They decided to inaugurate an award in Superman's name, which eventually snowballed into a ceremony declaring the "adoption" of the Man of Steel, complete with a declaration from the Illinois legislature designating Metropolis as the "Home of Superman." After some highly ambitious plans involving a theme park fell through in the early 1970s, a museum was built in 1973, but it closed the next year. Despite some false starts, today the annual Superman Celebration, held each June, draws large crowds to the site of the 15-foot bronze *Superman* statue in the town square, and together with the annual encampment at the reconstructed Fort Massac (not to mention the riverfront casino owned by Harrah's), tourism has become Metropolis's main economic force. Perhaps, it can be said that, as he did so many times in his comic books, Superman has in fact "saved" Metropolis.

One

Fort Massac

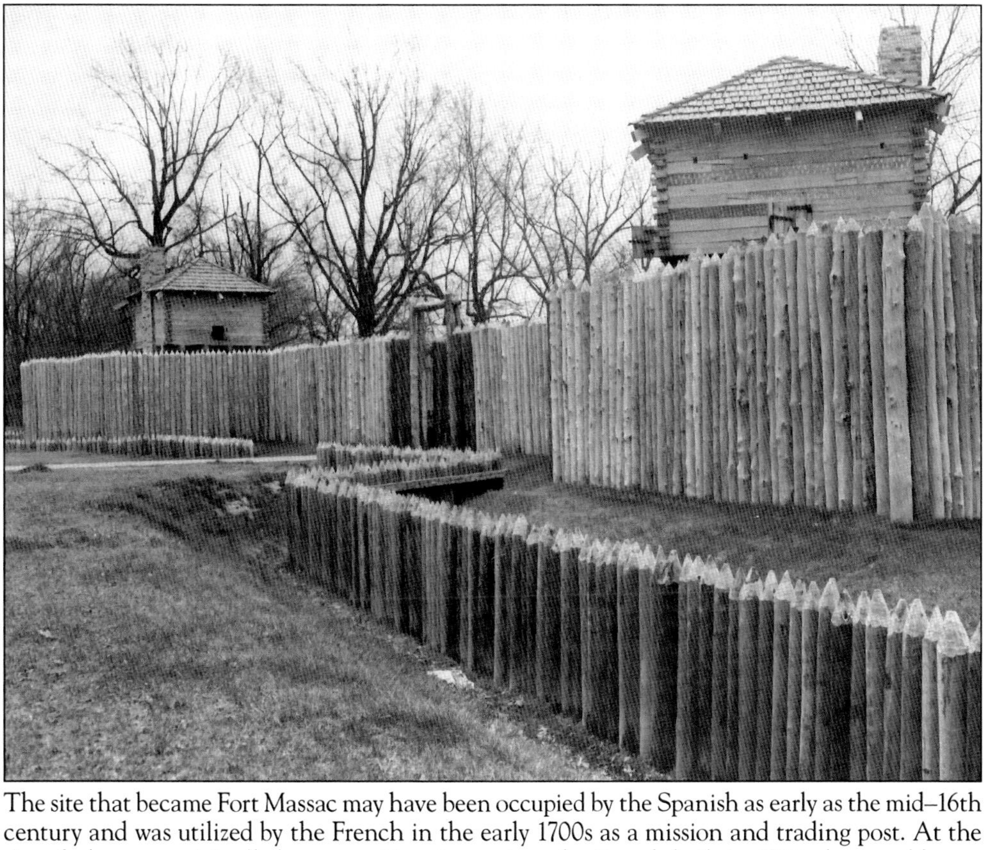

The site that became Fort Massac may have been occupied by the Spanish as early as the mid–16th century and was utilized by the French in the early 1700s as a mission and trading post. At the site of what was originally known as Fort Ascension, the French built in 1757 what would soon become Fort Massiac, which was later called Massac by the English. A modern reconstruction (pictured) depicts the fort as it appeared around 1795 after being rebuilt by the Americans.

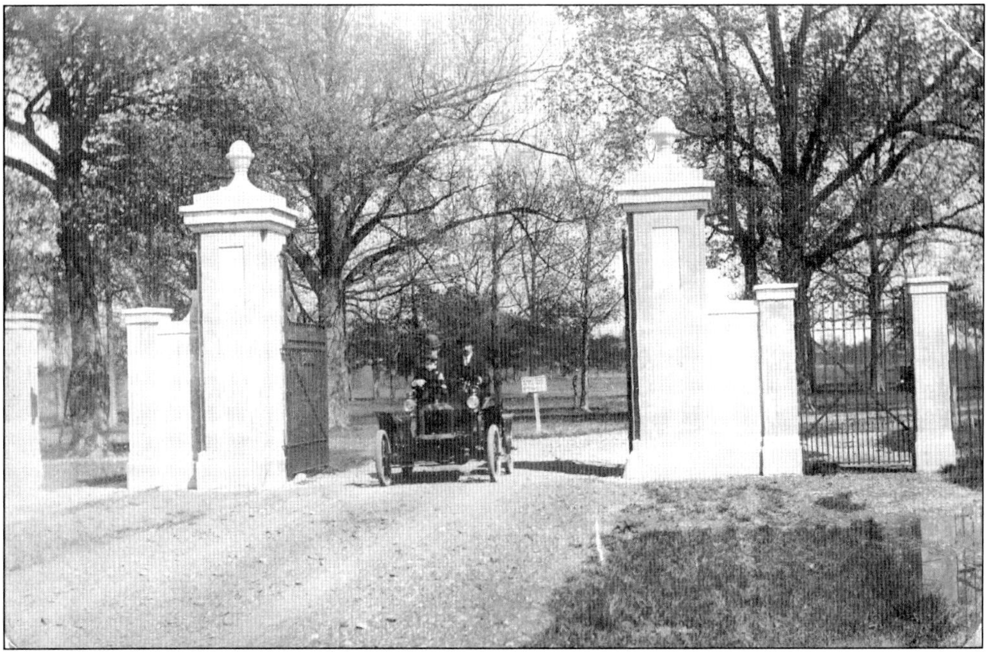

Two men and a young boy ride in their automobile between the old gates at Fort Massac. After becoming a state park in 1908, the area was a popular recreational destination.

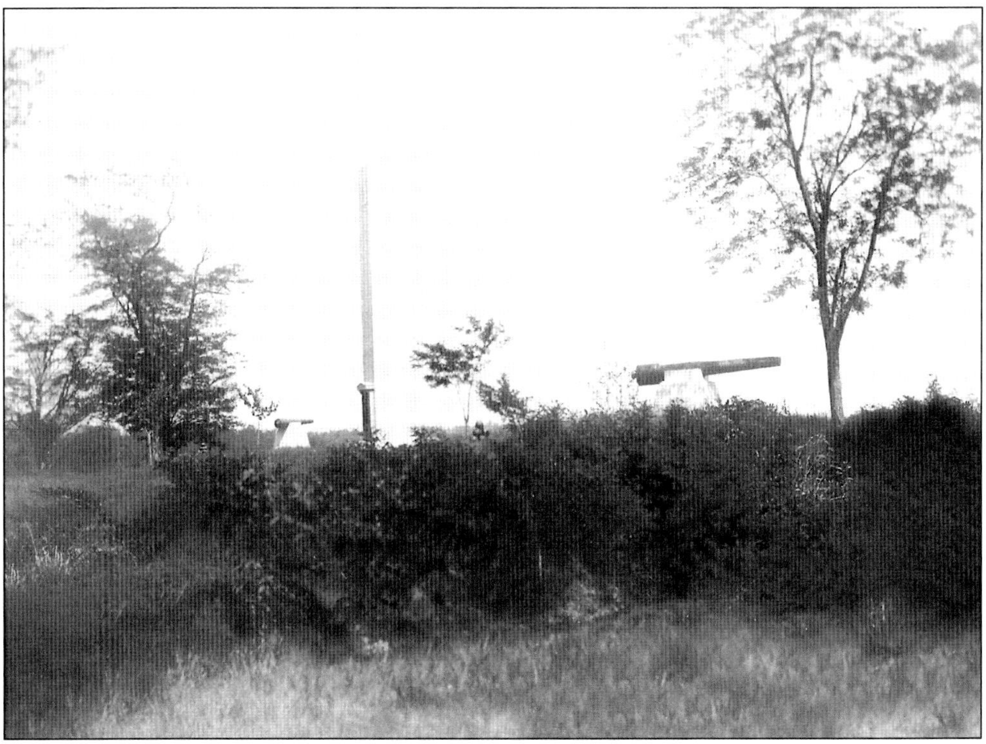

Two of four Civil War–era cannon emplacements at Fort Massac are shown in this photograph, with the Clark Monument in the background. The cannons were brought to the site from another location sometime prior to the fort grounds becoming Illinois's first state park in 1908.

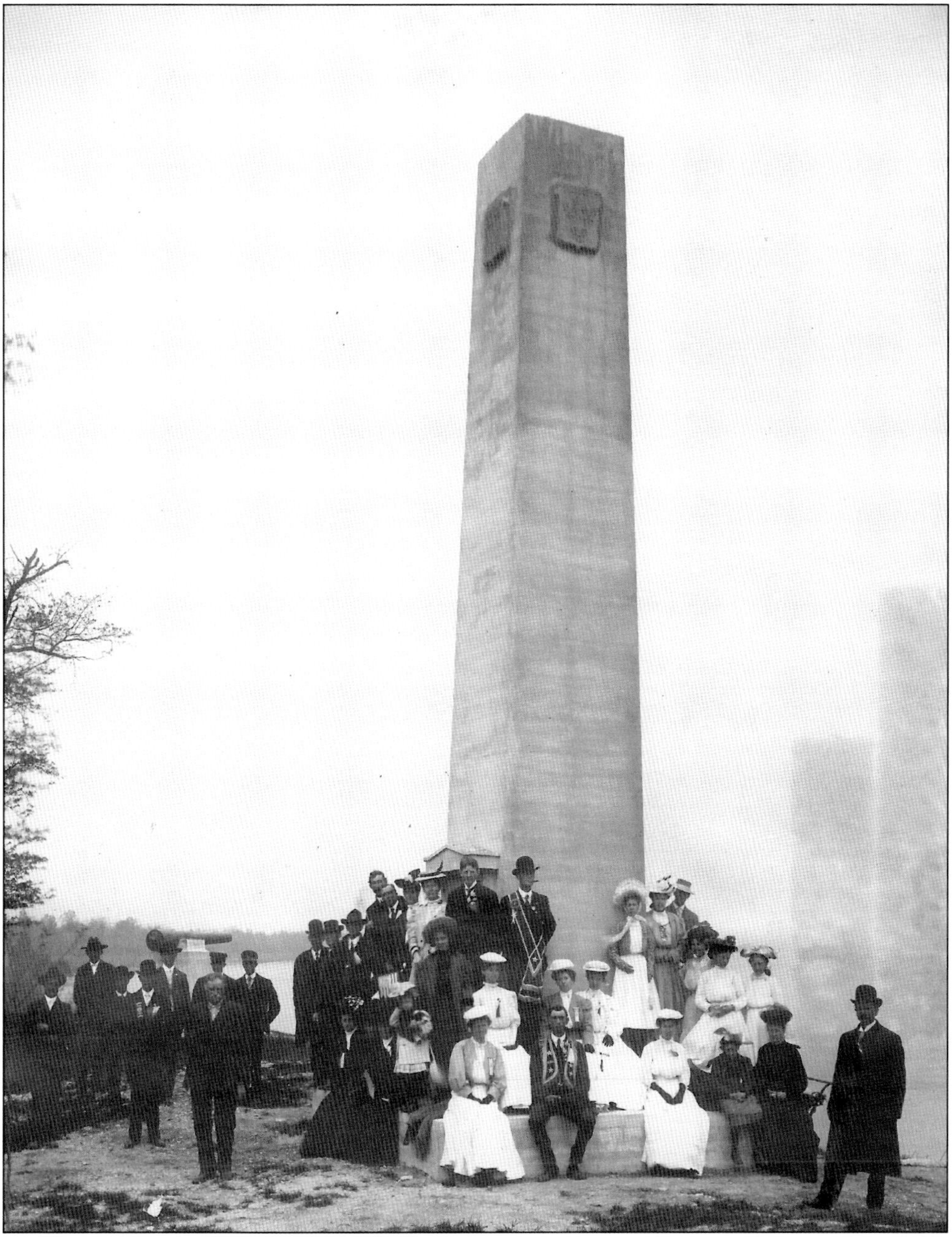

In a scene from 1908, members of a fraternal order pose under the first marker honoring George Rogers Clark at Fort Massac prior to the official dedication on November 5 of both the monument and the park. Note that the monument's cap had not as yet been put in place. These people could be members of the Independent Order of Odd Fellows, judging by the symbols on their sashes and vests (compared to those in the photograph of that group in chapter nine).

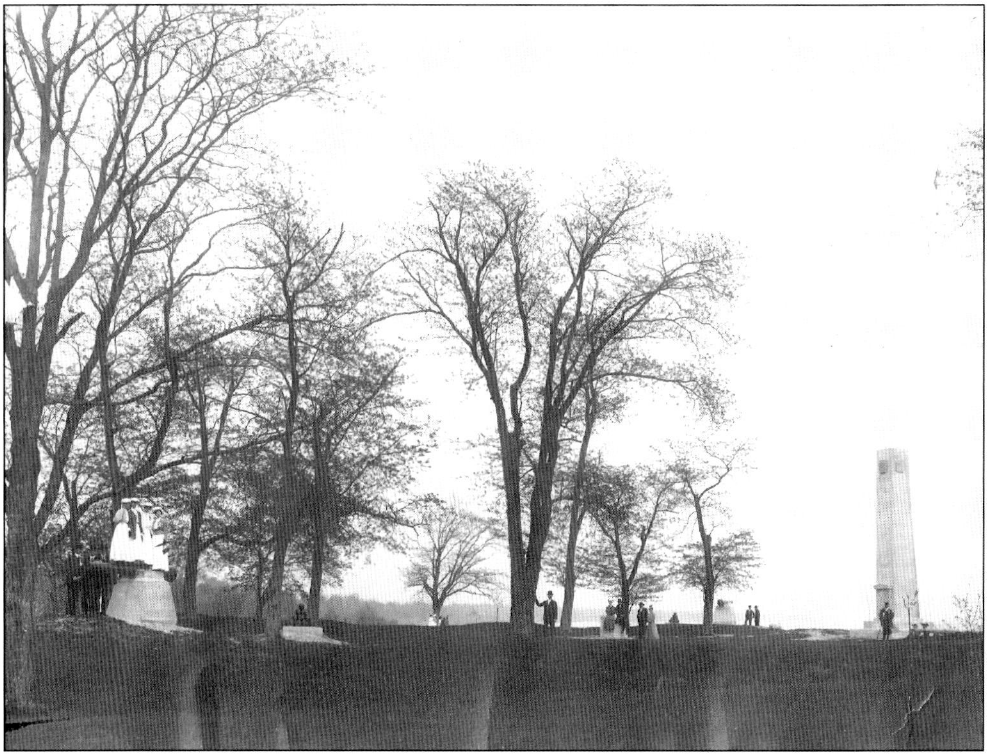

The same group as in the previous photograph is seen here posing on and around the cannons. During World War II, after a citywide vote, the cannon and cannonballs were donated to the scrap drive effort.

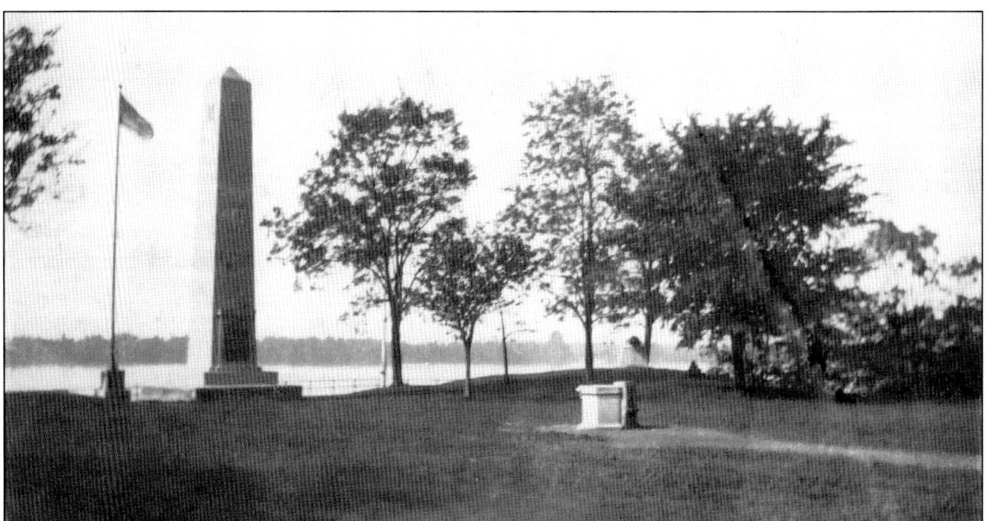

Taken after the 1908 dedication, this photograph of the George Rogers Clark Memorial shows the monument's cap now in place and a flagpole installed. After the fort was abandoned by the French, burned to the ground by Chickasaws, and sporadically occupied by the British, General Clark was allegedly the first American to raise the flag of the new nation over Illinois soil.

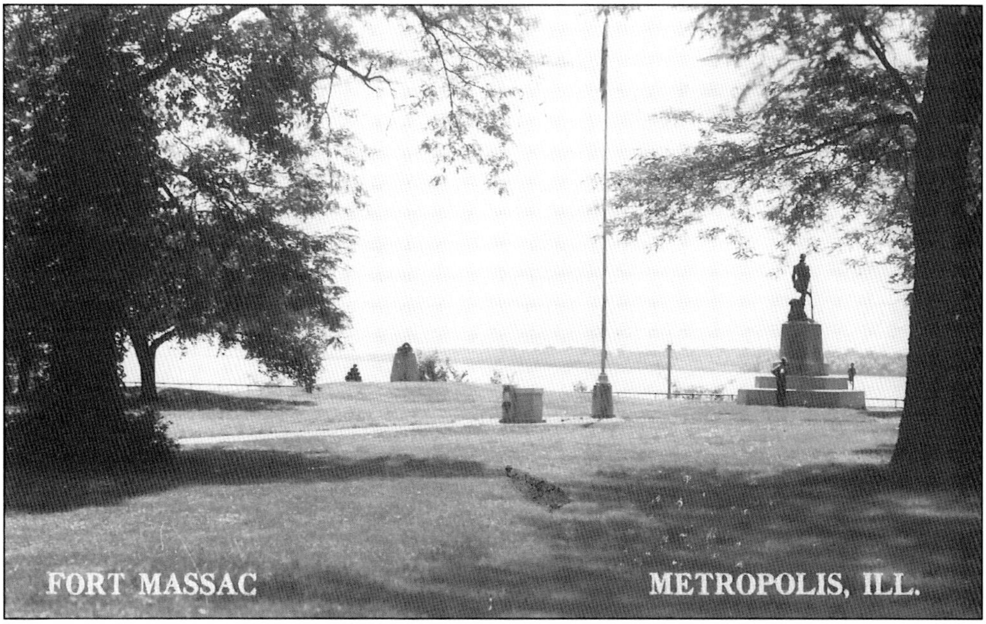

The statue of George Rogers Clark, shown in this postcard, replaced the older monument in 1932.

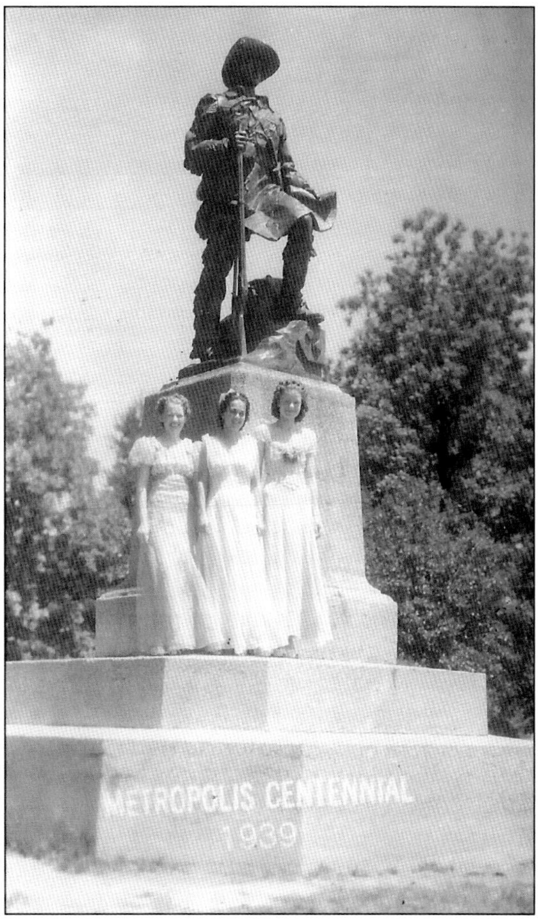

These unidentified young beauties are celebrating the Metropolis Centennial of 1939 in front of the statue of Clark at Fort Massac. Whether or not he raised the American flag there, it is known that General Clark and his men stayed the night at the abandoned fort in late June 1778 on their march to capture Kaskaskia. Unsure whether or not British soldiers still occupied the site, they entered the territory upstream.

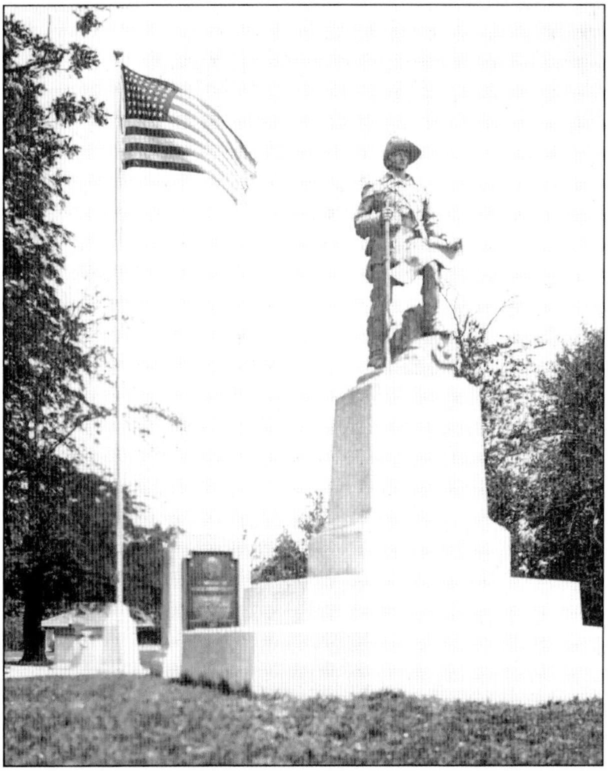

The edges of the old Fort Massac pavilion can be seen here behind the flagpole and drinking fountain around 1935. General Clark met with younger brother William Clark and Meriwether Lewis to discuss his knowledge of the western territories as they began preparations for their famous expedition in 1803. Later, they stayed at Fort Massac from November 11–13 that year, gathering supplies and recruiting men.

After decades of painstaking excavation and research, the reconstruction of Fort Massac and building of its accompanying museum were started in 1971 and completed by late summer of 1973. Shown here in 2010, the site has hosted the annual Fort Massac Encampment since 1974. (Courtesy authors' collection.)

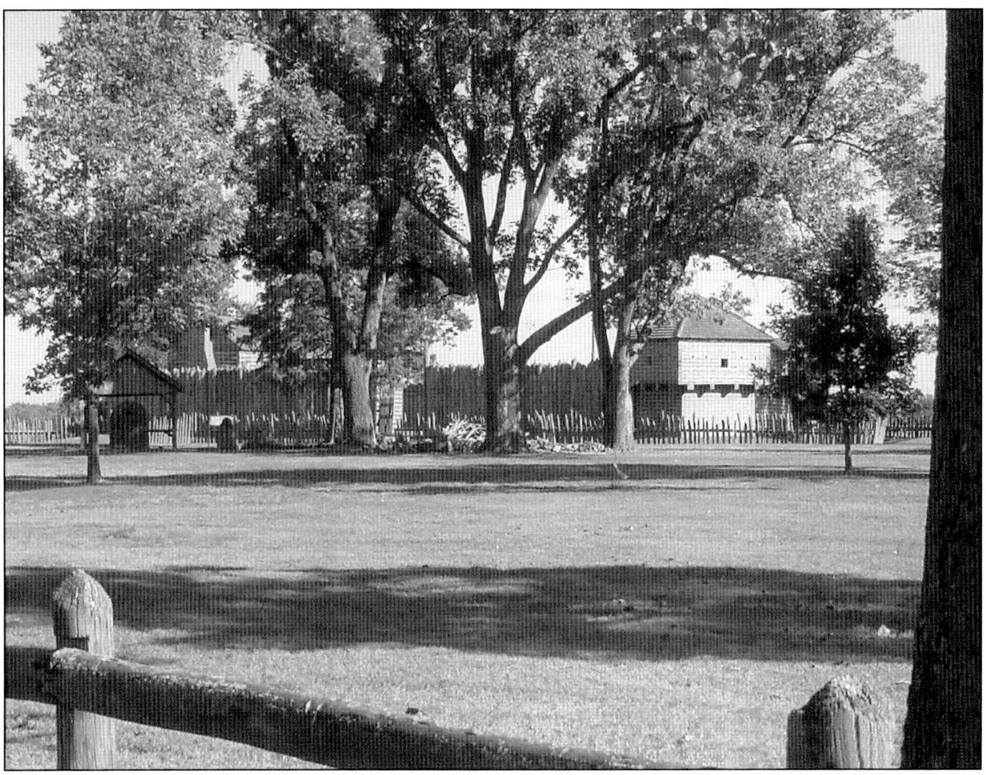

Two

River City

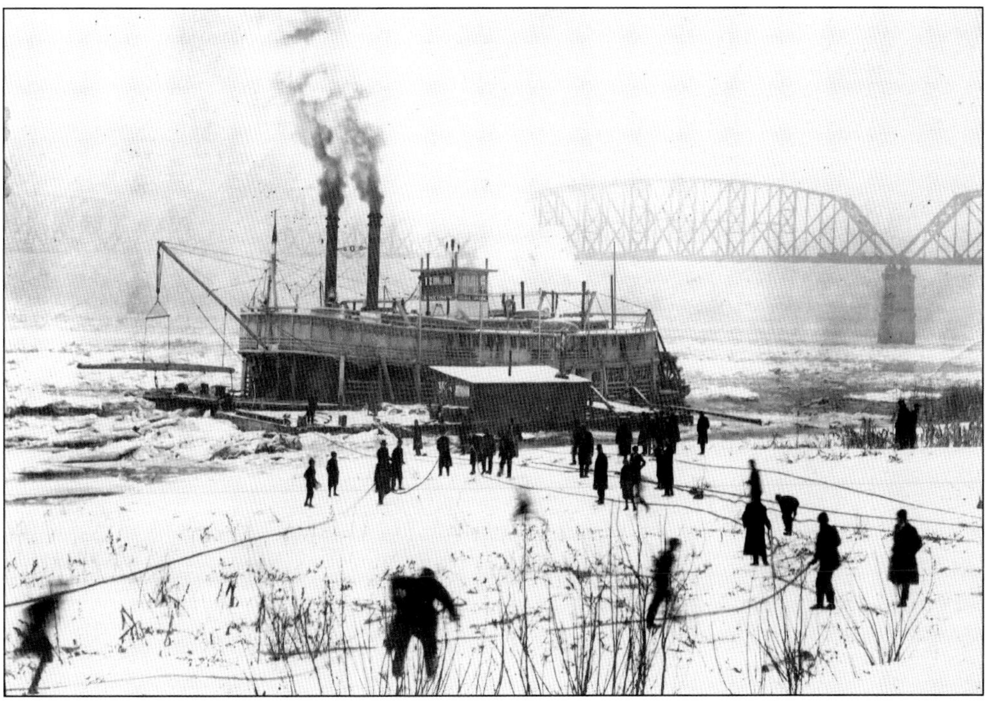

In January 1918, the Ohio River was frozen solid at Metropolis for the first time since 1876. When the ice gorge broke upriver, boat after boat careened by the Metropolis dock, where the *George Cowling* was moored. A huge block of ice was headed right for the boat, prompting Capt. Edward Cowling to order the crew ashore, but instead of destroying the boat, the block became lodged upriver, protecting the vessel from the rest of the ice that rushed past. This photograph is alleged to depict the moment when crew and townspeople came together to hold the lines, and the boat was saved.

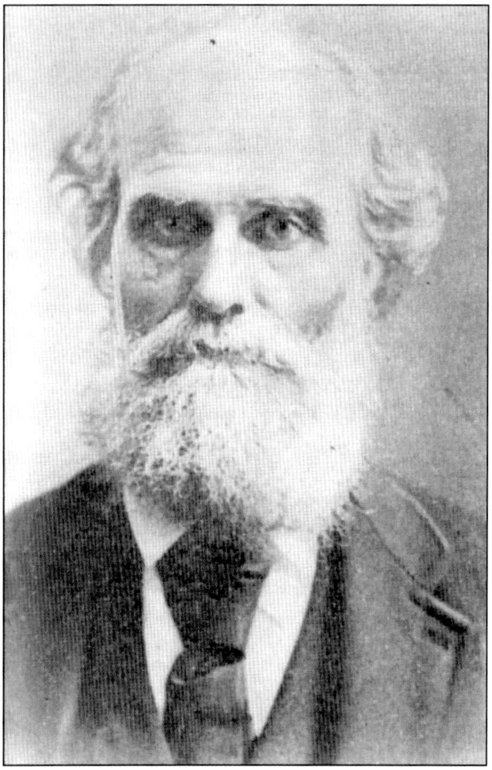

William A. McBane, the young merchant who dreamed of a new great city, is shown here in his later years. McBane is often referred to as William McBane Sr., although it was a nephew who was his namesake. Living with and caring for his elderly mother, Catherine (for whom a street in town was named), McBane was never married and left no progeny. He donated a great deal of land for civic and religious purposes, including Courthouse Square and Washington Park.

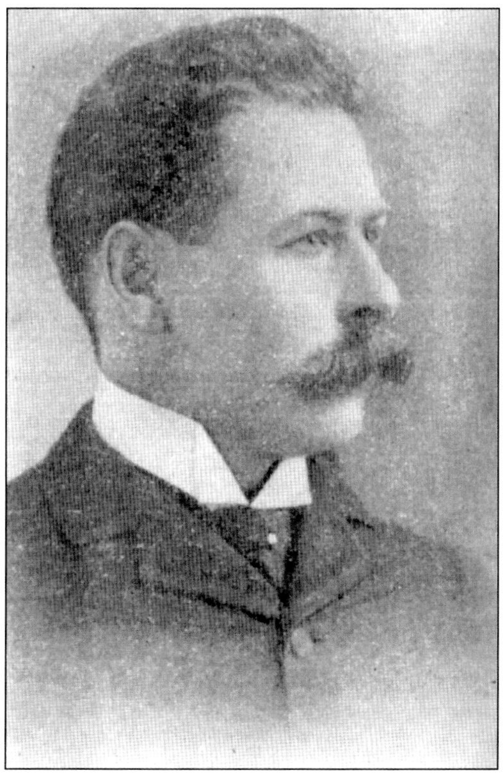

James Hendricks Gains Wilcox, cofounder of Metropolis, owned about 1,000 acres and ran a ferry business in the area when William McBane approached him about a partnership. McBane eventually bought out Wilcox's ferry concern and ran it for some 30 years. Wilcox moved to a farm outside of town several years before his death. The portrait here is apparently from a different era than the one above, as by all accounts Wilcox was the elder of the gentlemen.

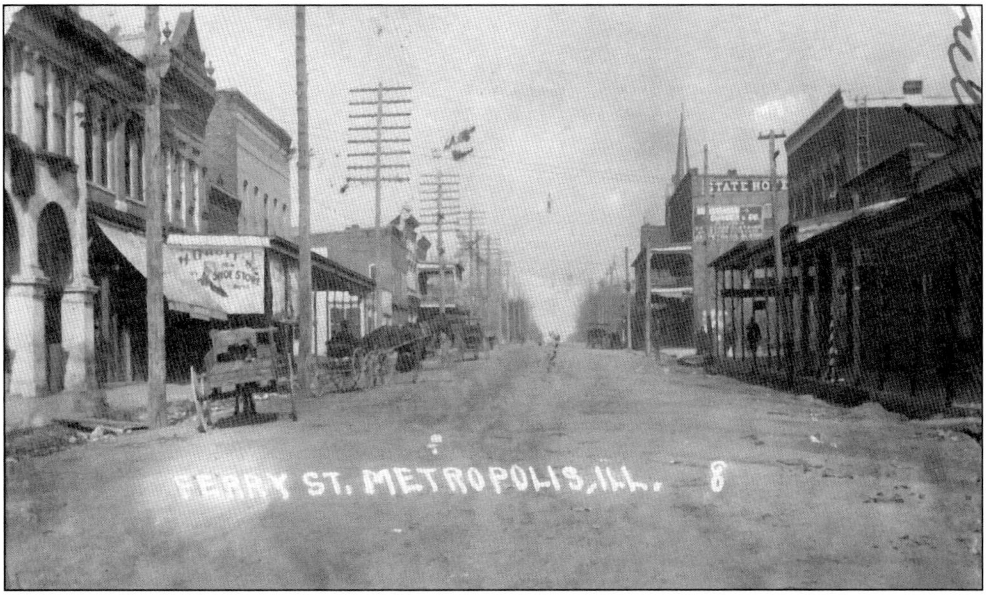

Found on a penny postcard sent in 1909, this view of Ferry Street shows the State Hotel on the right, with the spire of the First Methodist Church visible behind it. Addressed to W. K. Baker of Pine Bluff, Arkansas, the message reads as follows: "We are having such a nice visit here, everyone is very cordial. We have seen so many places that are quite familiar to you & mamma, and so many ask about you both. Aunt Fannie took us out in auto yesterday. We went out to the cemetery, it is so pretty there. Theresa."

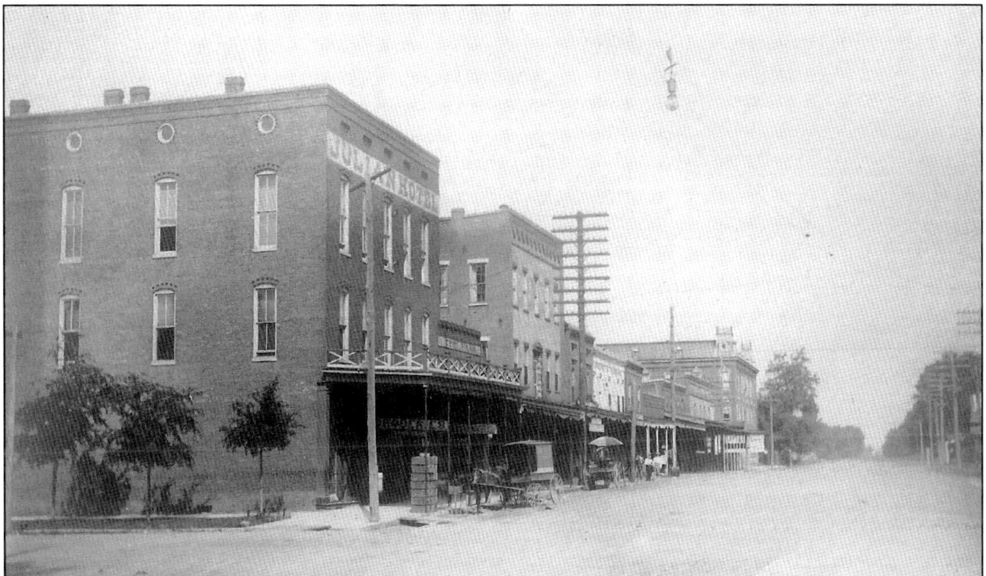

This scene is looking west on Third Street from Metropolis Street around 1910. The Julian Hotel is in the left foreground, with the Odd Fellows Hall/Miller's Dry Goods Store in the background at the end of the block. The Julian was constructed in the early 1880s and remained in use until the late 1960s, when a fire damaged it beyond repair, at which time it was taken down. The hotel got its name from Julia, the wife of Judge Robert McCartney.

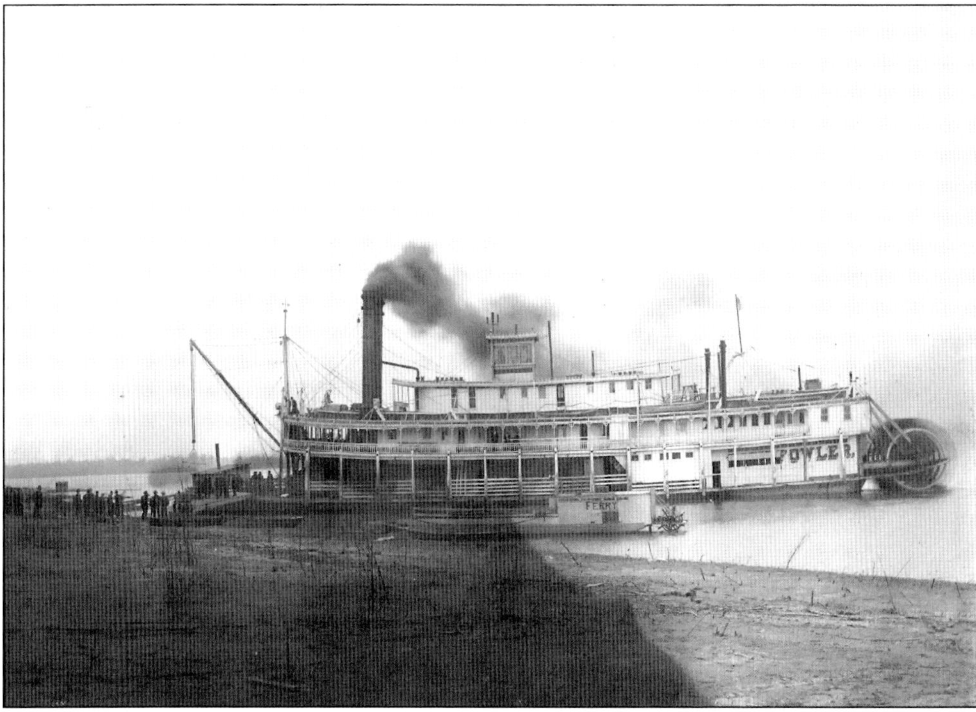

Operated out of Paducah by the Fowler family, the *Dick Fowler* docked in Metropolis every morning at around 9:00, then stopped there again on its way back from Cairo, Illinois. Seen here around 1905, it was soon after sold at auction, where Edward Cowling acquired its whistle for use on the second of the two boats he named for his father.

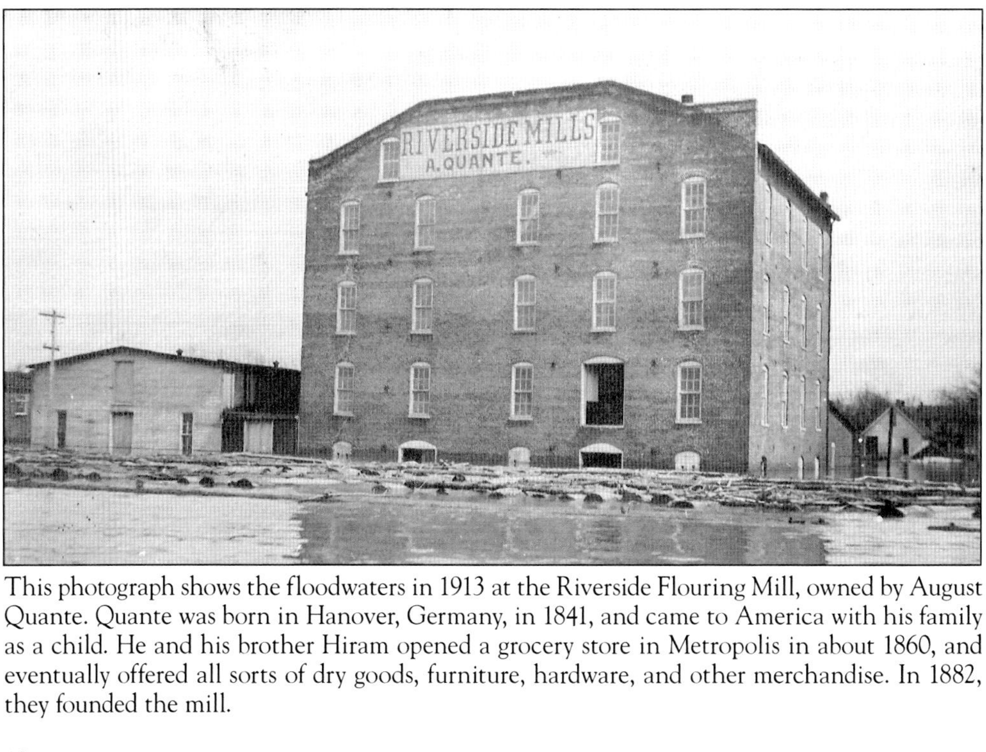

This photograph shows the floodwaters in 1913 at the Riverside Flouring Mill, owned by August Quante. Quante was born in Hanover, Germany, in 1841, and came to America with his family as a child. He and his brother Hiram opened a grocery store in Metropolis in about 1860, and eventually offered all sorts of dry goods, furniture, hardware, and other merchandise. In 1882, they founded the mill.

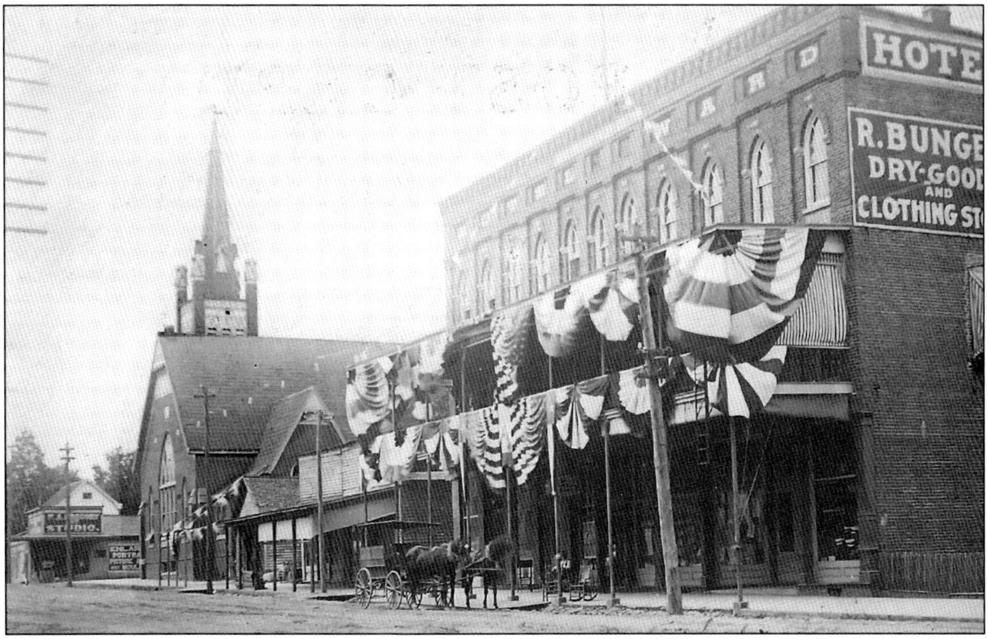

The Ward Hotel on Ferry Street is decorated here in preparation for the Hustlers' Convention, held June 8–10, 1911. A gathering of traveling salesmen, the convention culminated in a parade, as did most every other occasion that could serve as an excuse for one. Shortly before this, the location had been known as the State Hotel. Beyond the hotel, the First Methodist Church can be seen, and on the next block is F.A. Gregory's photography studio.

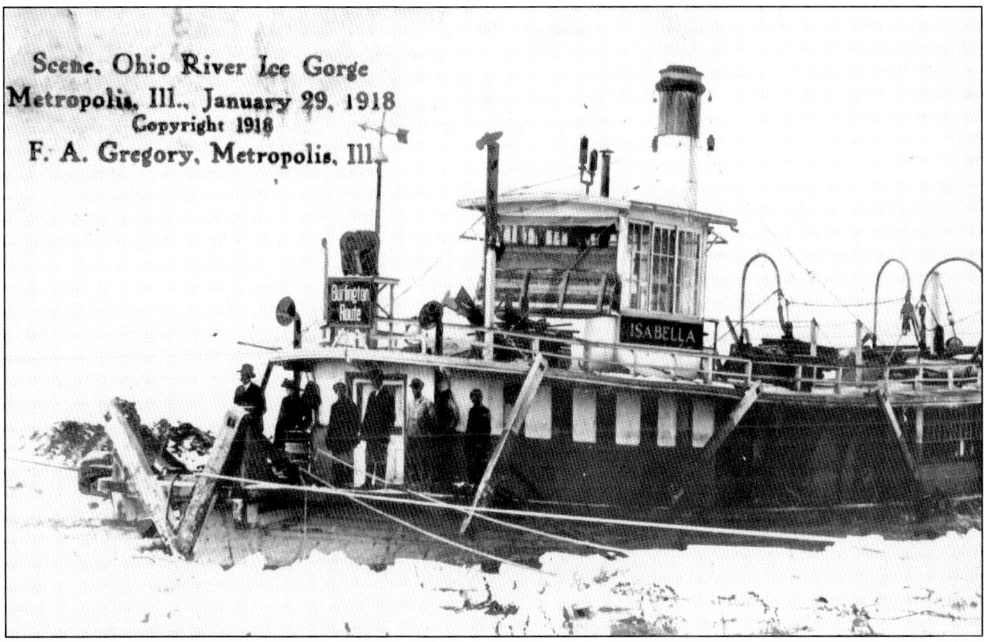

An ice gorge seems to engulf the Burlington Railroad tugboat *Isabella* on the Ohio River in this postcard by F.A. Gregory's studio. Before the railroad bridge was built, railcars were loaded onto either ferryboats or barges, the latter pulled by tugs like this one, for transport across the river. This practice lasted into the 1920s—even after the bridge was completed.

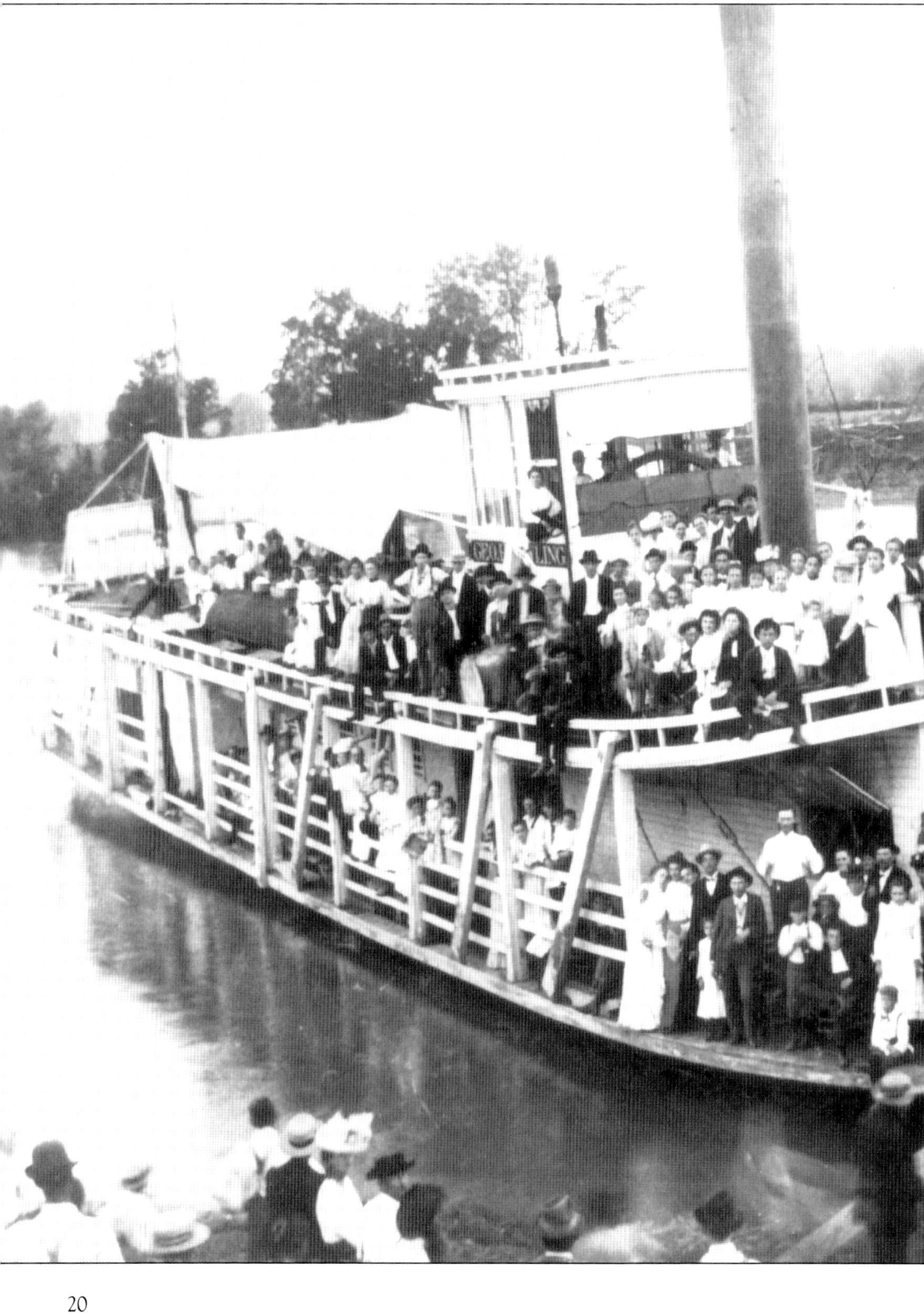

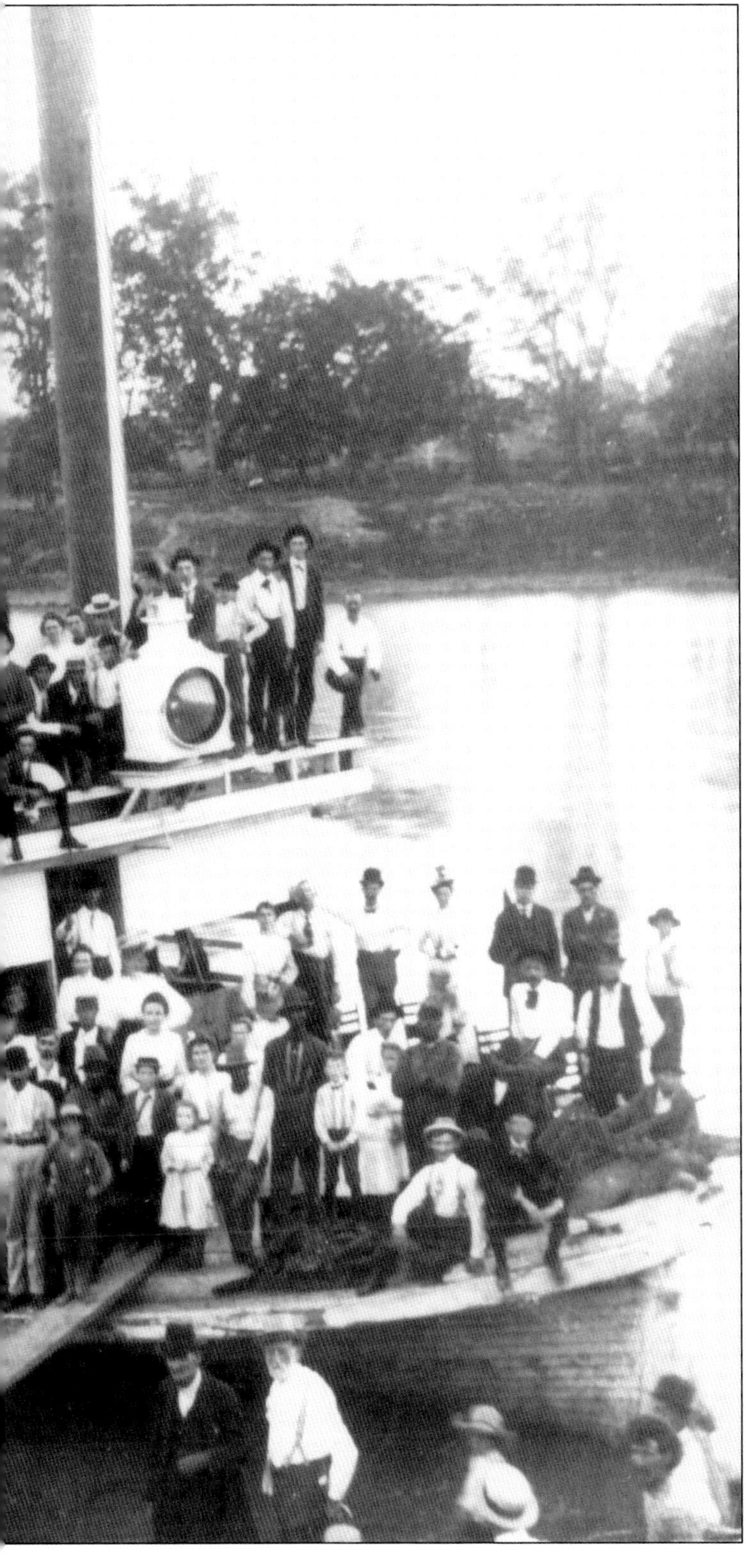

Appearing somewhat overloaded, the riverboat shown here is the *George H. Cowling*, an 88-ton, 120-foot-long stern-wheeler built in Metropolis in 1896. It was the first boat of two that Edward Cowling had built to honor his father. The younger Cowling owned the business for nearly 30 years after his father's death.

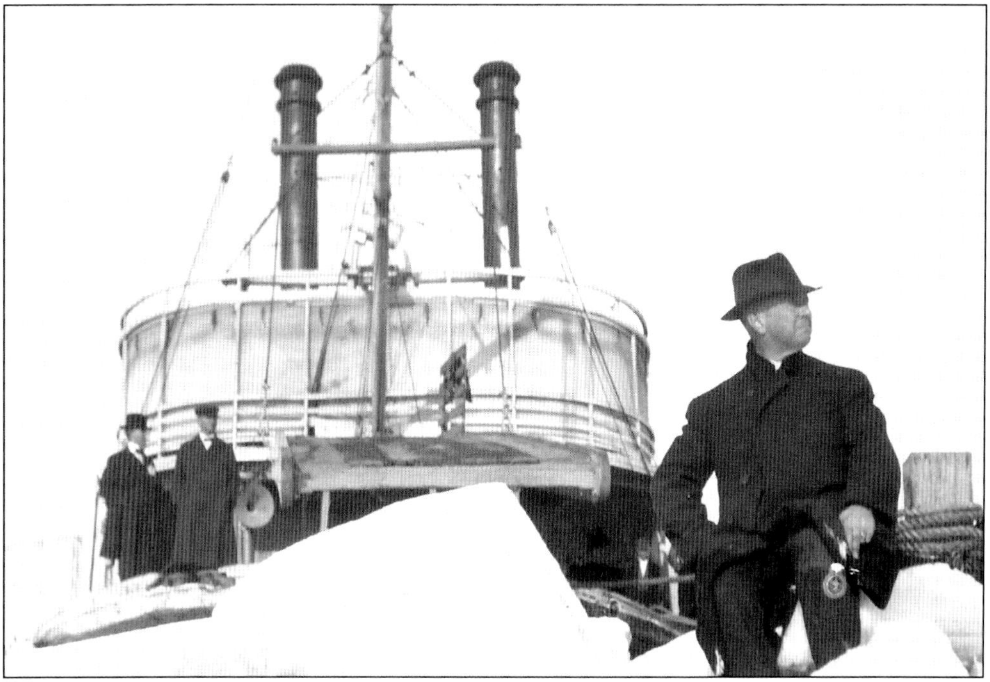

Capt. Edward J. Cowling poses in front of the *George Cowling*, possibly around the time of the events of January 1918 detailed at the start of the chapter, judging by the apparent ice blocks jutting from the river. It is said that the close call, along with the emerging competition of the railroads, led Captain Cowling to his decision to sell the business.

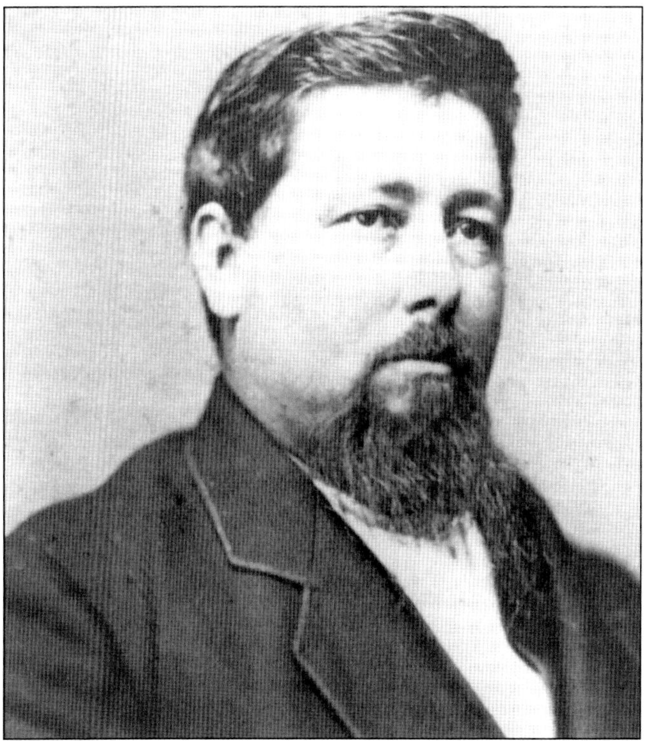

Capt. George Henry Langston Cowling was born in 1841 in London, and immigrated with his parents to Pennsylvania, where his father was a successful tailor. After his mother's death, George worked his way down the Ohio on the riverboats, eventually starting his own riverboat business in Metropolis in 1882. He died in 1894, leaving his son Edward to run the business while still in his early 20s.

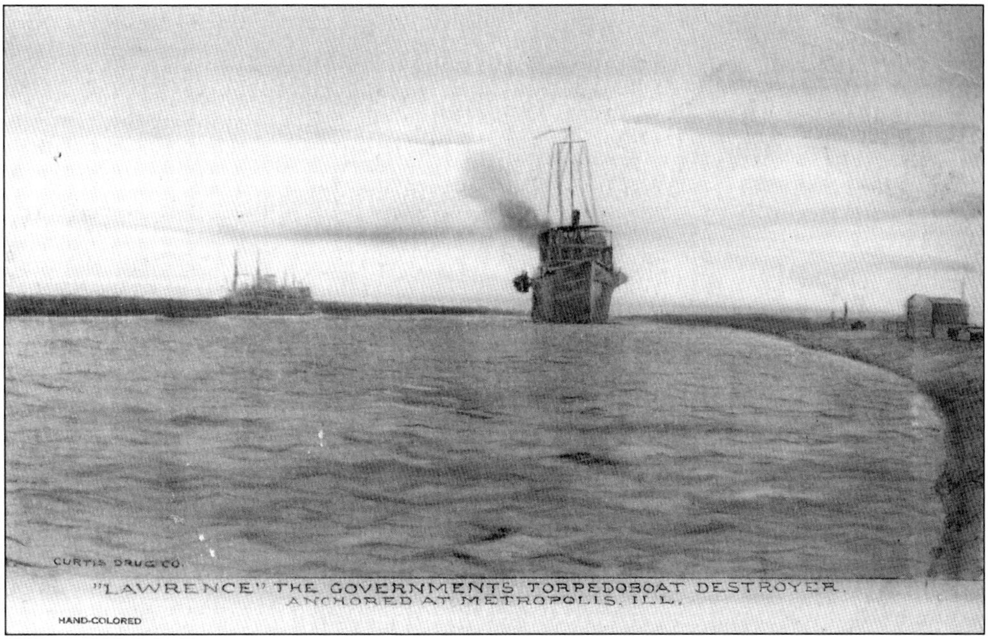

Shown in a Curtis drugstore postcard, the USS *Lawrence* is anchored at Metropolis in 1908 while on a recruiting tour for the US Navy. The third vessel to be named for Capt. James Lawrence (1781–1813) was a torpedo boat destroyer of the Bainbridge class and one of the earliest destroyers commissioned by the Navy. The ship later operated in the Panama Canal Zone during World War I.

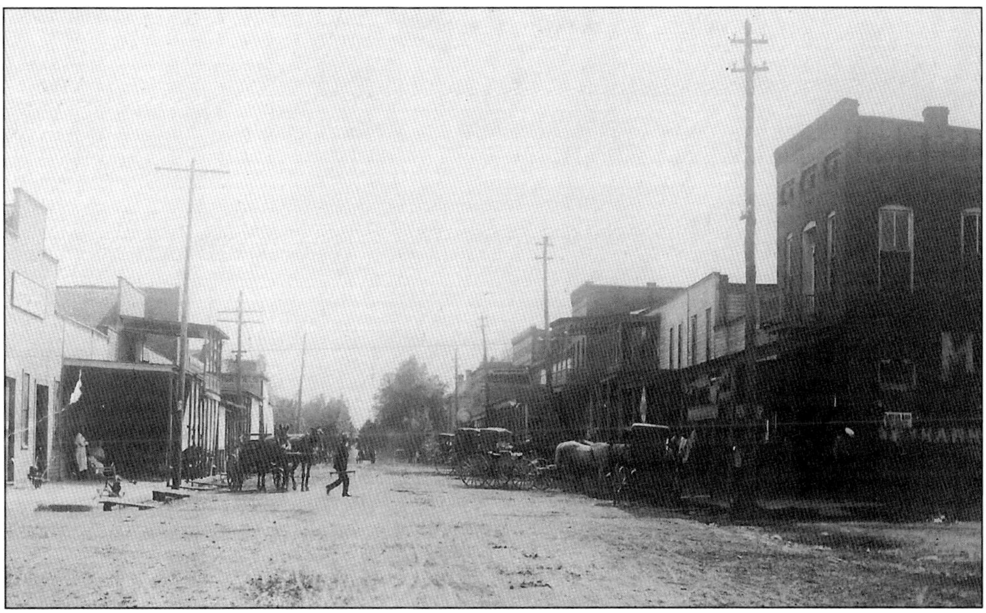

This view is looking north on upper Market Street from Seventh Street around 1912. The frame building on the left is a blacksmith shop, and the brick building on the right is Miller's Grocery and Harness Store. Perhaps on his way to Miller's to have it repaired, the man crossing the street is seen carrying a singletree, used to harness horses to a plow or wagon. (Courtesy Metropolis Public Library.)

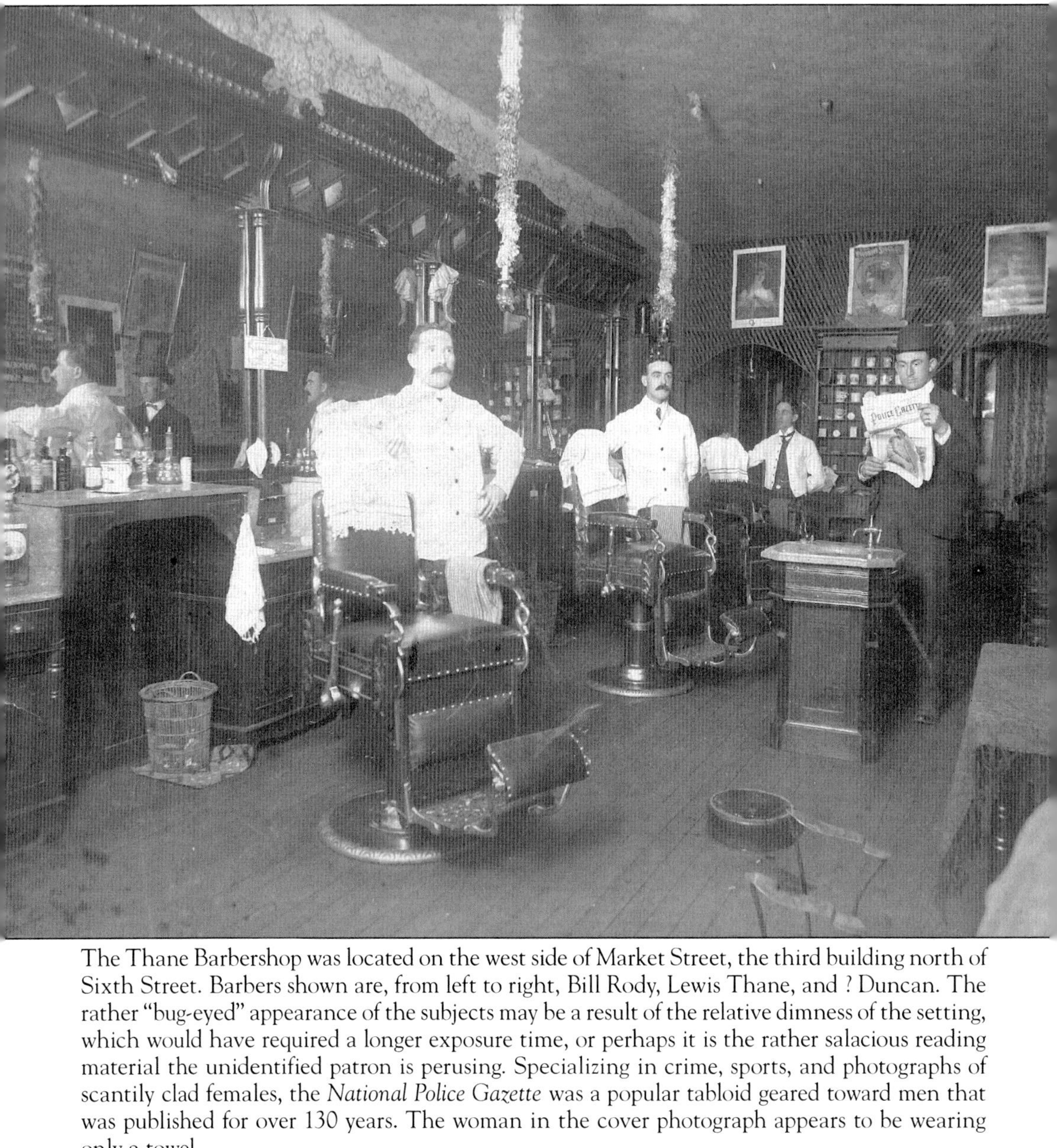

The Thane Barbershop was located on the west side of Market Street, the third building north of Sixth Street. Barbers shown are, from left to right, Bill Rody, Lewis Thane, and ? Duncan. The rather "bug-eyed" appearance of the subjects may be a result of the relative dimness of the setting, which would have required a longer exposure time, or perhaps it is the rather salacious reading material the unidentified patron is perusing. Specializing in crime, sports, and photographs of scantily clad females, the *National Police Gazette* was a popular tabloid geared toward men that was published for over 130 years. The woman in the cover photograph appears to be wearing only a towel.

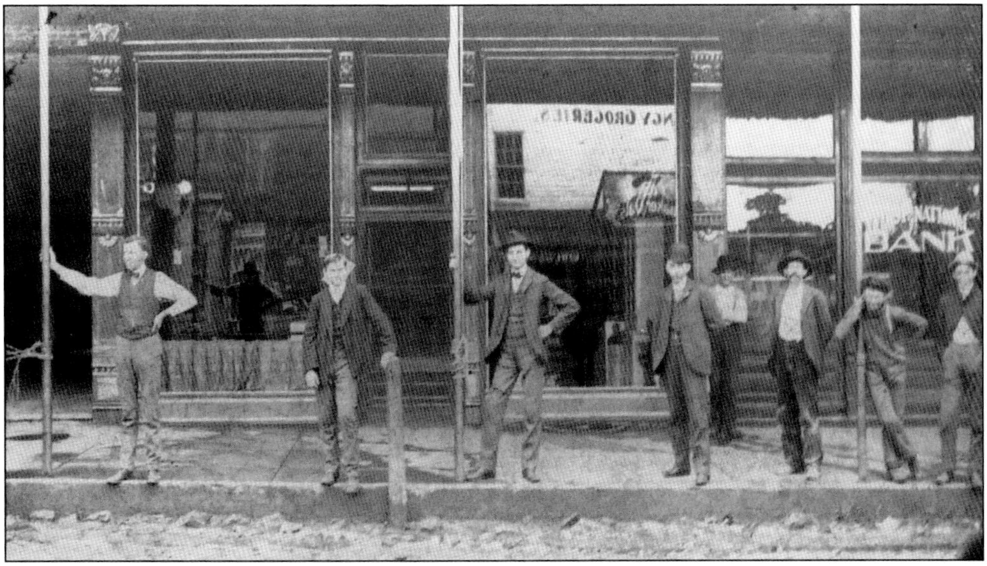

Humma's Drugstore is pictured here around 1895, with the First National Bank next door, in the Fritts Building, 302 Ferry Street. The man in the center with the jaunty stance appears to be Henry Humma, proprietor and pharmacist. Reflected in the store window, the Quante brothers' store across the street has a sign reading "Fancy Groceries."

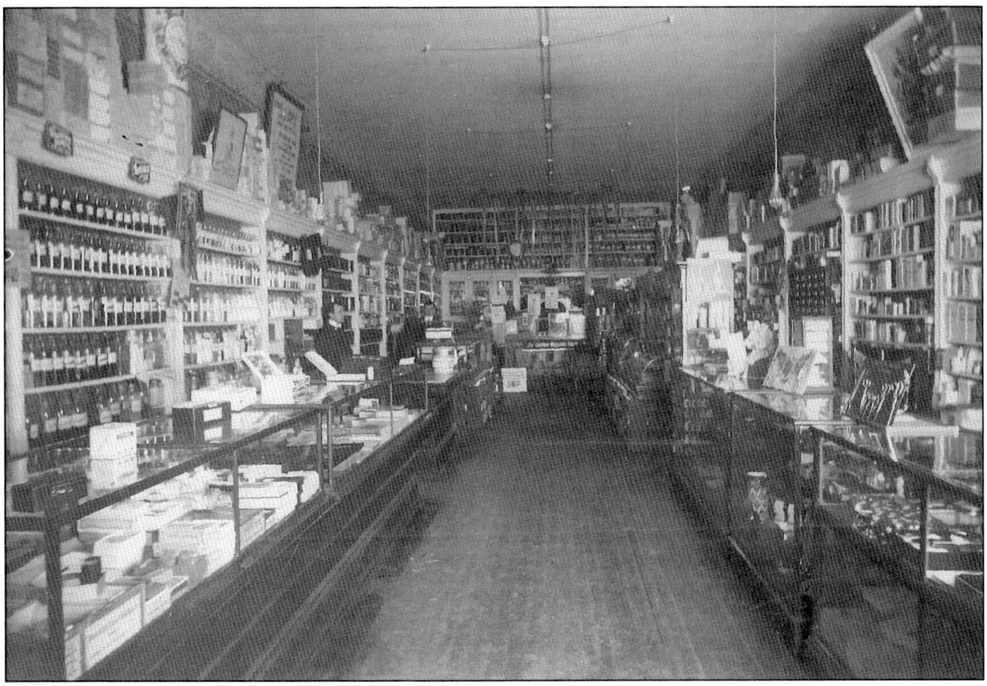

This photograph shows the interior of the original Humma's Pharmacy Fritts Building location, founded in 1892. The building, constructed in 1876, replaced the earlier Fritts Building, which burned in April of that year. It housed the Brown and Bruner Bank starting in 1892, but the bank collapsed during the panic of 1893. Despite the establishment's short duration, the structure is still often referred to as the Brown and Bruner Bank Building. In 1904, Humma moved across the street, along with the First National Bank, which had replaced the failed bank.

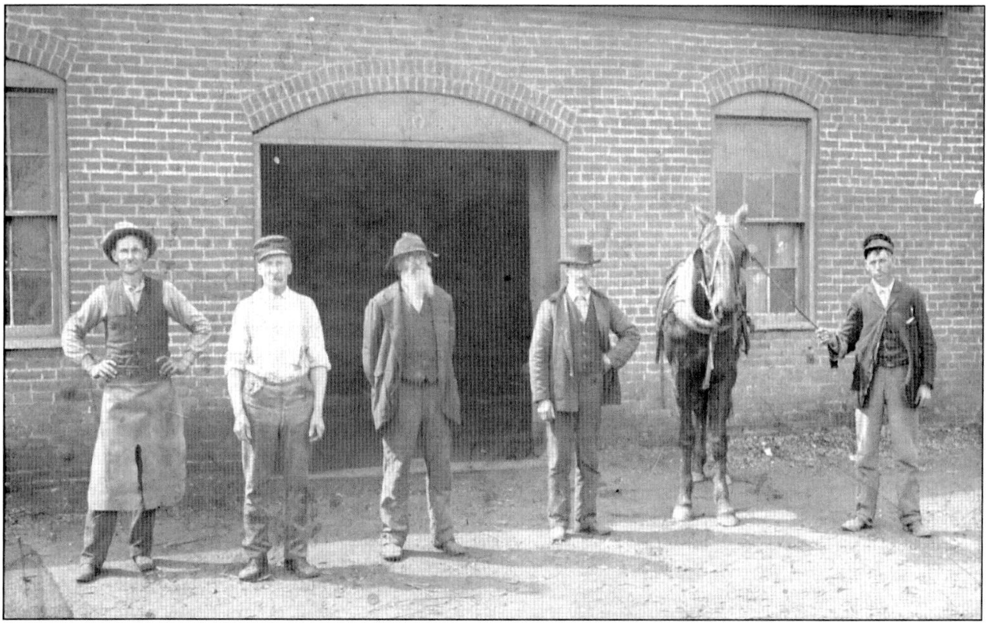

This photograph shows the front of C.C. Wittman's Blacksmith shop on the southeast corner of Fifth and Market Streets in 1890. The building was constructed in the 1870s and used by a taxi business in later years. In the photograph are, from left to right, John Bunchman, Henry Smith, C.C. Wittman, Henry Wittman, a horse (no doubt there to be shod), and an unidentified person holding the reins.

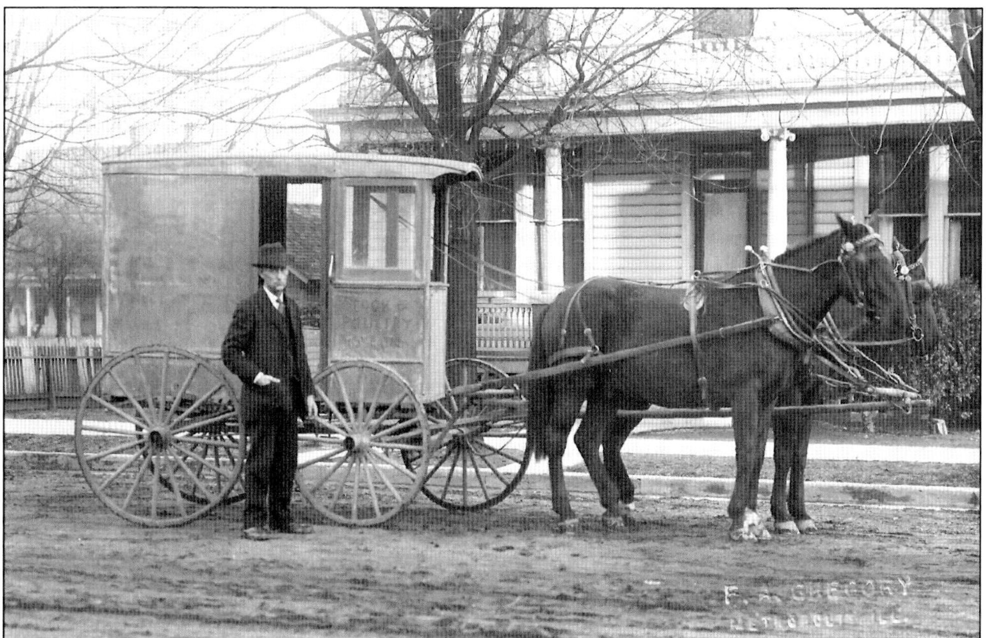

As a salesman for the Rawleigh Co. Chemists, Henry Miller was known as "The Rawleigh Remedies Man." According to the side panels of his wagon (illegible here), he sold "Stock & Poultry Preparations" as well as "Extracts, Spices, Toilet Articles." Miller had local competition in the Watkin's Remedies Man, who sold similar products in a similar manner.

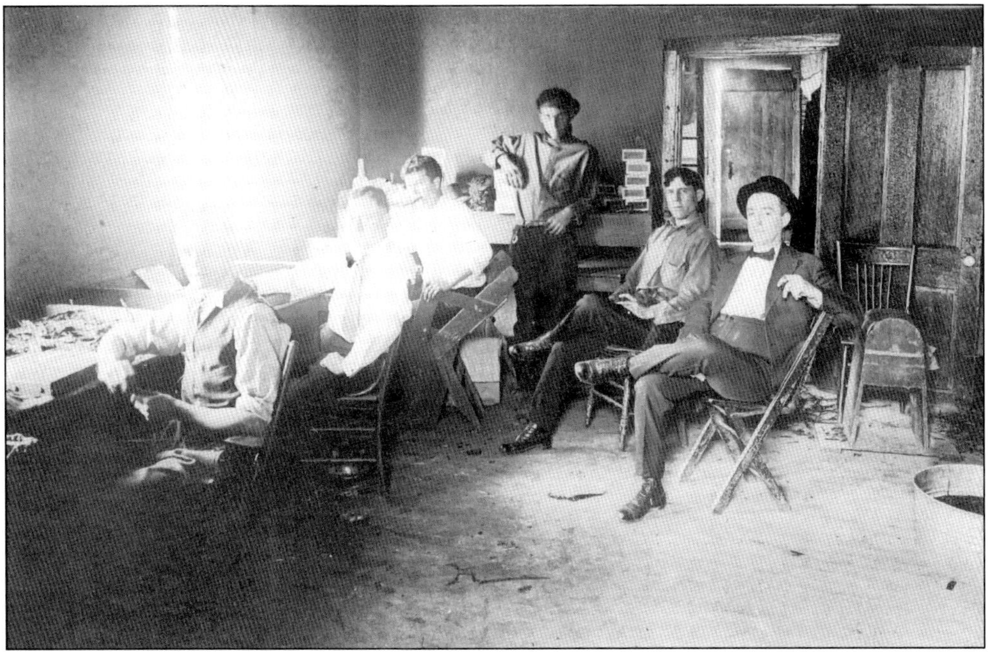

This photograph appears to be the secondary Kraper Cigar Company production facility, located behind the home of owner William H. Kraper (seated at far right), in the 400 block of Market Street. Between the company's two locations, it had 25 to 30 employees producing up to 1.5 million cigars a year.

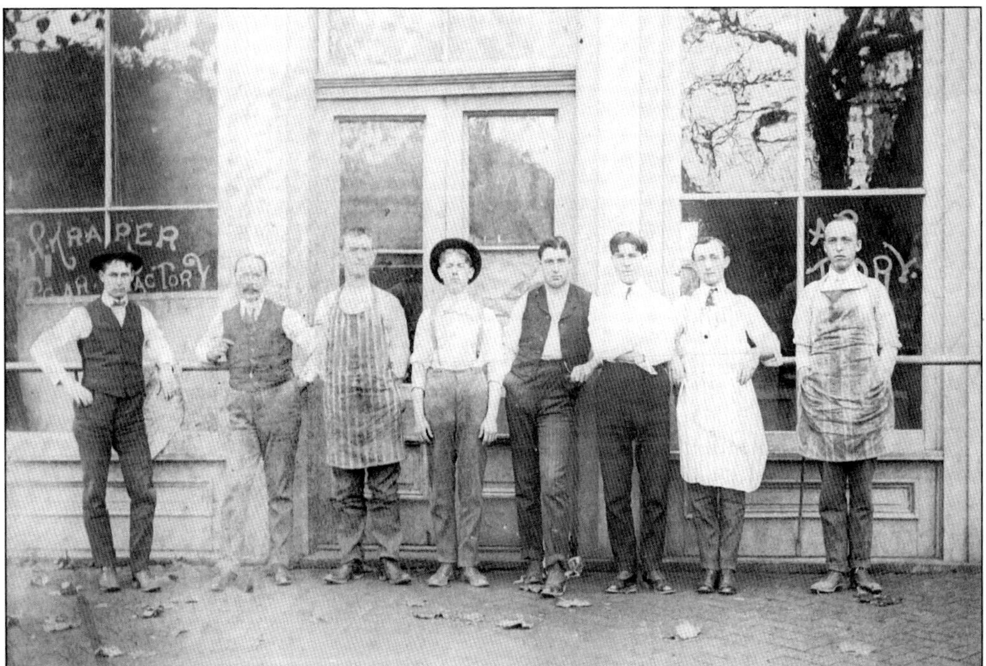

Workers and/or customers are seen outside the main Kraper Cigar Factory on the south side of Third Street, between Metropolis and Ferry Streets. The fourth man from the right is evidently named Charlie as a note on the card identifies him.

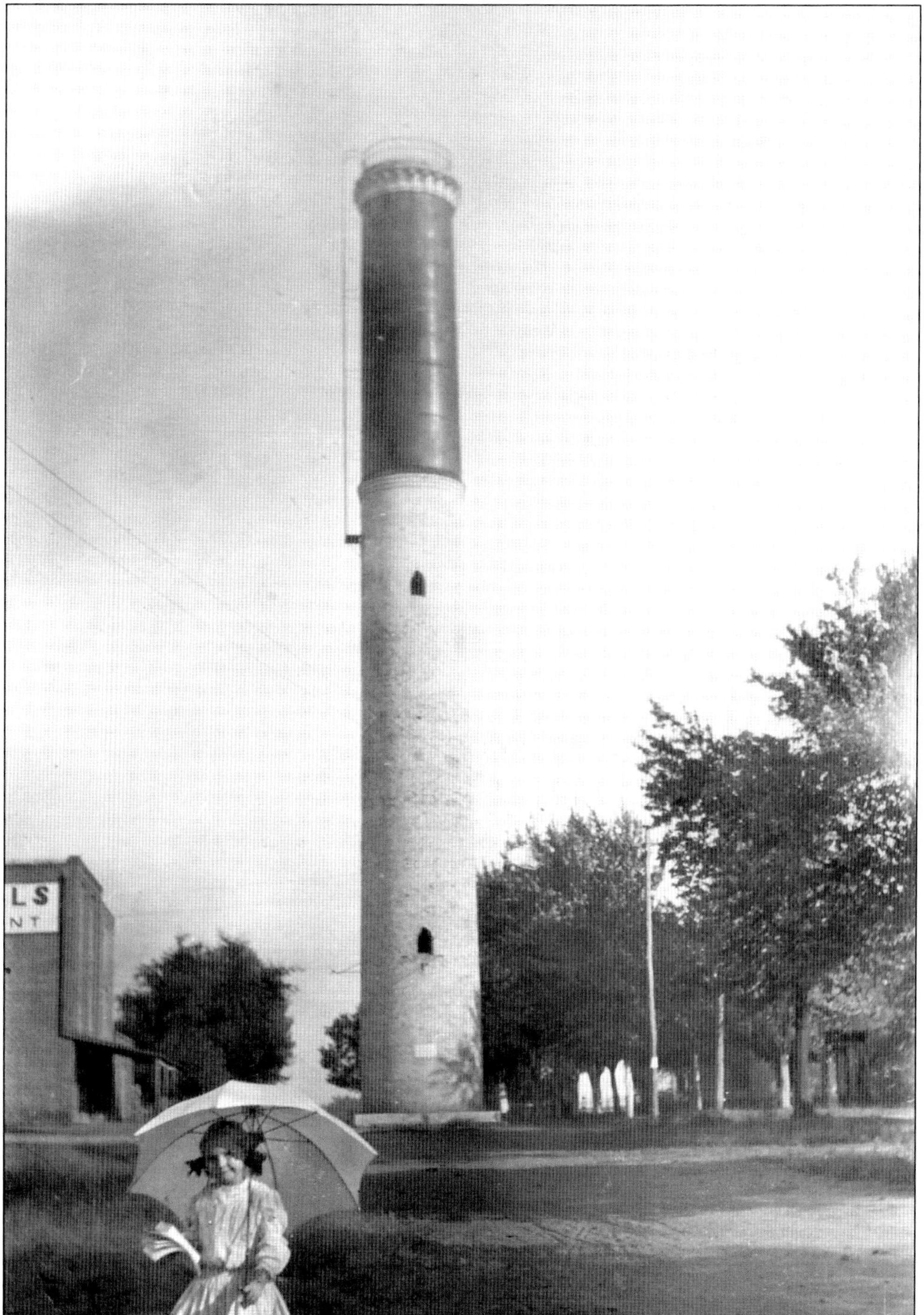

Standpipes were the standard for water towers before 1900, and Metropolis was no exception. This one, erected in 1892, helped with the pressurization of the city's water supply. It was in the center of the intersection of Ninth and Metropolis Streets, near the Empire Mill, which is seen in the photograph.

With advances in technology allowing for larger water towers, the standpipe had served its purpose and was taken down in 1910. The townspeople made an occasion of it. There are very few 19th-century standpipes still in existence in America.

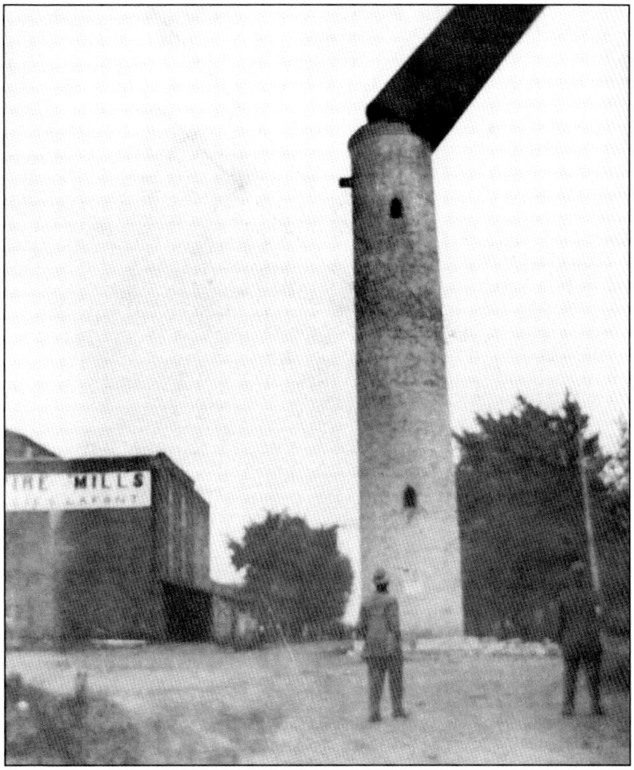

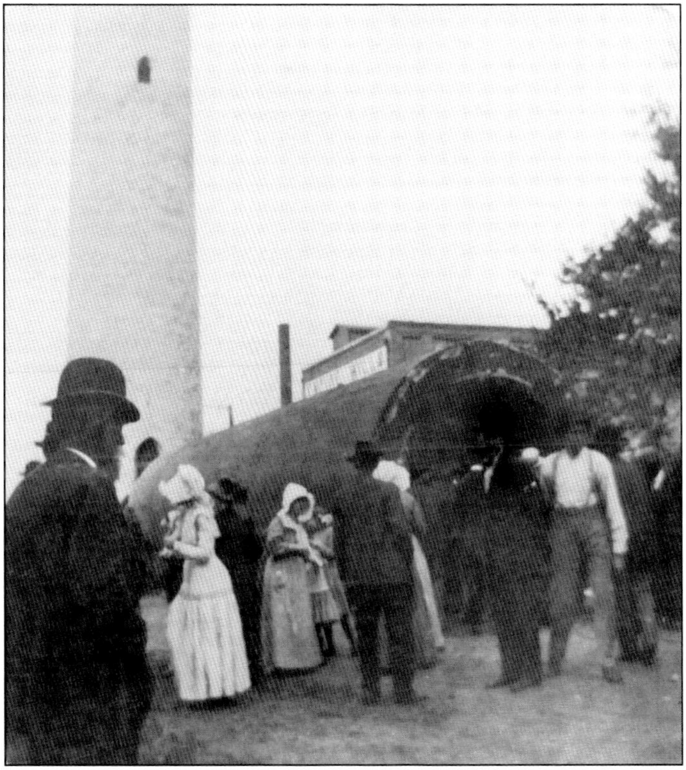

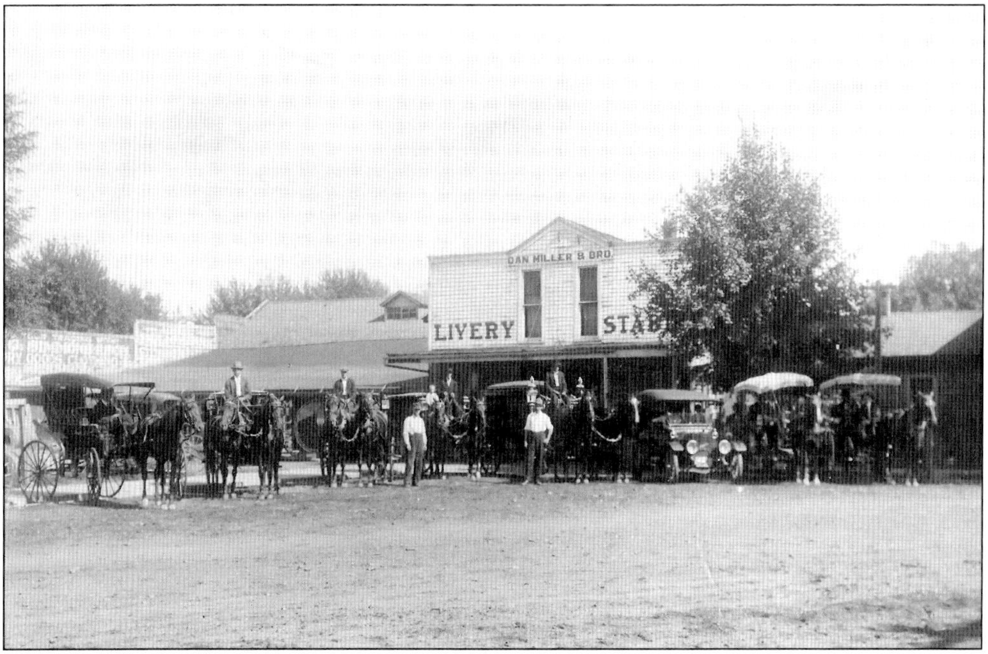

Dan Miller & Bro. Livery Stable is seen here on the northeast corner of the square in 1916. It was started as a livery stable in 1895, then later the Miller Brothers added taxi rental and automobile repair to their list of services. The building burned down in 1923, after which the Lindsey Lumber Company took its place.

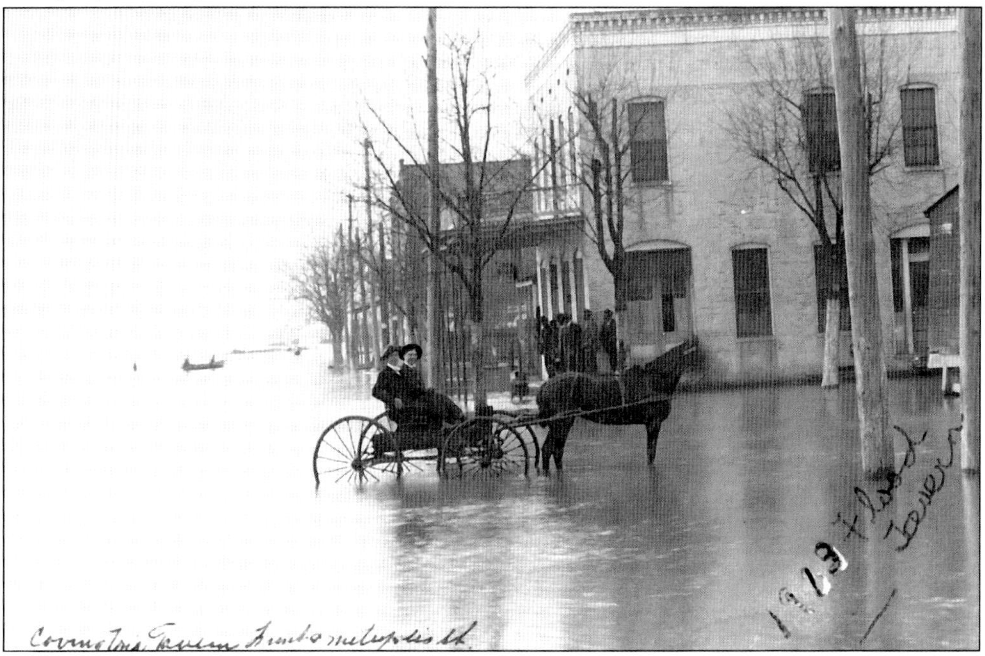

In front of the Covington Hotel/Doc's Tavern, located at Front Street and Metropolis Street, unidentified people are shown during the 1913 flood. Previously, it was known as the Palace Hotel and Saloon and was reputed to have served as a "house of ill repute" catering to river travelers. The structure was torn down in the 1960s to make way for a public park.

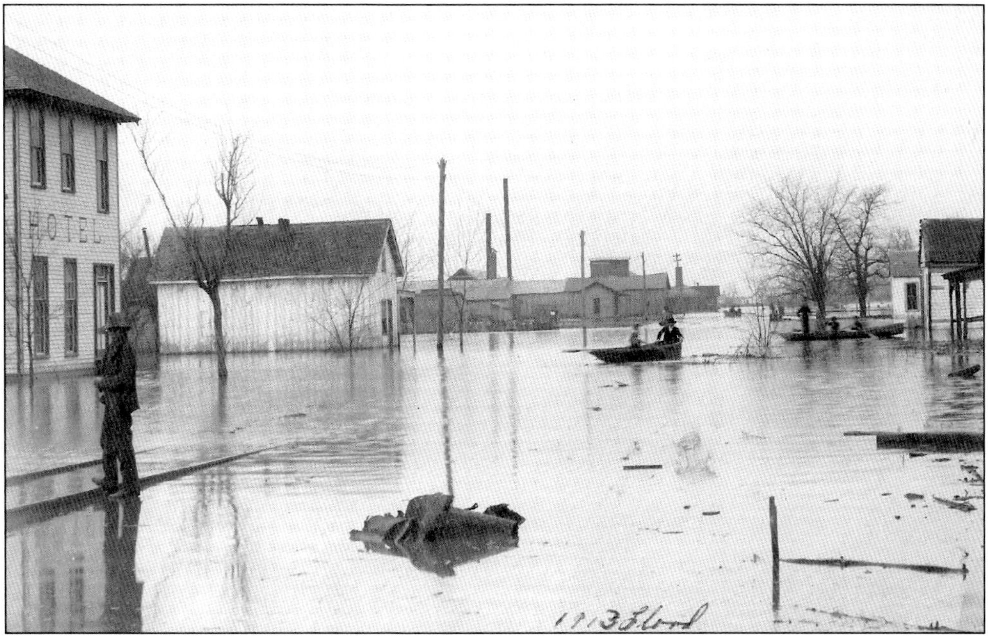

The flood of 1913 is shown covering Front Street and the railroad tracks. To assist in the flood efforts, Alfred Cutting Boat Works gave out 47 rowboats, some of which can be seen here in the background.

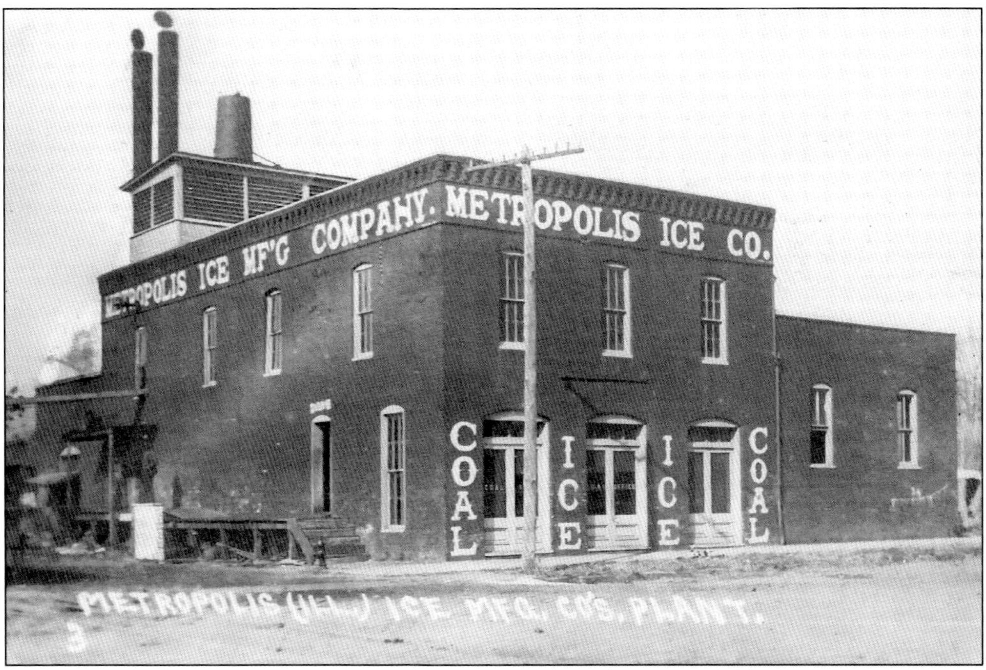

This postcard shows the Metropolis Ice Manufacturing Company, located just north of the Illinois Central Railroad Station. Founded in 1903, the company made up to 50 tons of ice a day, one-fifth of which was used for local consumption. CIPS bought the company in 1927. Postcards of the day, like this one, were often actual photographic prints on heavy paper that could withstand mailing. (Courtesy Phyllis Joseph.)

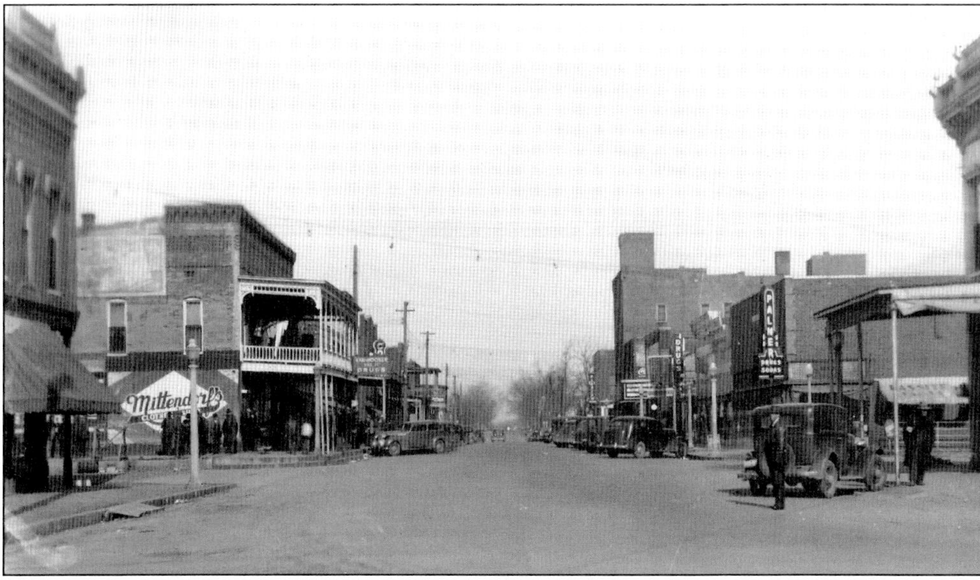

This 1937 photograph is of upper Market Street, looking north from just before Sixth Street. Palmer Drugstore is on the right. Mittendorf's Clothing and Van Hooser Drugs are on the left, with Cohen's located behind the drugstore sign that reads "Van Hooser Has It."

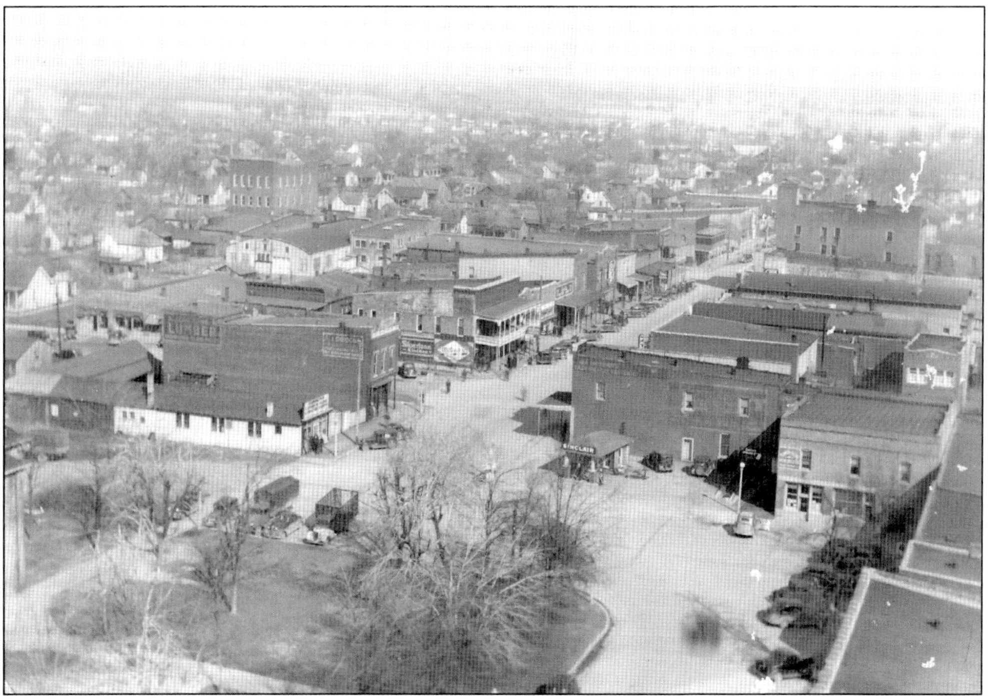

In this aerial view from the water tower, looking north on Market Street from the square, one can see the old courthouse on the extreme left, with Gibbons Lumber and Furniture, Mittendorf's, Van Hooser's, and Cohen's on the left side of the street. The tall brick building on the back left is the McAfee Building at Seventh and Pearl Streets. The New York Life Insurance Building on the right is no longer standing. On the right is a Sinclair Oil station, on a site where the First National Bank is today.

Three

THE RAILROAD

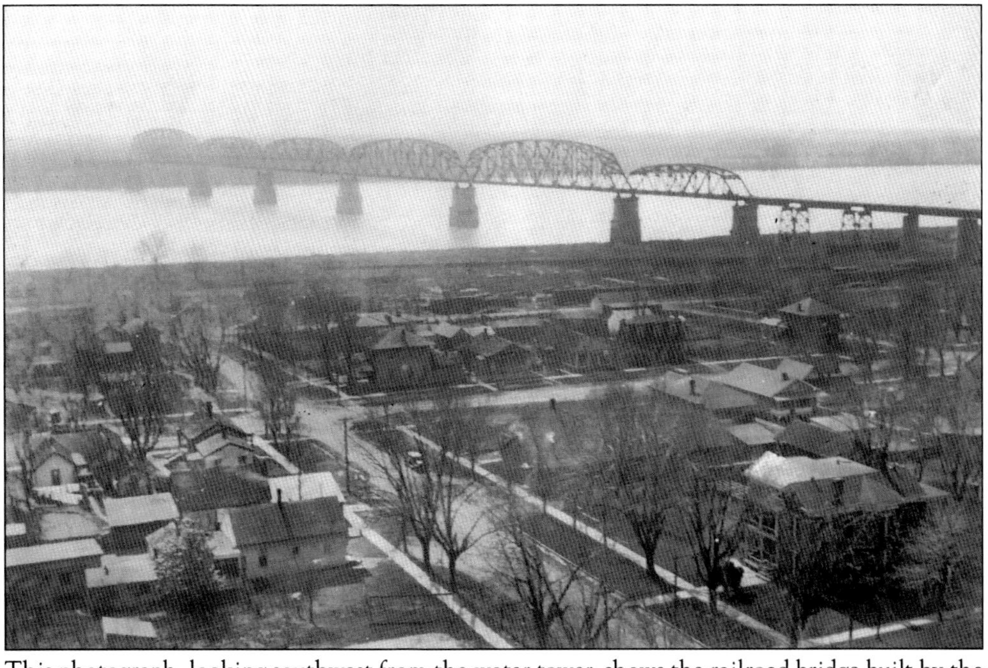

This photograph, looking southwest from the water tower, shows the railroad bridge built by the Chicago, Burlington & Quincy Railroad over a period of several years and completed in 1917 at a cost of over $4 million.

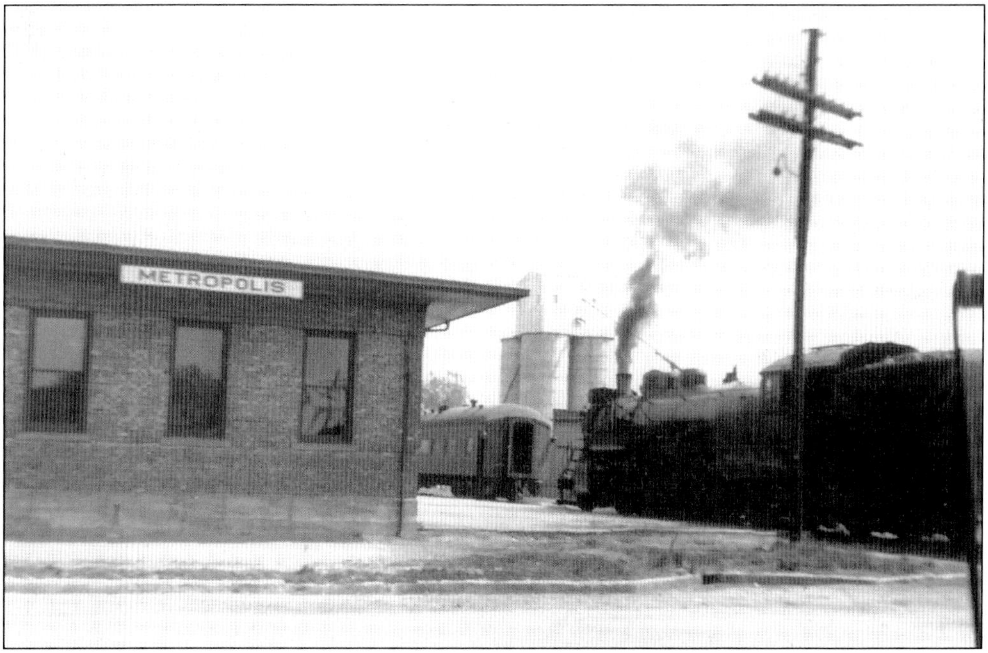

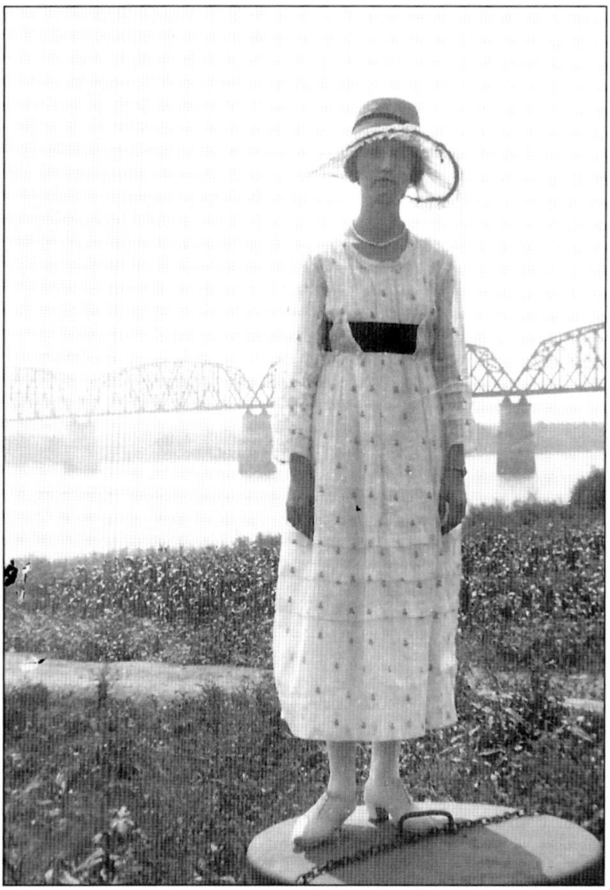

The Illinois Central Railroad depot, located at First and Metropolis Streets, is pictured around 1940. The concrete silos in the background are at the site of the Riverside (Quante) Mills.

Judging by the style of clothing, this lady is posing in front of the CB&Q Bridge sometime during the 1920s, just a few years after the structure's completion. At the time, the bridge was a major engineering feat. The longest span of the bridge, at over 700 feet, was and remains the largest of its type in the world.

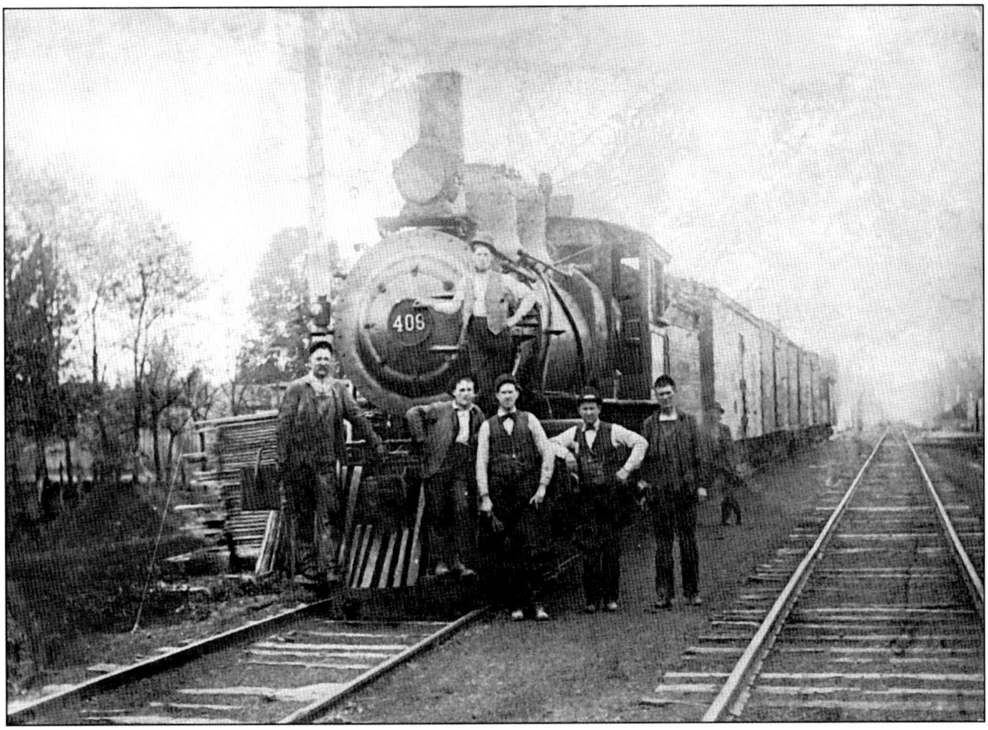

This photograph, dating from about 1905, shows an Illinois Central Railroad freight train and crew in Metropolis.

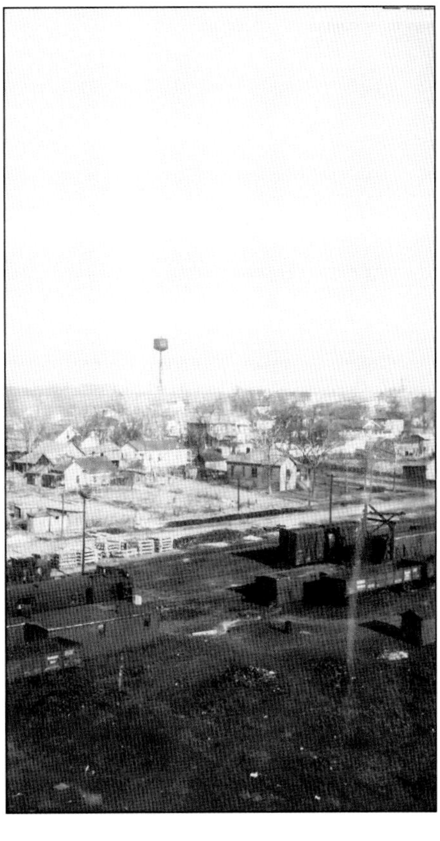

This view of Metropolis is looking southeast from the railroad bridge approach, through the Chicago, Burlington & Quincy rail yard.

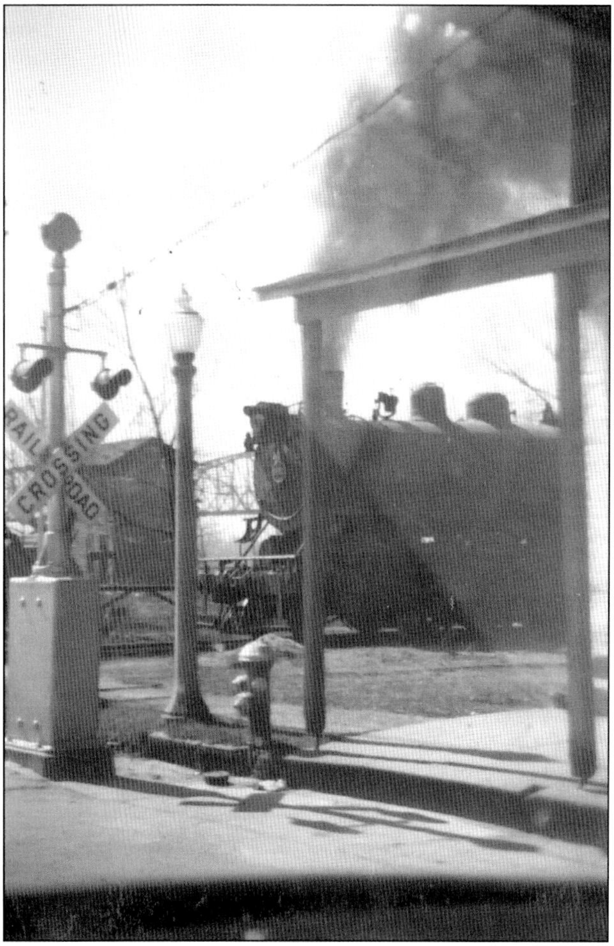

Here, an Illinois Central Railroad train crosses Ferry Street at First Street around 1940.

The Illinois Central Railroad depot is shown here. It should be noted that the Chicago, Burlington & Quincy Railroad (CB&Q) also had a depot for passenger and freight traffic, but it was demolished by the tornado of 1935.

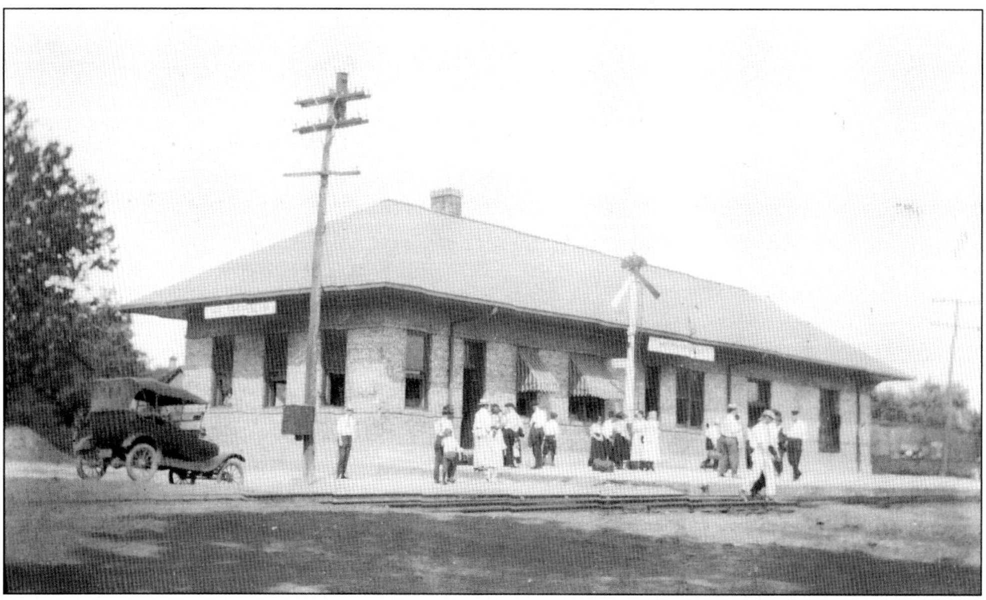

Four

Industry and Commerce

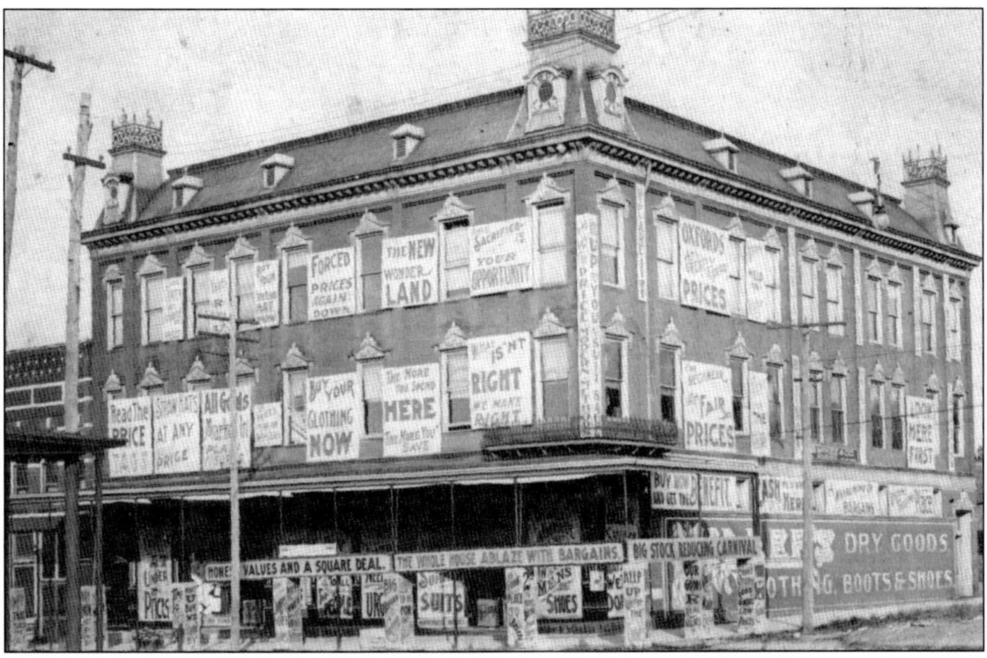

It is unknown whether Miller's Dry Goods, shown here in 1909, is having a really quite exceptional sale or if the hype lasted year-round. One sign reads, "The Whole House Ablaze with Bargains." The building, also home to the Odd Fellows Lodge, was located on the southwest corner of Third and Ferry Streets. It was built in 1894 and torn down in the early 1980s.

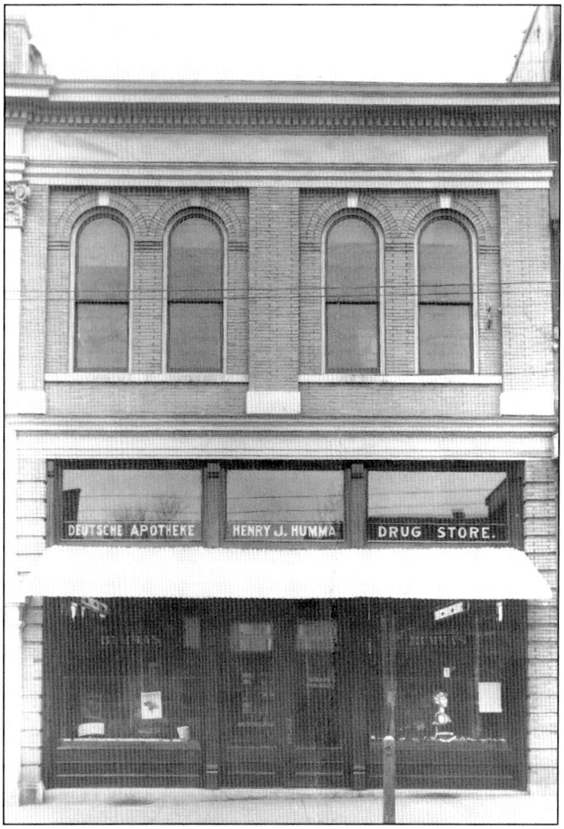

Humma's Drug Store, at 317 Ferry Street, is pictured here in 1904. This is its second location, across the street from the Fritts Building. Note the use of German on the storefront ("*Deutsche Apotheke*," which means "German pharmacy"). At that time, many stores and newspapers in American towns that had large German populations used the German language.

This is a photograph of the interior of Humma's second Ferry Street location in the early 1900s. There are many photographs of Humma's stores because Henry Humma was an amateur photographer, and then, as now, drugstores were the most accessible places to offer photograph-developing services. The store also carried a variety of photographic prints and postcards.

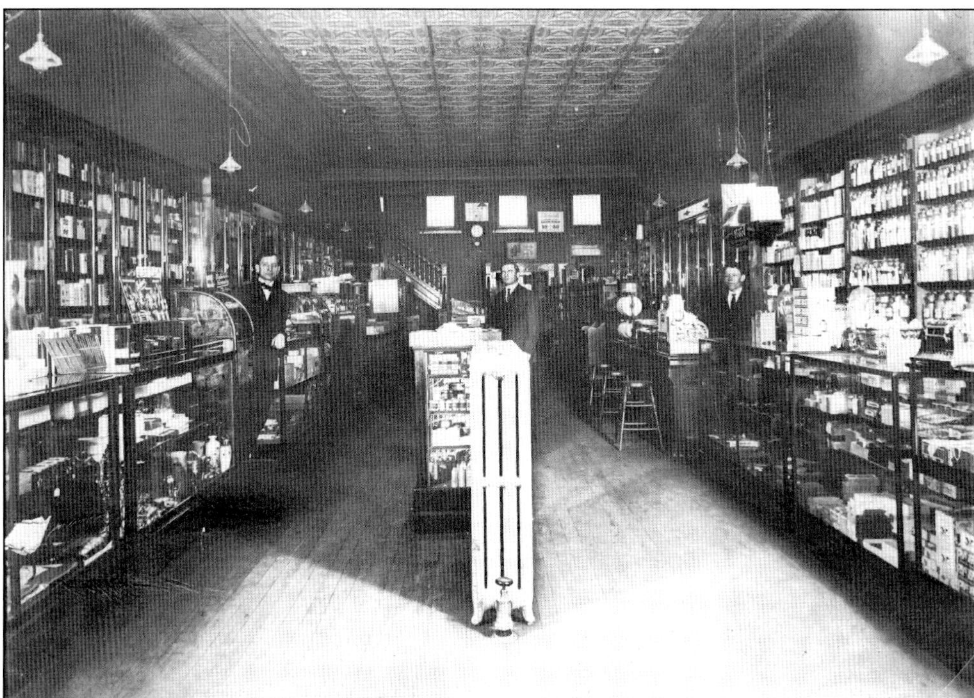

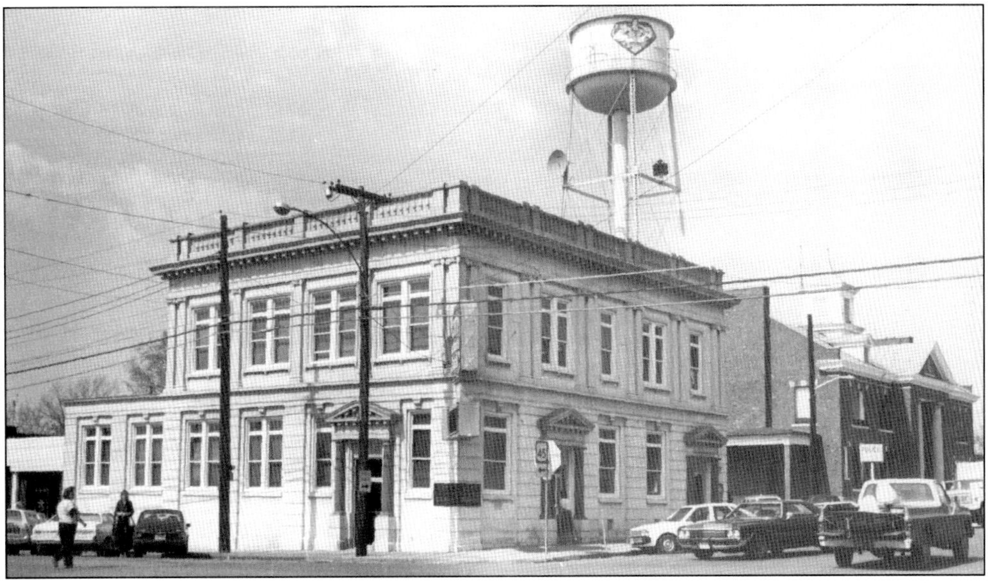

City National Bank opened for business on July 1, 1907, initially in the W.H. Kraper Building at Sixth and Market Streets. Approximately two years later, a building was opened at the corner of Fifth and Ferry Steets (shown here in the 1980s), where the bank remains. The first Superman water tower can be seen in the background. A new water tower, again adorned with the Man of Steel, was later located closer to the interstate.

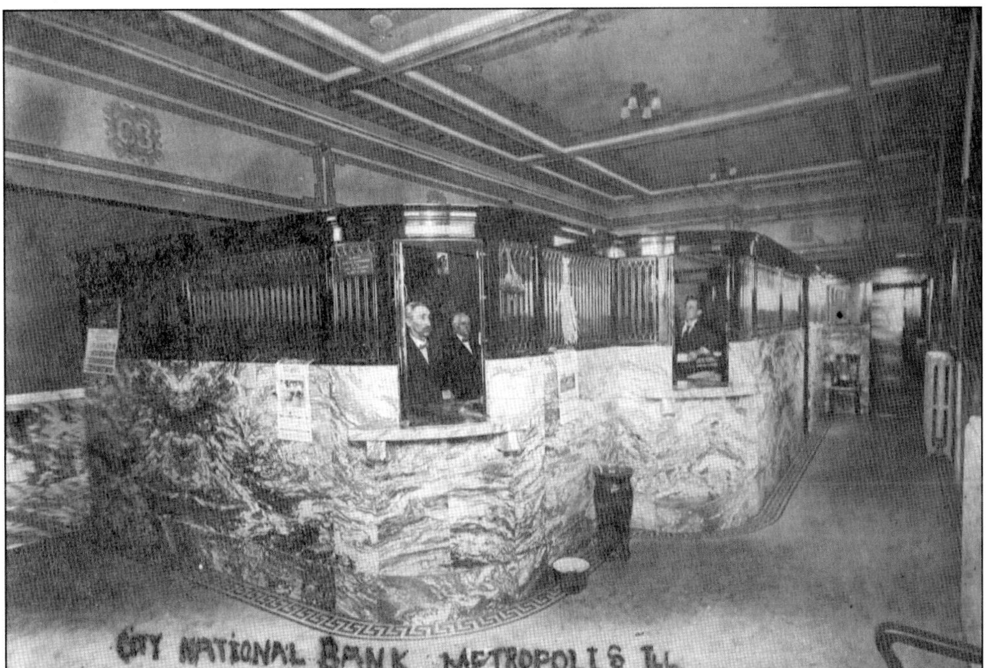

The new City National Bank Building had two marble teller cages, a vault, and a work area behind the cages, shown here probably shortly after it opened in 1909. The lot had been purchased for $800, while construction was contracted for $14,200. Over the years, it has been renovated and modernized numerous times.

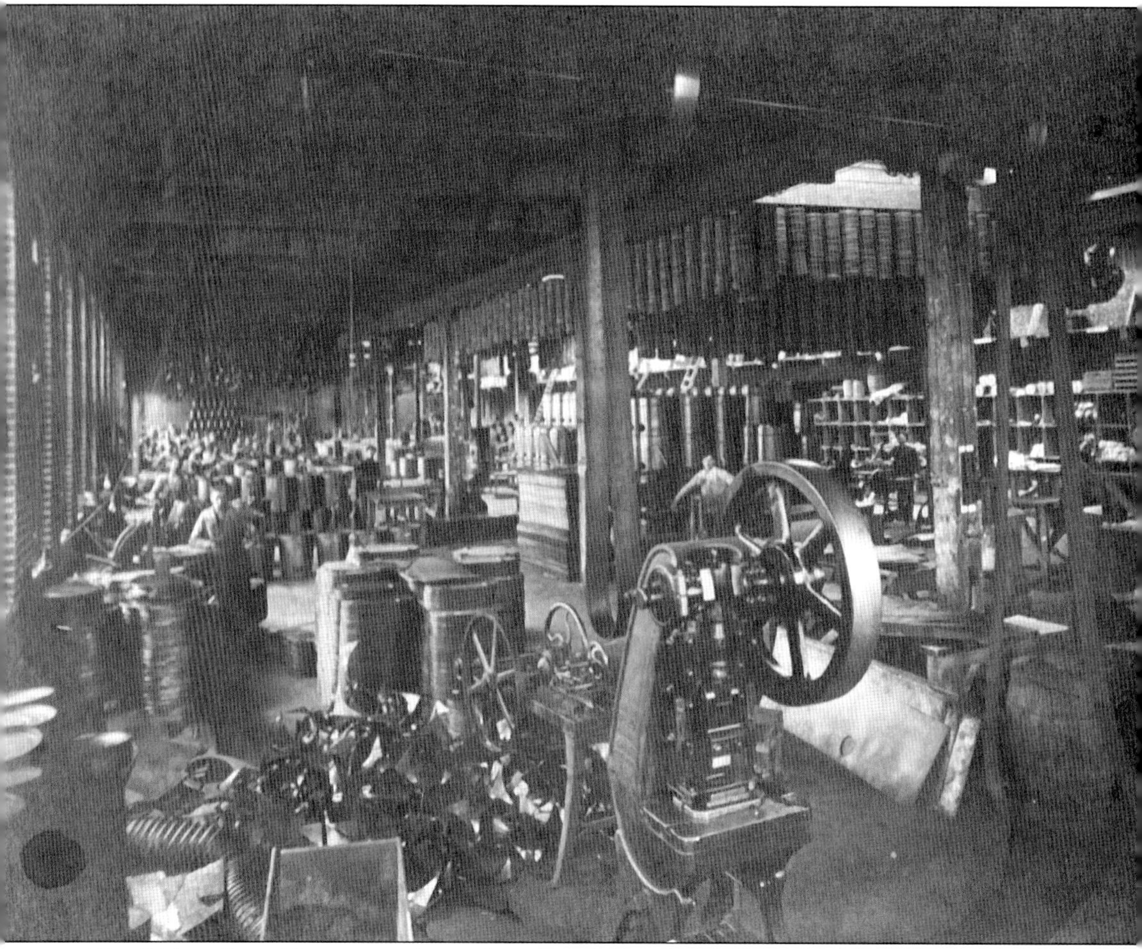

The Wilson Stove Factory was located on 53 acres on the west side of the railroad bridge and started operations in 1916. The plant employed about 300 workers until 1932, when it was sold. If one looks closely at this photograph, a few workers can be seen at their posts. The building became the location of a duck decoy maker, then later burned.

Humma's Drug Store is shown here in 1950 at its third location at 606 Market Street. It had opened in 1936, after Henry Humma's two sons, Harry and Benny, bought the business from him. They operated it concurrently with the Ferry Street location for a number of years. Though out of the Humma family for some time, the site remained a drugstore until December 2011, when it ceased operation as a pharmacy after nearly 120 years.

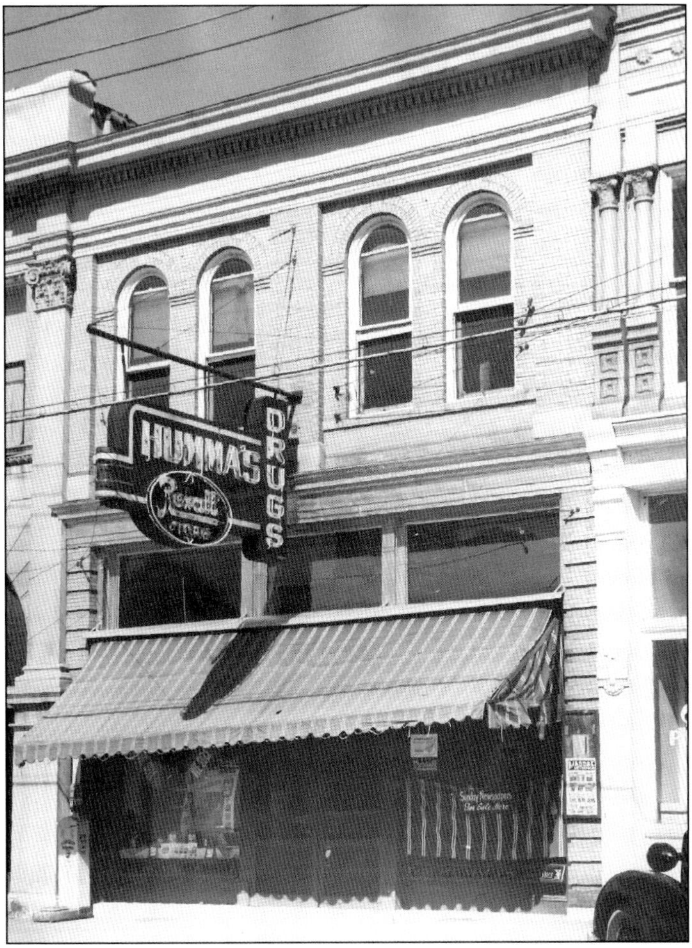

CIPS, or Central Illinois Public Service Company, delivered ice in a Model T Ford truck, as in this 1929 photograph by C.G. Hutchison. The business was located at First and Metropolis Streets after the Metropolis Ice Plant was bought by CIPS in 1927.

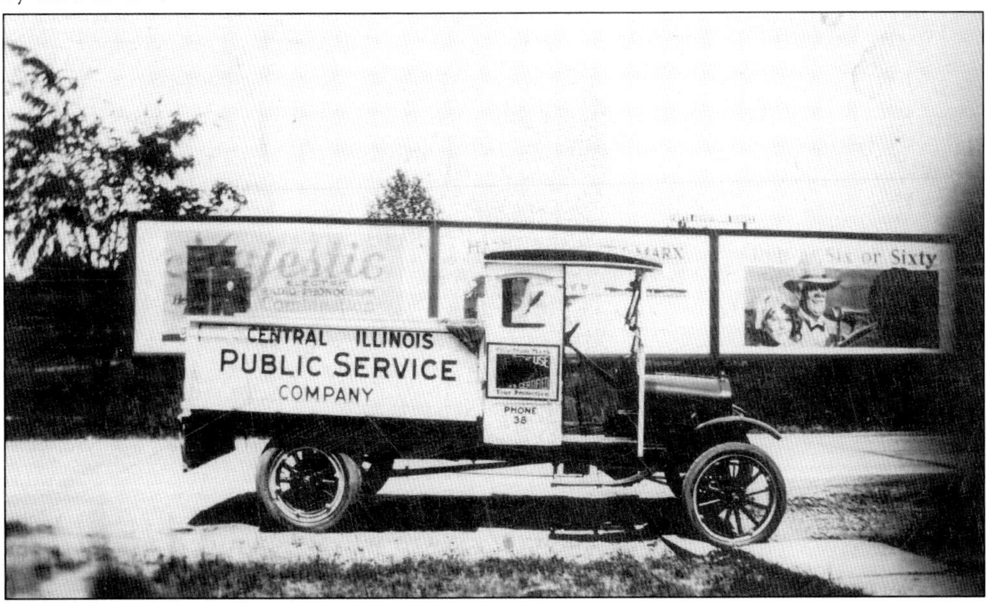

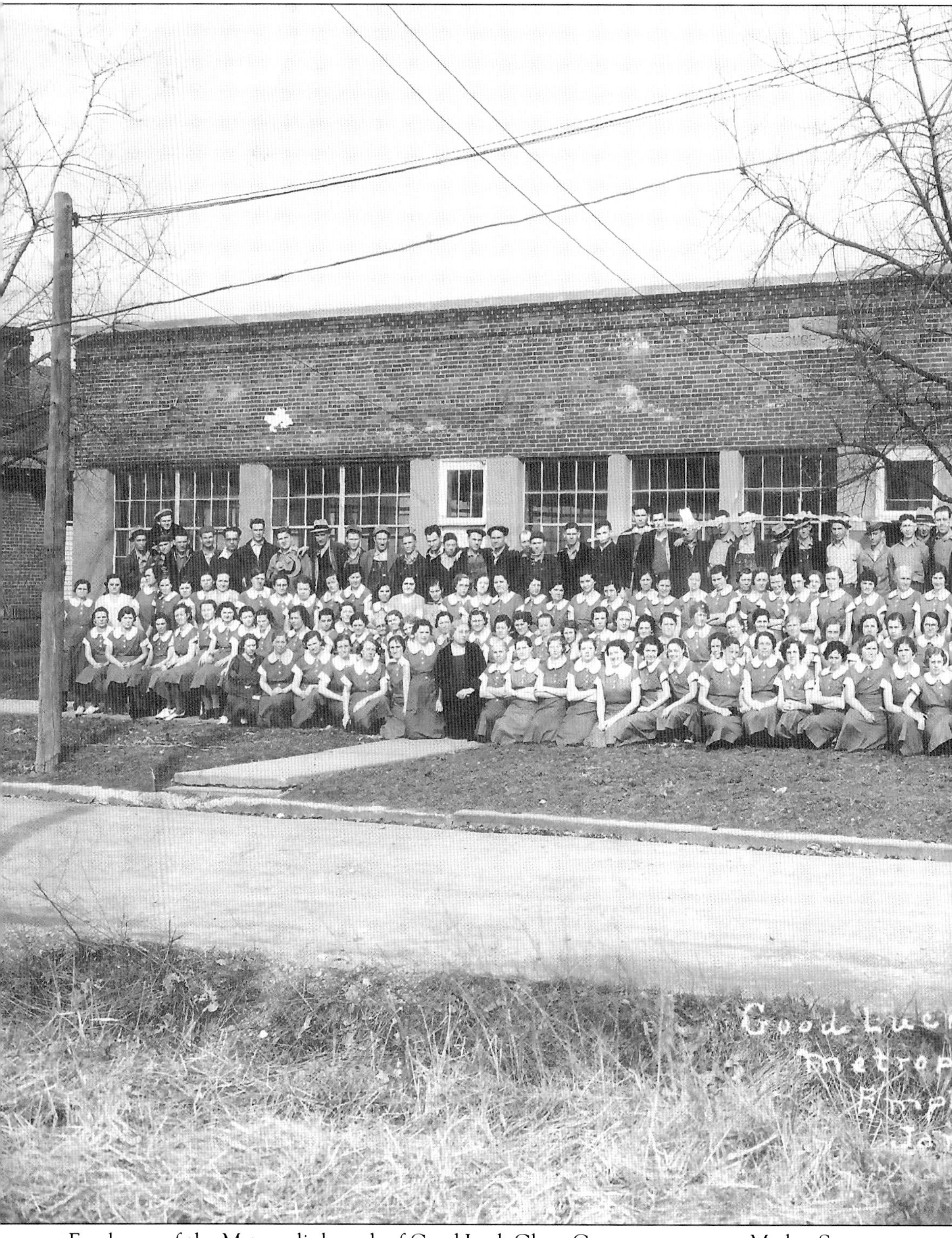

Employees of the Metropolis branch of Good Luck Glove Company, on upper Market Street at Seventeenth Street, pose for photographer Cliff Brindle on January 28, 1935. Good Luck Glove started in Columbus, Ohio, as C.T. Houghton Glove Factory in 1909, and the company's Detroit,

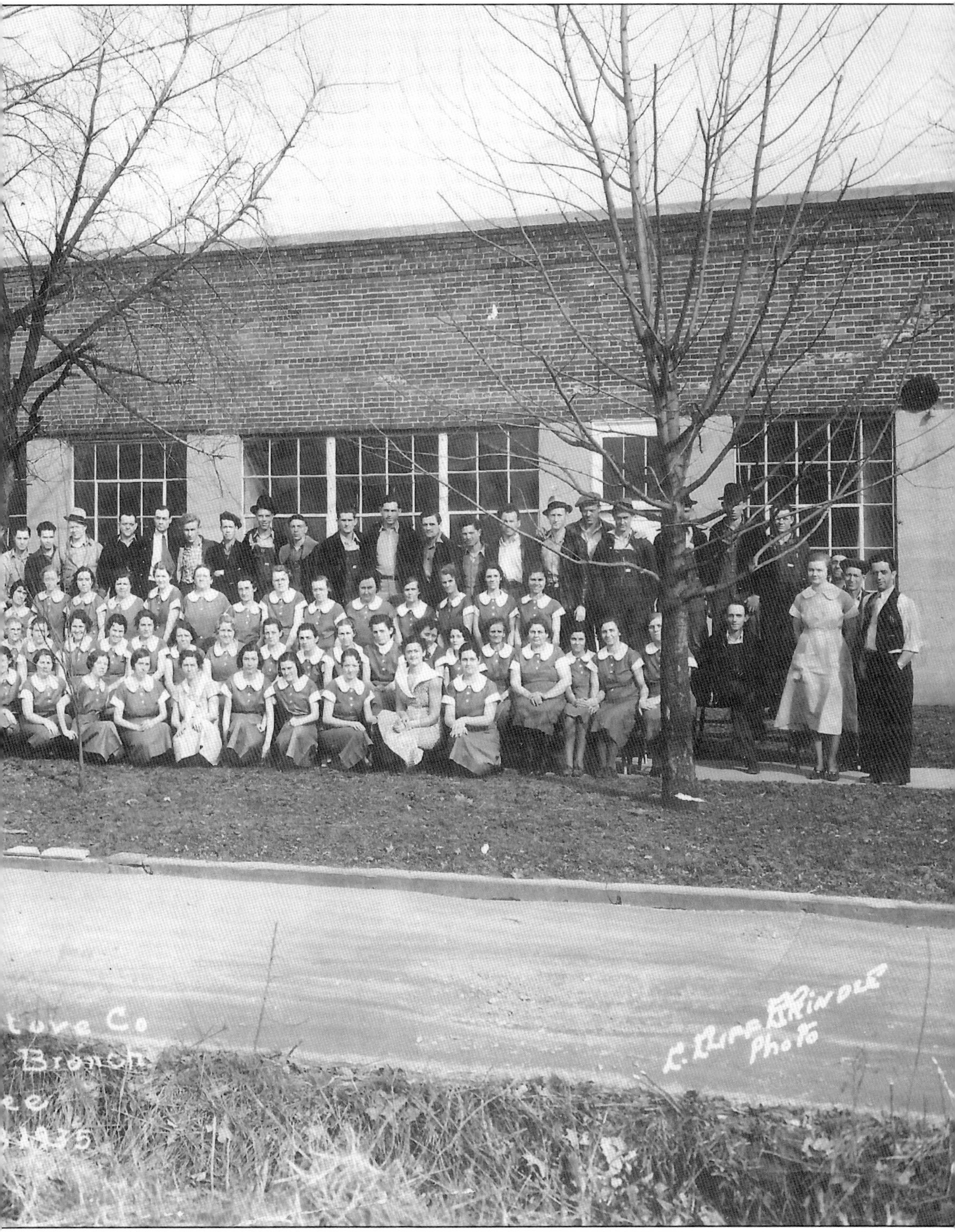

Michigan, plant was moved to Metropolis in 1916. It started with 160 girls who each earned $3.20 per day for making four dozen pair of gloves. Annual output grew to 10 million pairs. When the Carbondale, Illinois, plant closed around 1965, some employees moved to Metropolis.

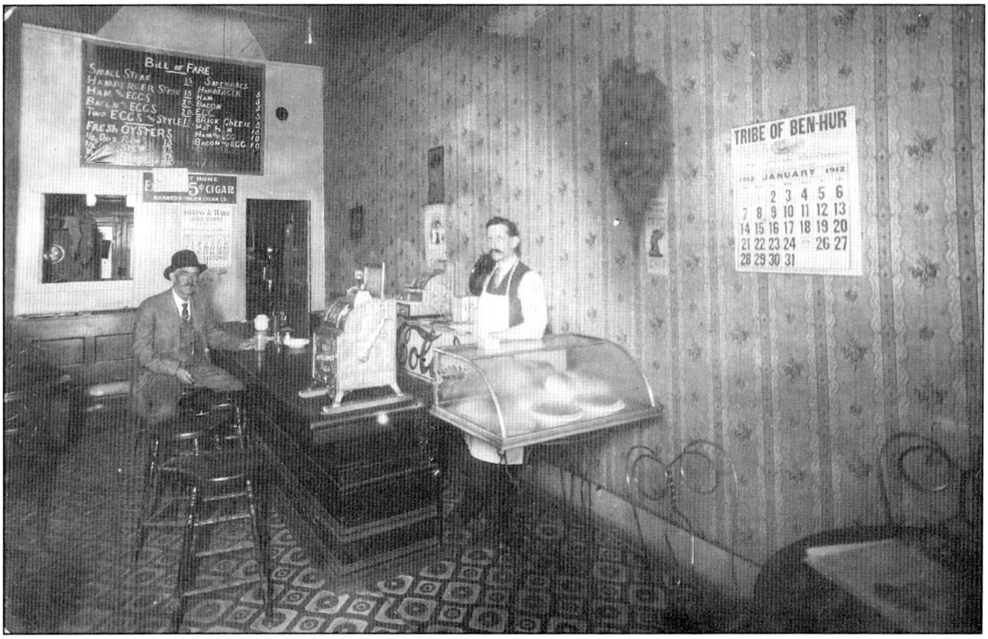

The Woodward Café on lower Ferry Street is shown in 1912. The bill of fare on the back wall shows hamberger (*sic*), ham, bacon, egg, or brick cheese sandwiches for a nickel each; raw oysters are 15¢. And, yes, they do have a good 5¢ cigar. The calendar title, "Tribe of Ben-Hur," refers to a fraternal order named after Lew Wallace's book *Ben-Hur: A Tale of the Christ*. The group had a local chapter.

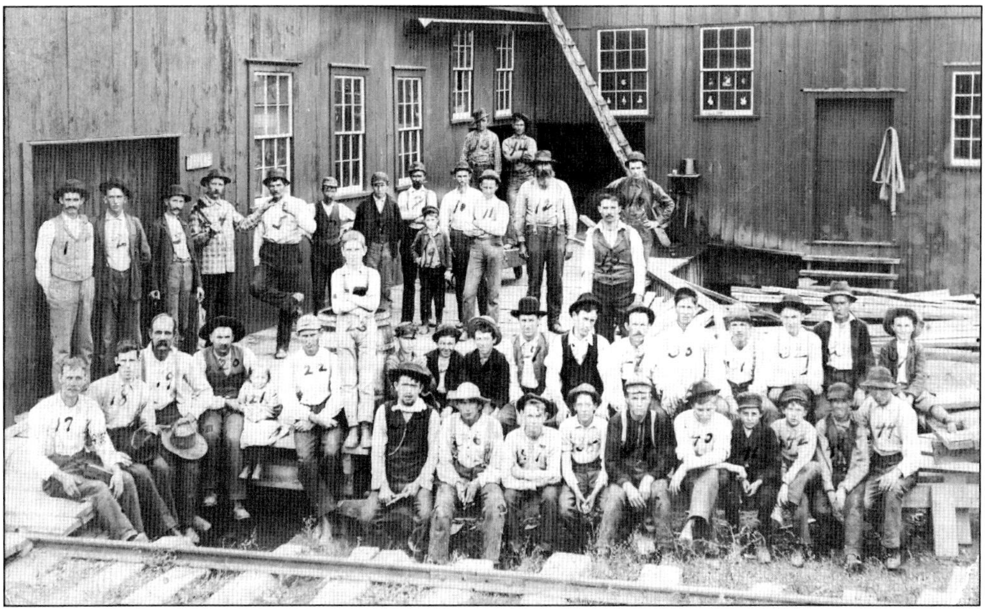

Here is a photograph from 1896 of the J.N. Roberts Mfg. Company, later known as the Roberts-Liggett Company and locally called "the box factory," since it made wooden containers. C.C. Roberts, whose house is still on the southeast corner of Metropolis and Third Streets, was the manager from 1893 to 1910. After it became the Roberts-Liggett Company, the managers were Frank B. Liggett (1910–1930) and Walter R. Liggett (1930–1948.)

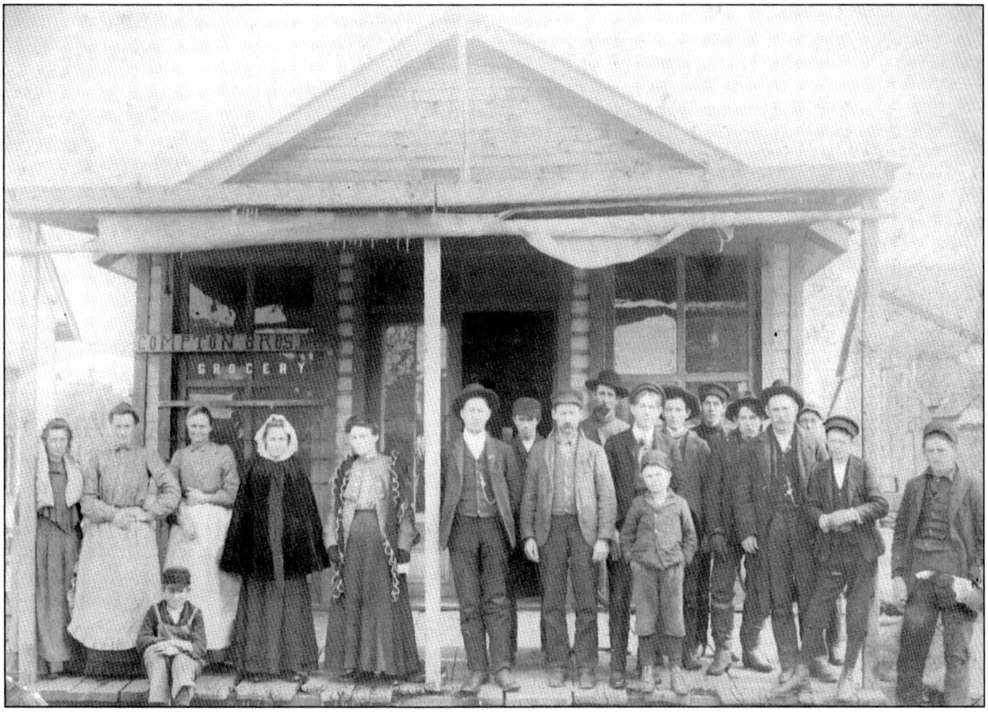

Compton's Grocery, at 212 Scott Street in East Metropolis, was owned and operated by William and Ed Compton. Formerly, it had been Rehlmeyer's Grocery. Other groceries in Metropolis during this period were Cromeen's on upper Market Street; Stalcup's on Ferry Street, between Second and Third Streets; and Barger's, which was on lower Ferry Street in the 1940s.

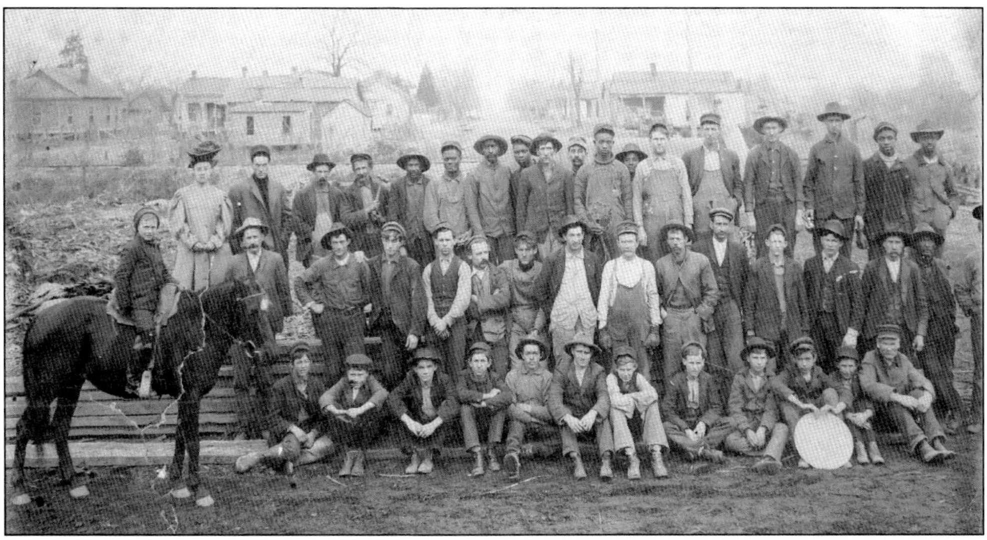

H. Rampendahl & Co. was located at the foot of Scott Street, just below First Street, in East Metropolis. A family concern founded in 1890, it manufactured barrel heads and staves and was said to have employed over 100 men, though it is clear from the workers seen in the first row that not all of them are quite men yet. Child labor was neither rare nor remarkable before the enactment of child labor laws, and several child laborers can also be seen in the box factory image on the facing page.

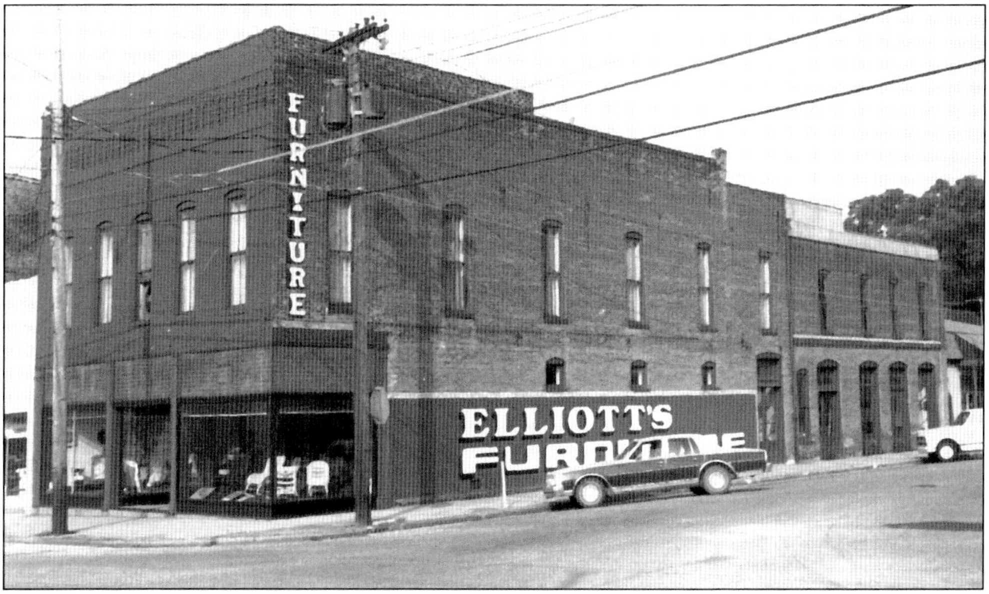

This scene is of the southwest corner of Fourth and Ferry Streets, where the Elliott family operated Elliott's Furniture for 124 years. The oldest business in Metropolis before it closed, it was placed on a list of Illinois's Centennial Businesses in 1984. The location was sold in 1992 and is now the home of Willy Jak's, a restaurant and bar. Like other furniture stores at the time, Elliott's also sold caskets and did undertaking in its early years. (Courtesy *Metropolis Planet*.)

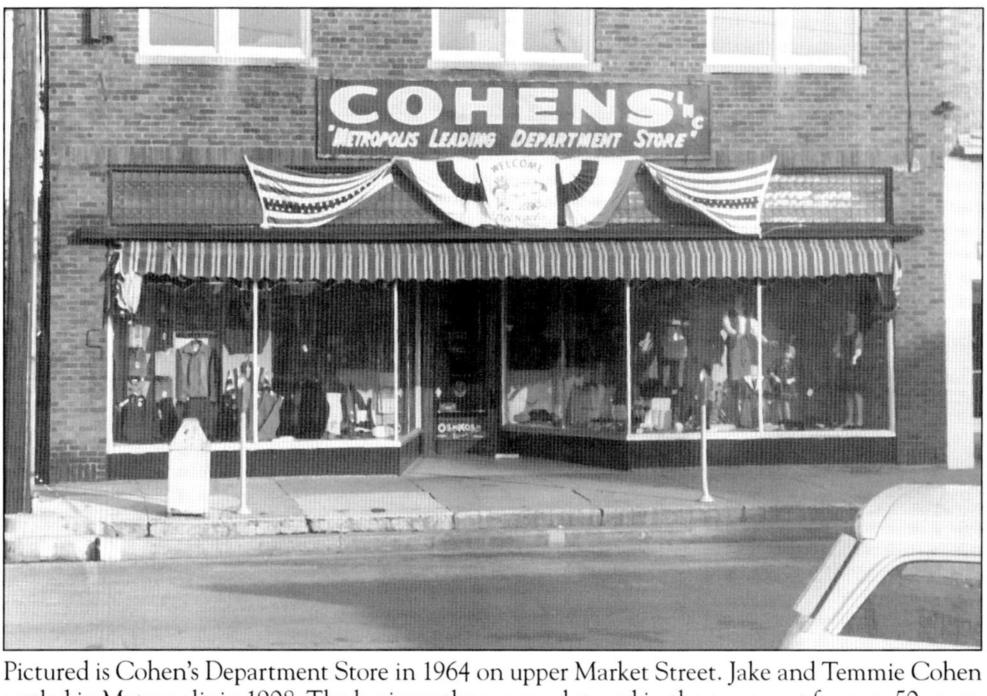

Pictured is Cohen's Department Store in 1964 on upper Market Street. Jake and Temmie Cohen settled in Metropolis in 1908. The business they opened stayed in the same spot for over 50 years. Only age and illness forced the daughters to close the store some time after they had taken it over from their parents. In 2012, this is, and has been for years, the location of Farley's Cafeteria.

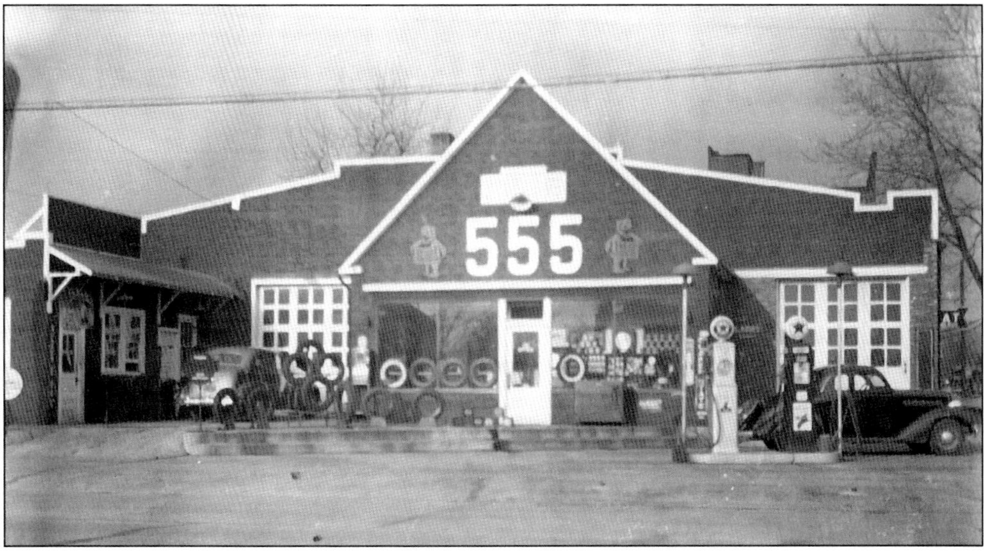

This c. 1937 photograph shows Bonifield Brothers Truck Lines, located on the southwest corner of Seventh and Ferry Streets at the 555 Texaco service station. According to local lore, the station originally was named 666 Texaco, until protests by customers had the brothers change the sign to 555. Today, the address is 619. Brothers Fred and Alfred later joined with brothers Reuben and Clarence, and the line was moved to Carbondale in the 1960s. Sadly, it has been defunct for many years. At its zenith, the line had terminals from Chicago to Paducah and St. Louis to Evansville, in southwestern Indiana.

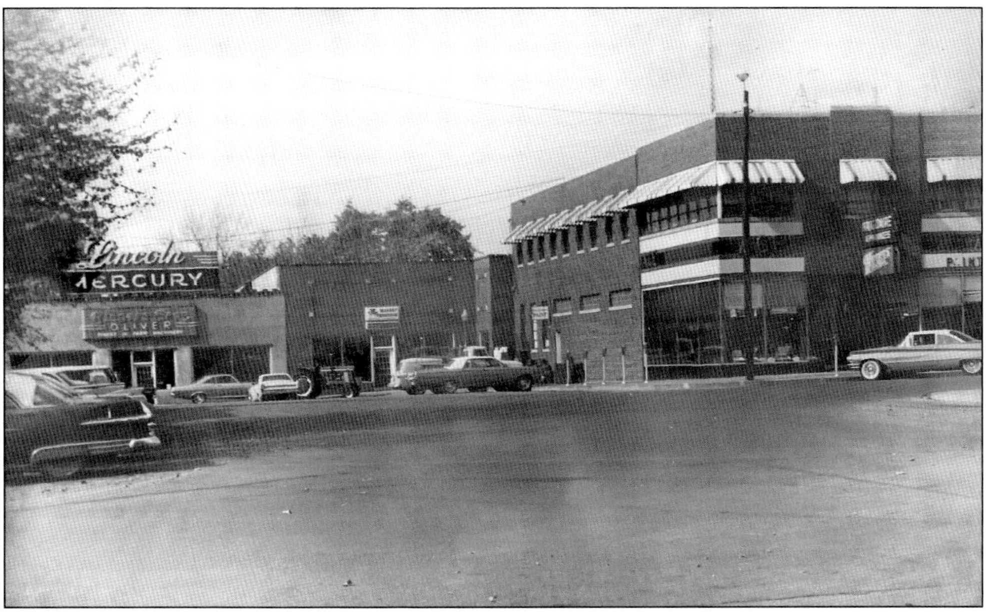

A typical business partnership in Metropolis was that of the Hinner brothers (Ed and Noah). At the northeast corner of the square in the 400 and 500 blocks of Market Street, the Hinners operated a Lincoln-Mercury dealership, dealt in Massey-Ferguson farm equipment, and ran a hardware and appliance store. The hardware store building is now the home of the Super Museum, and the site of the car dealership and farm equipment store is occupied by the Massac County Law Enforcement and Detention Center.

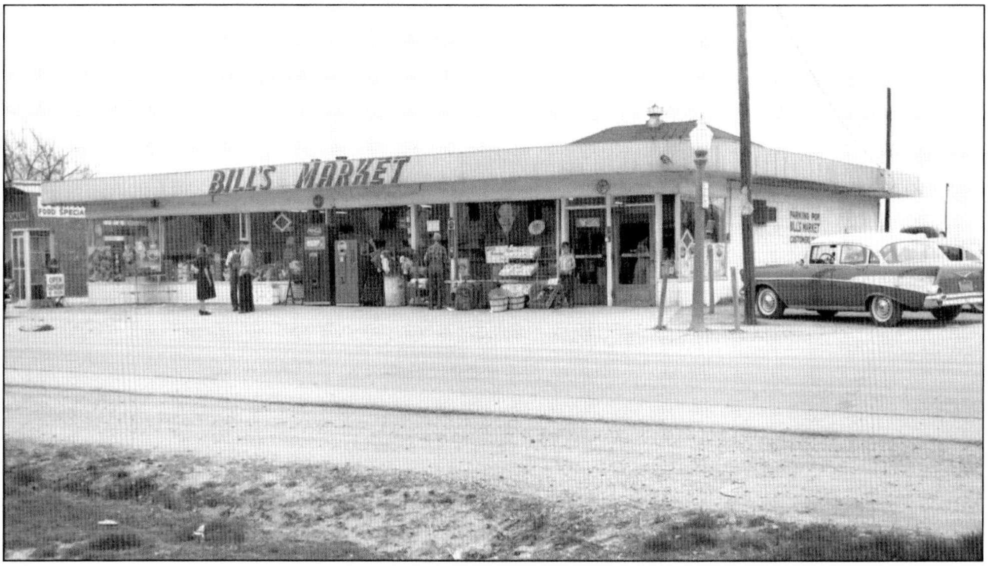

By the 1950s, shopping habits had changed, and small downtown grocery stores gave way to larger, self-contained supermarkets, such as Bill's Market, which, as the sign on the left indicates, was even open on Sundays (though not until noon).

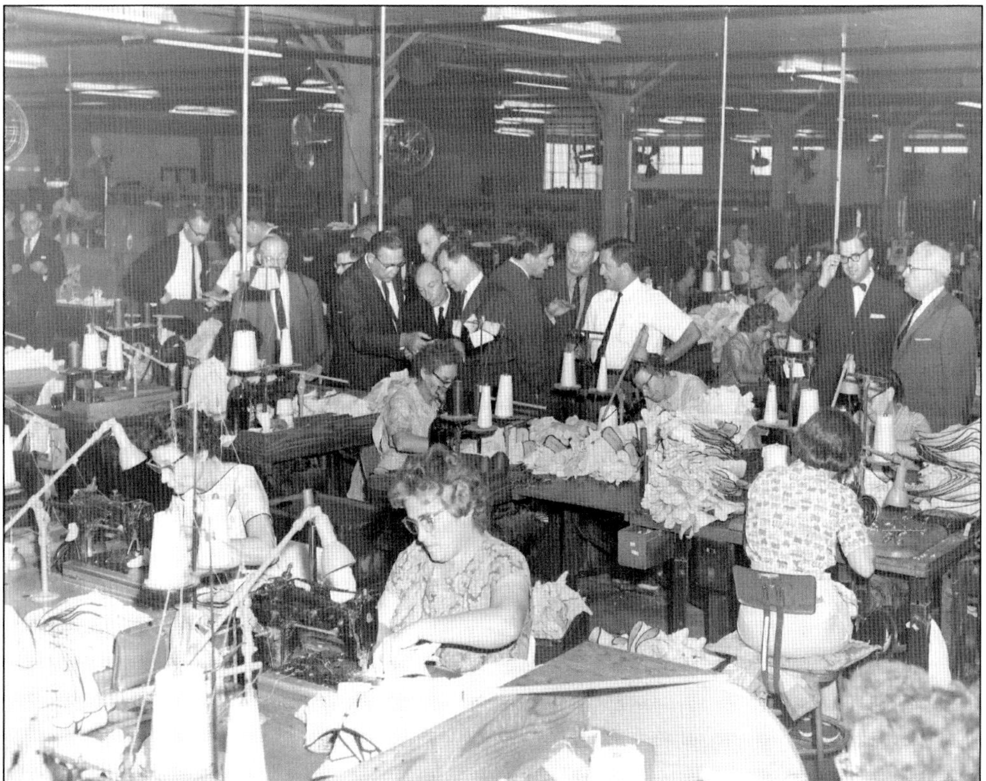

This is a look inside the Good Luck Glove Company factory in the early 1960s. A group from Norway is seen touring with sales representatives and co-owner Bernard Lurie. The business was sold in the late 1970s and became the Nationwide Glove Company. (Courtesy *Metropolis Planet*.)

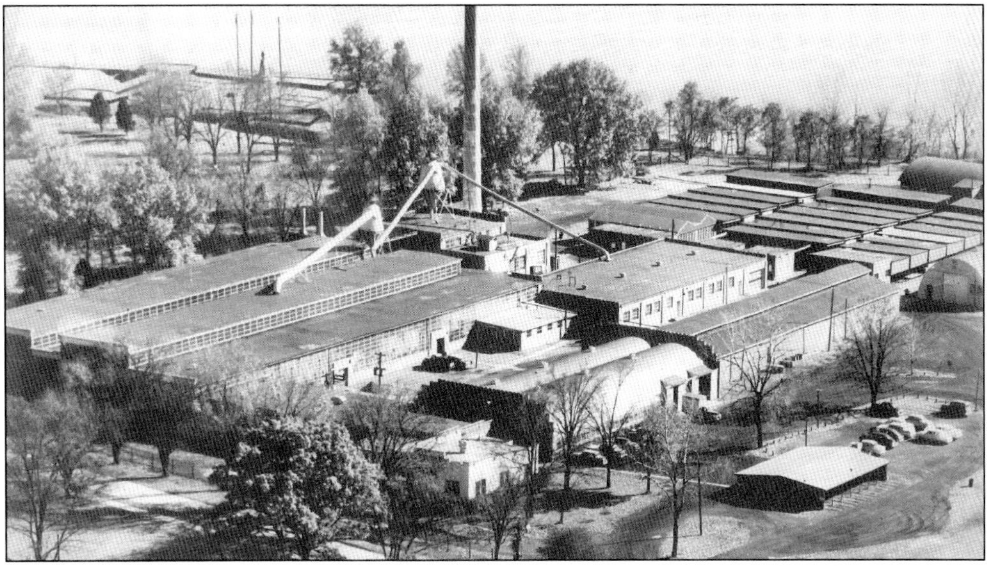

In 1903 the Metropolis Bending Company bought the site of the Cleveland Bending Company, next to Fort Massac, where it made wooden parts for buggies and, later, automobiles. Through the 1940s and 1950s, the company manufactured infant furniture, card tables and chairs, house trim, and, during the war, liners for aircraft gas tanks. In the background, the *George Rogers Clark* statue and flagpoles can be seen on fort grounds.

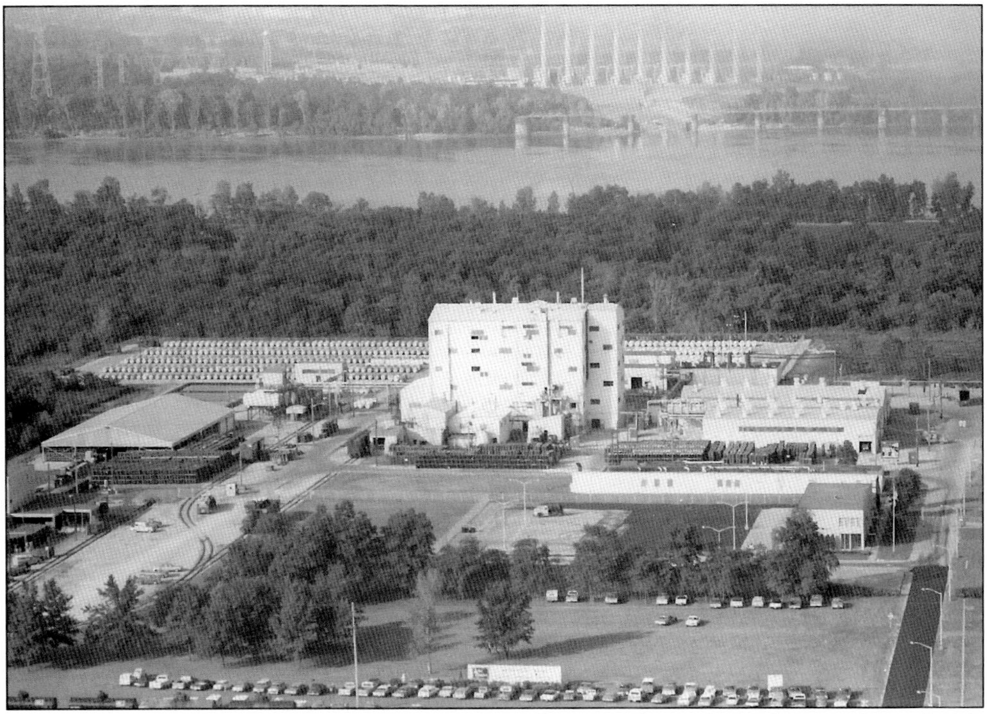

Allied Chemical Corporation, about a mile north of Metropolis, is shown here in the mid-20th century. Built in the late 1950s to fulfill a government contract to process uranium ore, the company now operates privately under the Honeywell name. In the background is the Martin Marietta plant.

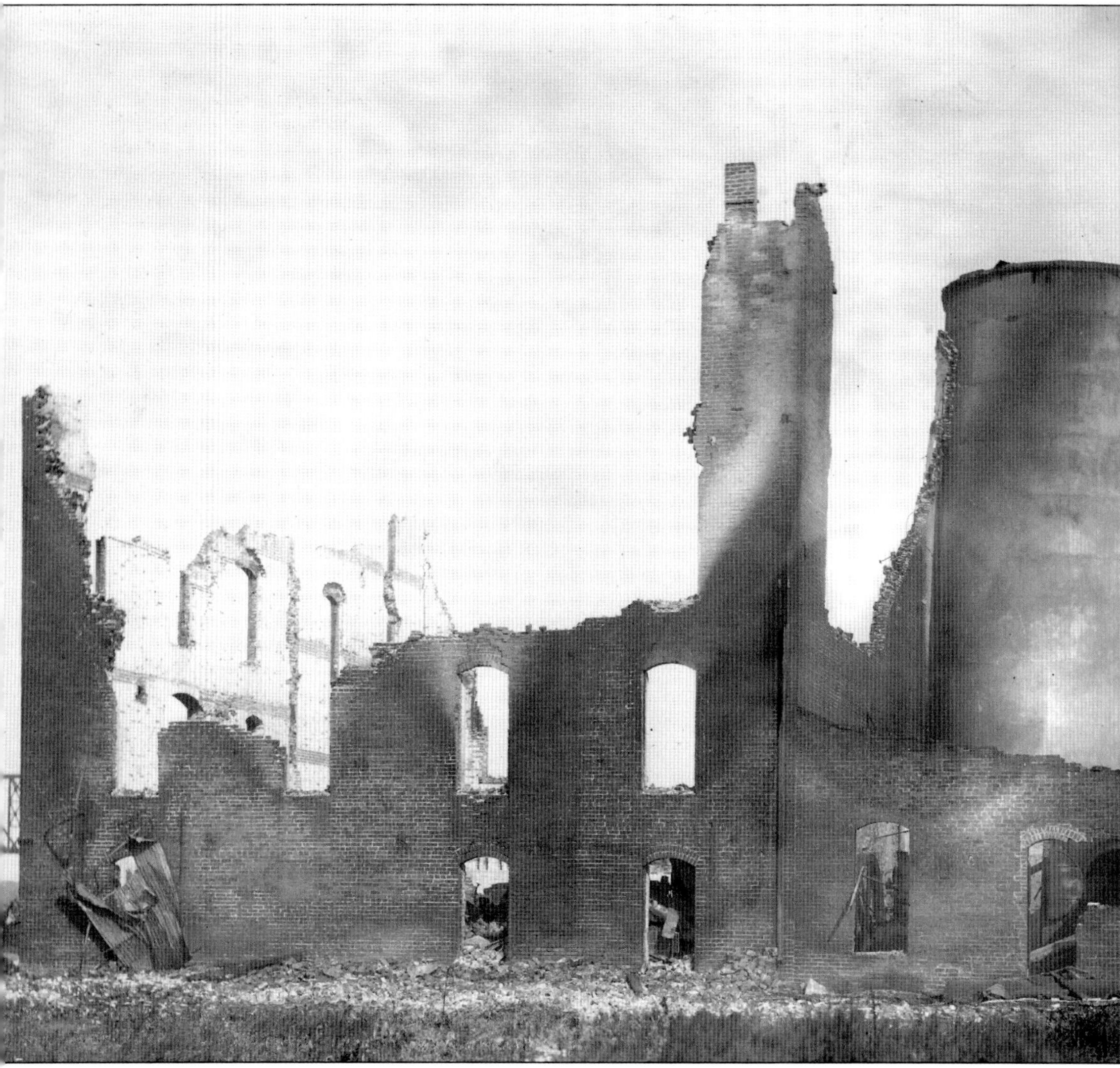

August Quante sold his flour mill in 1919, then died in 1922. In 1932 the four-story mill suffered a disastrous fire, after which, due to increasingly difficult times, the decision was made by the new owners not to rebuild. The mill was at the foot of Girard Street, near the Metropolis Power House on the Ohio River, and was replaced by a grain elevator.

Five

DISASTERS

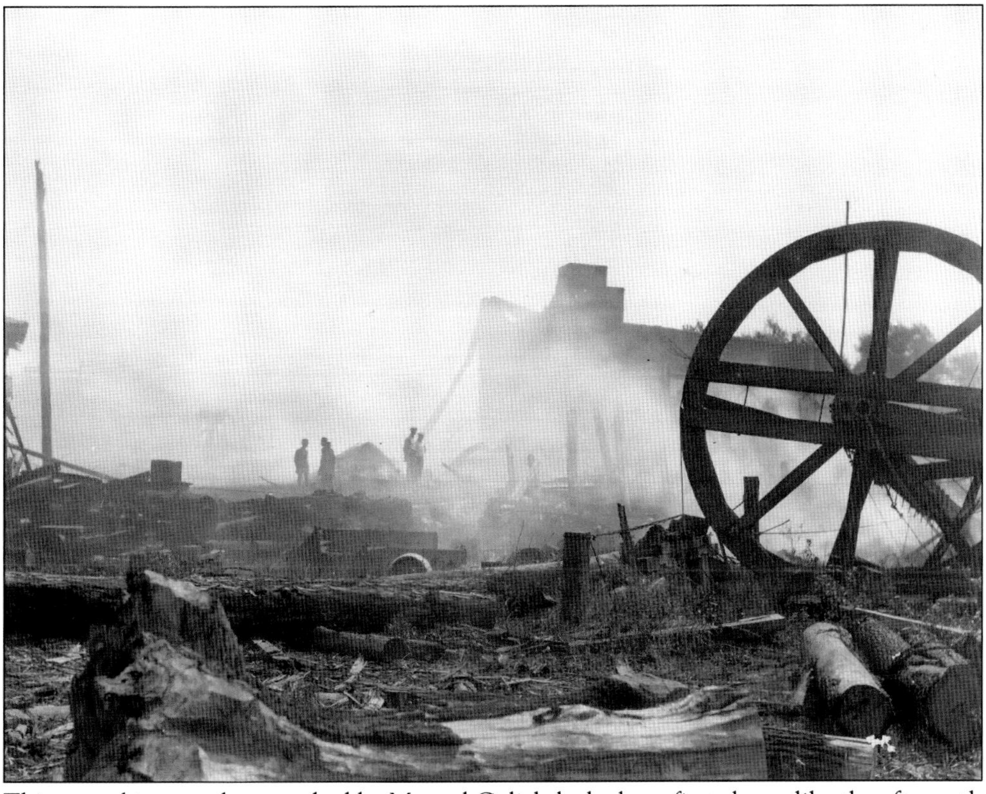

This surreal image, photographed by Manuel Golightly, looks at first glance like the aftermath of some 18th-century war zone but is, in fact, the smoking remains of the Artman Lumber Mill, which burned in 1928. E.C. and J.E. Artman constructed the mill in 1912–1913 and also rebuilt it after the fire.

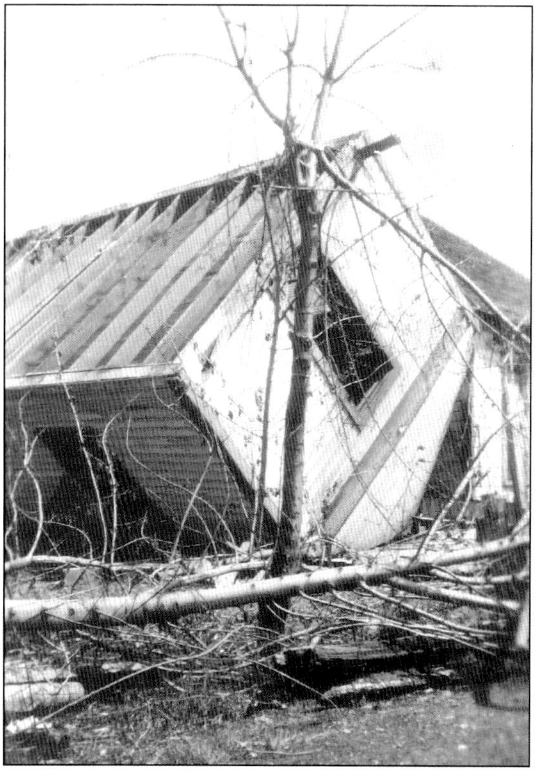

Tornado damage in 1935, near the Empire Mill, at Ninth and Metropolis Streets, is seen in this photograph. It is most probably north of Tenth Street in the residential section.

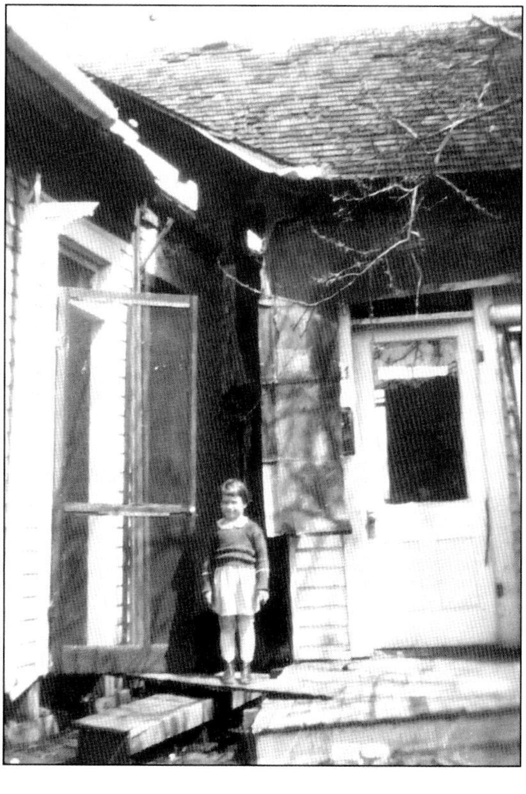

This photograph, also taken near the Empire Mill, at Ninth and Metropolis Streets, shows a child standing by the front door of a badly damaged house after the 1935 tornado. While still in the residential section, the exact location is not known, but happily, though the child is not identified, she is alive and unhurt.

At Seventh and Market Streets, the Chevrolet dealership was damaged after the devastating cyclone struck on March 25, 1935, at 3:30 p.m.

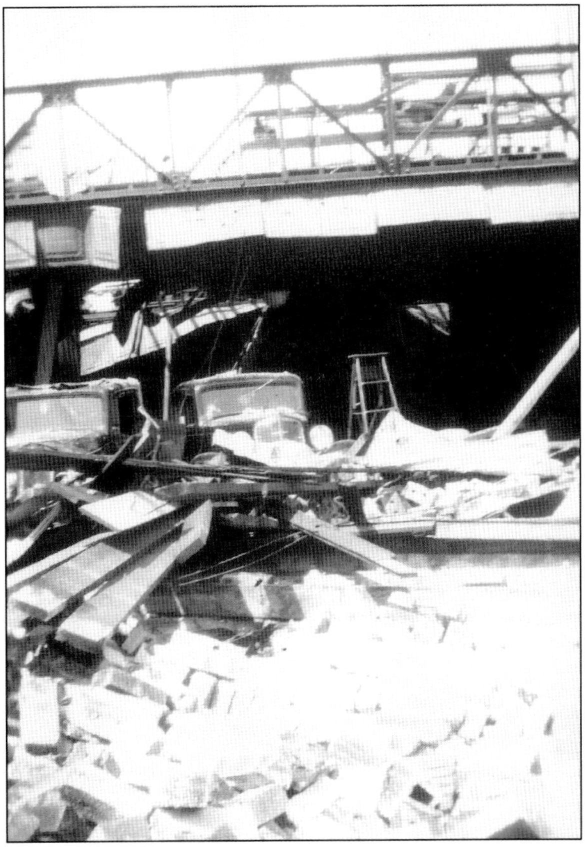

The damage from the March 1935 tornado was extensive. The injuries were few, but one death is one too many. Sam Abell, the owner of the Chevrolet agency, died when a falling beam struck him as he attempted to leave the building. This scene is at the rear of the dealership, where onlookers gathered to see the damage.

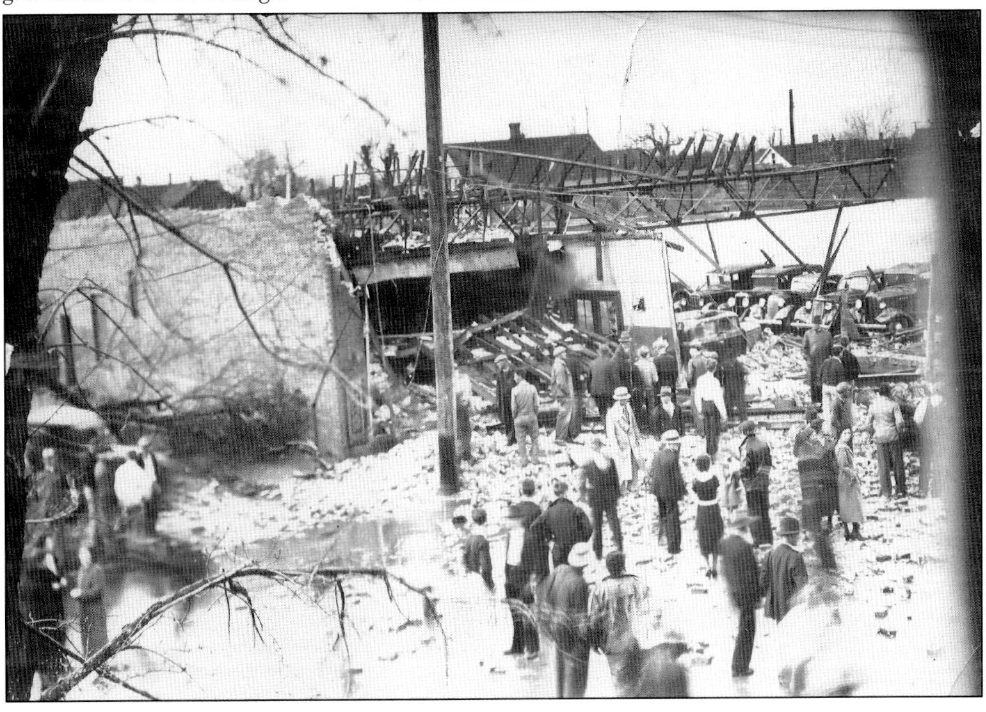

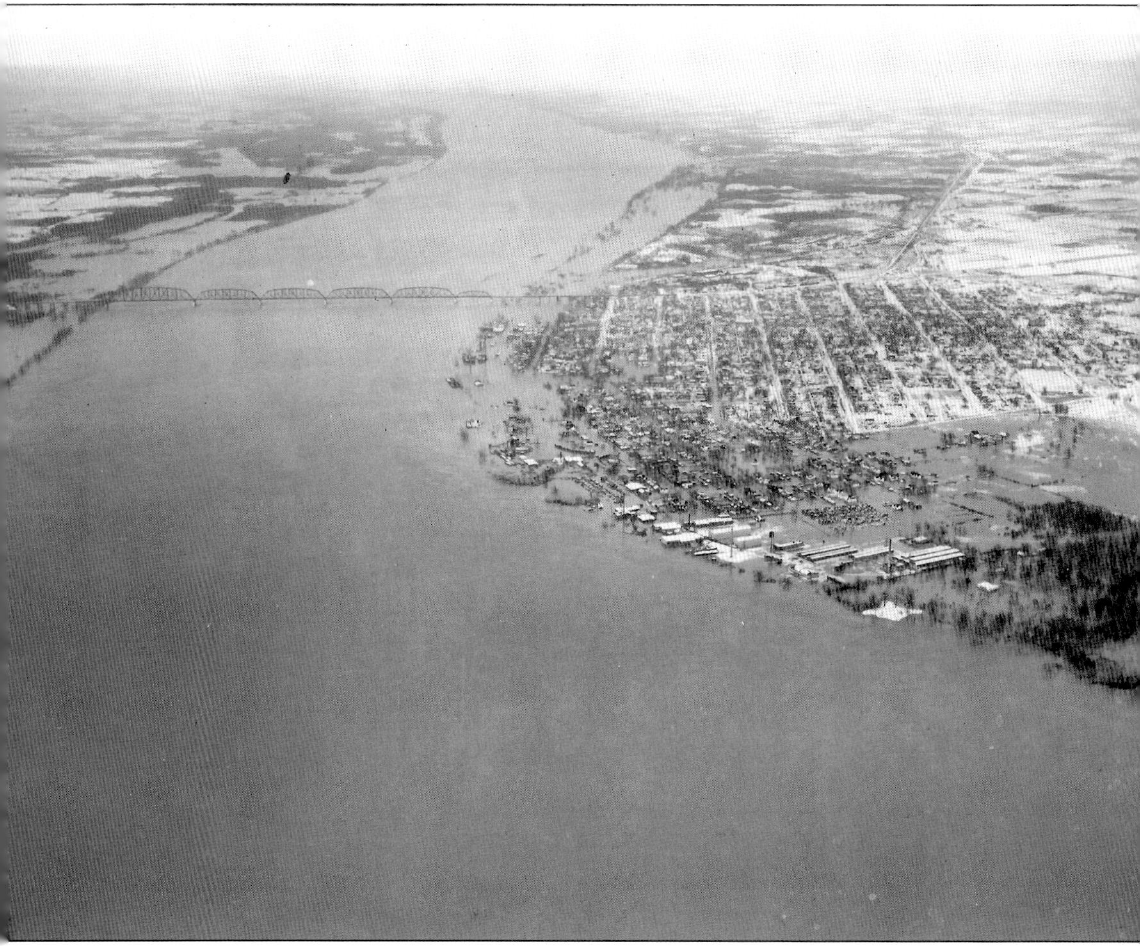

This aerial photograph, taken by the US Army Corps of Engineers, shows the extent of flooding as of January 25, 1937. It displays the severity of the inundation, which at its worst covered much of East Metropolis, as well as Washington Park, extending about two thirds of the way up Metropolis Street toward Fourth Street. The flooding along the Ohio River that year was so severe that it caused Shawneetown, in Gallatin County to the northeast of Metropolis, to be relocated.

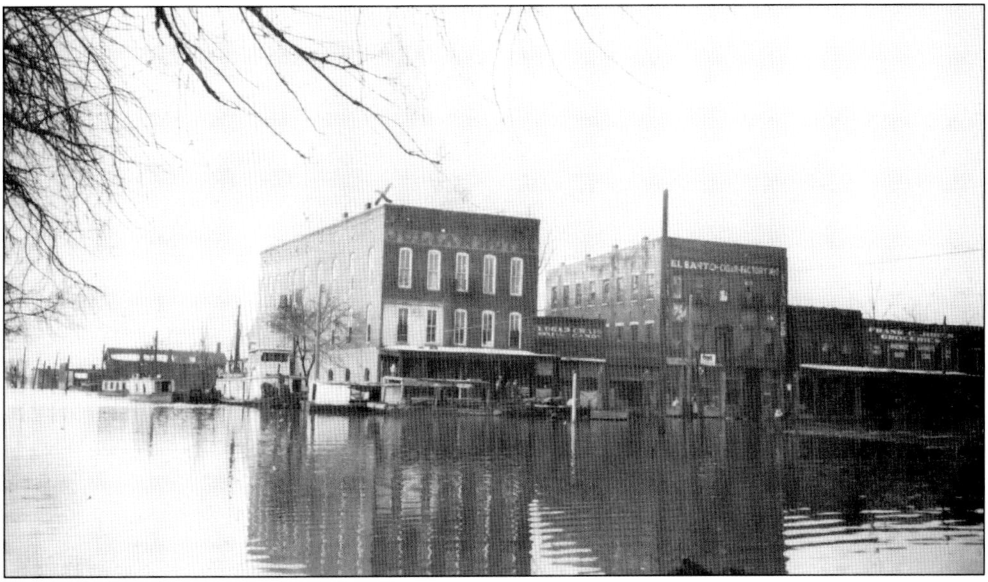

This photograph shows the 1937 flood at Third and Metropolis Streets. The Julian Hotel (left), Edgar Craig Candy (center), and El Barto Cigar Company are shown with water covering the streets to such an extent that boats could go up and down them. To the left (just off camera) was the home of C.C. Roberts, which is still standing in 2012.

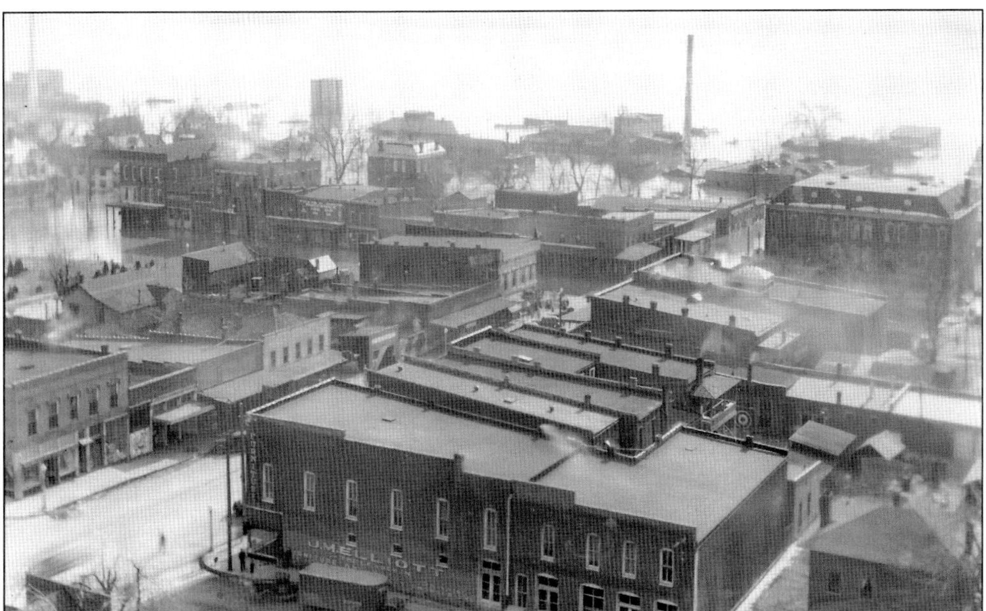

The 1937 flood makes its way up toward Fourth Street on Ferry Street. The building in the lower center is Elliott's Furniture. The photograph was taken from the old water tower, located between Market and Ferry Streets and Fourth and Fifth Streets.

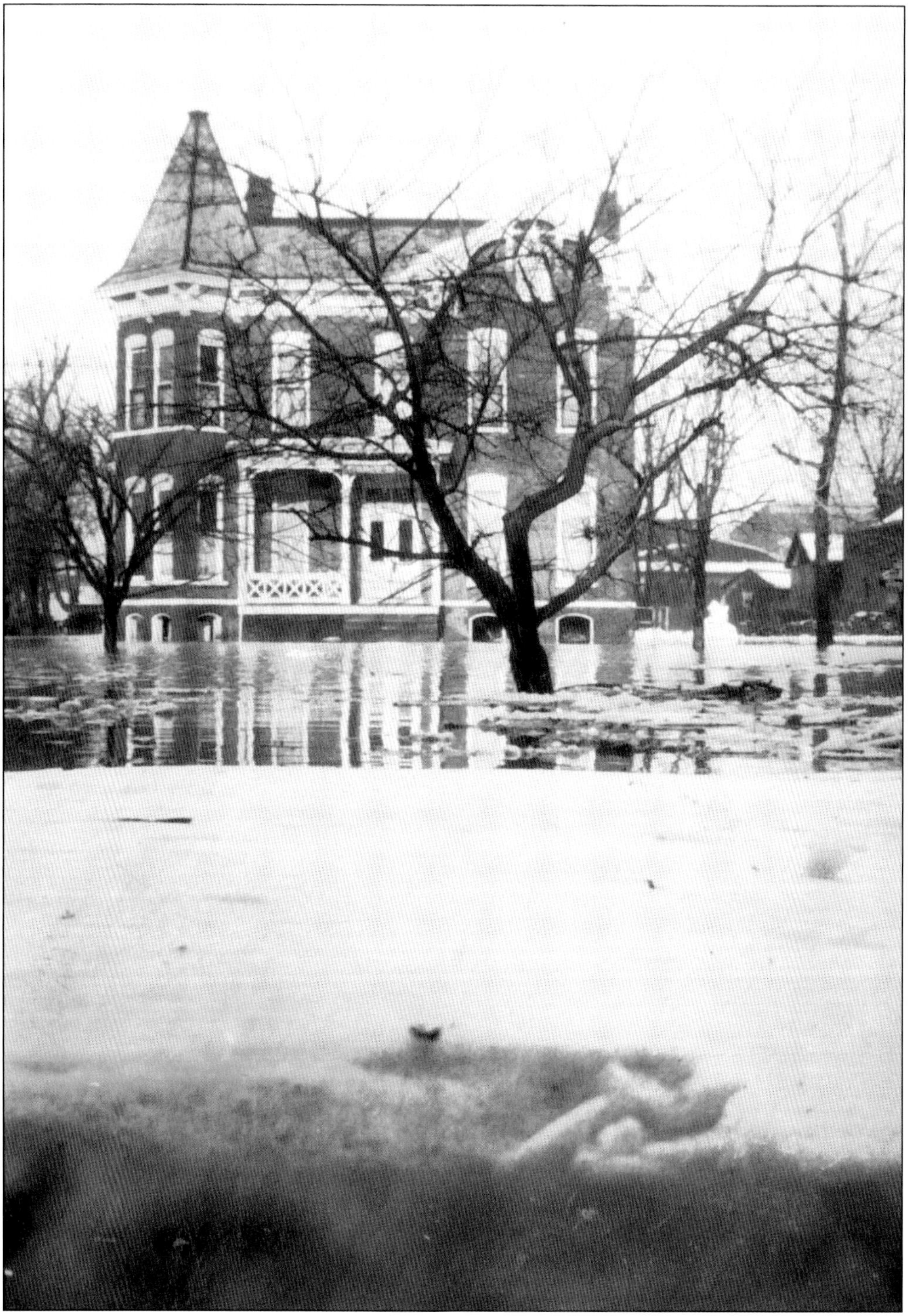

As can be seen in this photograph of the Quante house, heavy snows had hit the area before the January 1937 flood. Besides being a beautiful house, its location causes it to be frequently threatened by floods. These two factors make it one of Metropolis's most photographed landmarks This year, it was in more danger than usual.

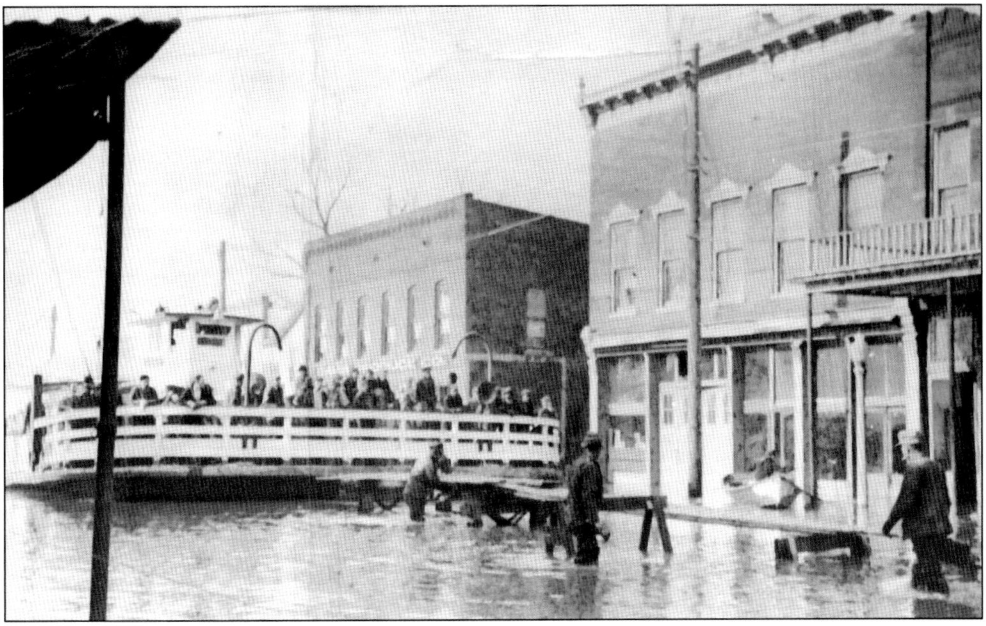

This scene shows a possible rescue of residents of Brookport, Illinois, which was devastated by the 1937 flood. The area is lower Ferry Street, south of Third Street on the west side, where the water was so high that, even loaded with passengers, boats could travel freely. The site is just north of where Harrah's riverboat is today. (Photograph by Cardinal Studio.)

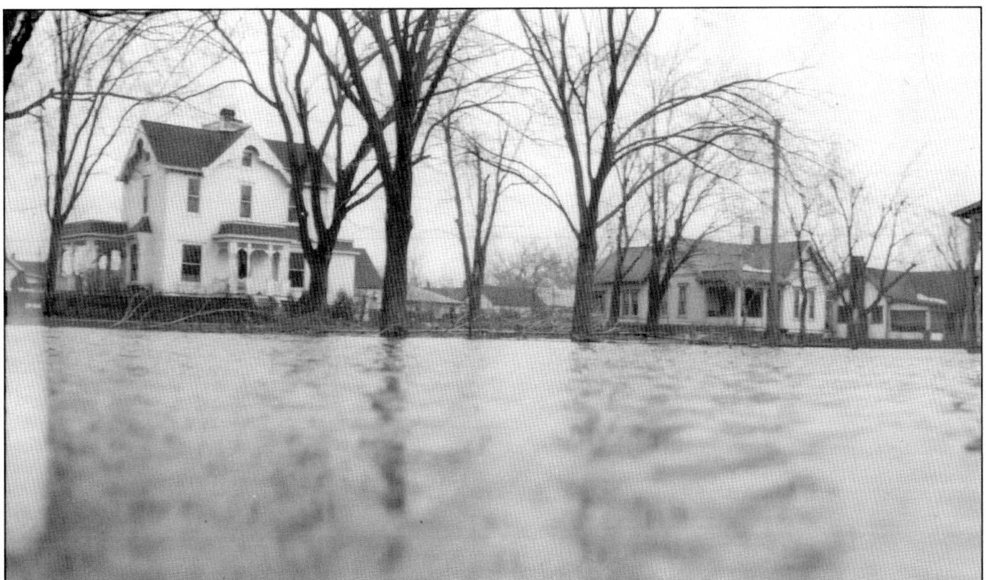

The Armstrong, Speckman, and Morris homes, located at Sixth and Catherine Streets, are pictured here amidst looming floodwaters on January 31, 1937, two days before the flood's crest.

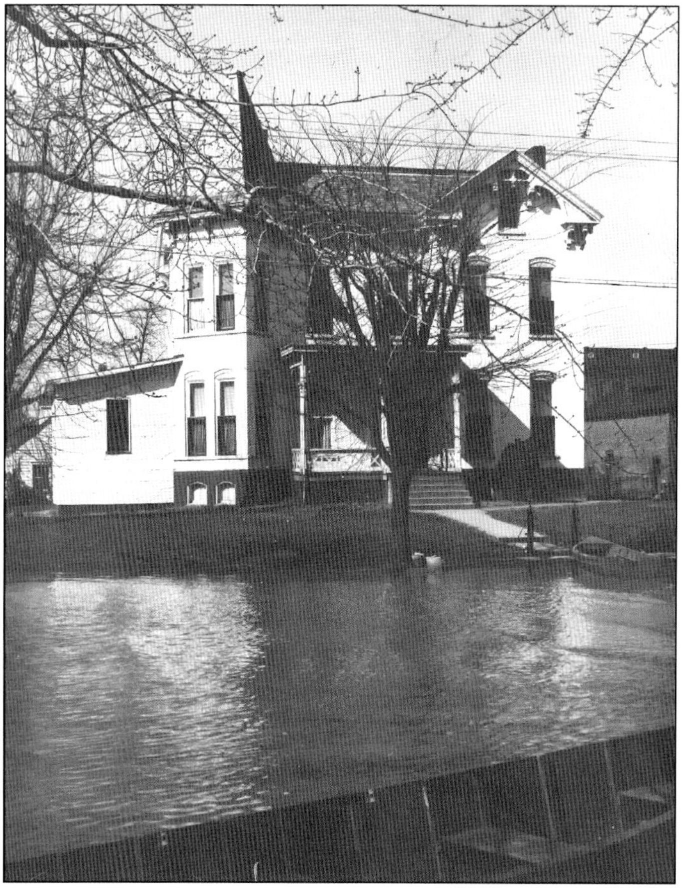

This shows the Quante house when it was Fisher Hospital during the 1952 flood.

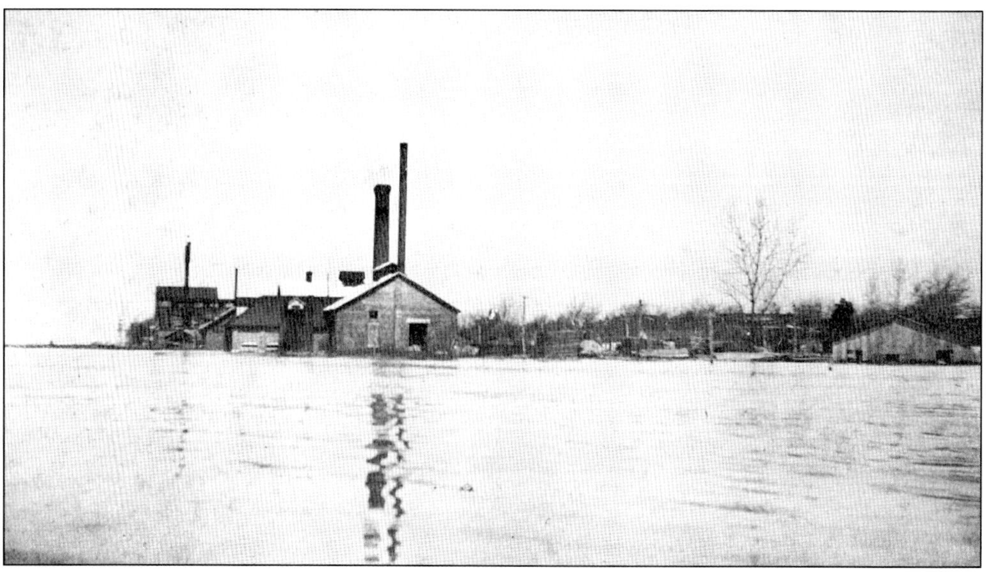

The power plant is seen in the middle of floodwaters in 1937. The plant had a brick wall all the way around it that, when properly sandbagged and braced, helped keep out the worst flooding. Coal was brought in by boat, and amazingly, Metropolis never lost power throughout the ordeal.

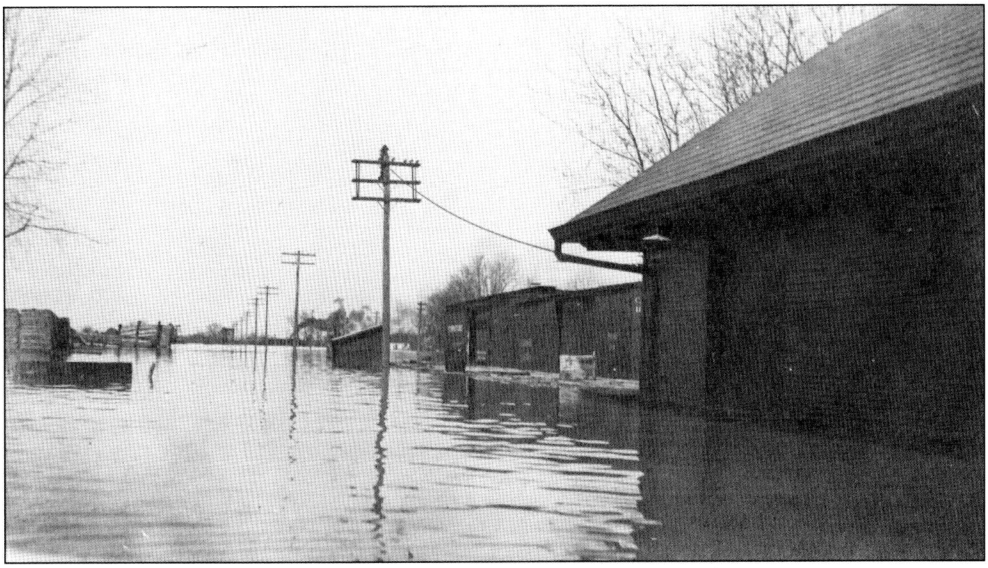

The tracks by the depot are impassable in this photograph from the 1937 flood.

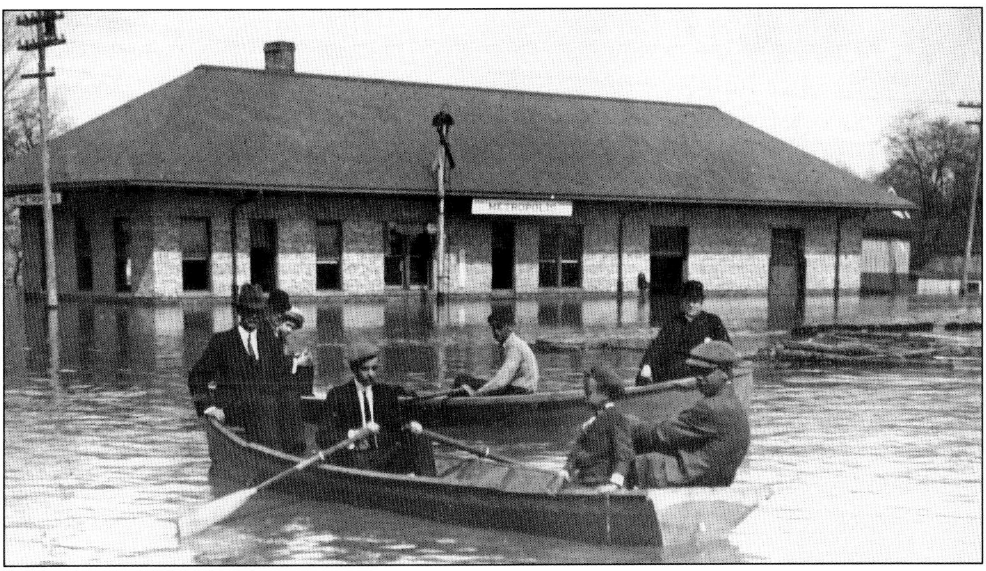

The first flood for which extensive photographs survive was in 1912–1913, and this picture of the Metropolis Illinois Central Depot shows the depth of the water. Alfred Cutting is shown seated in the bow of the boat, in the front. Owner of one of the boat works in East Metropolis, he had donated a number of rowboats to help citizens cope with the flooding. It is said that Martha Beideck, age 24, gave birth to a daughter on April 15, 1913, in an Alfred Cutting rowboat.

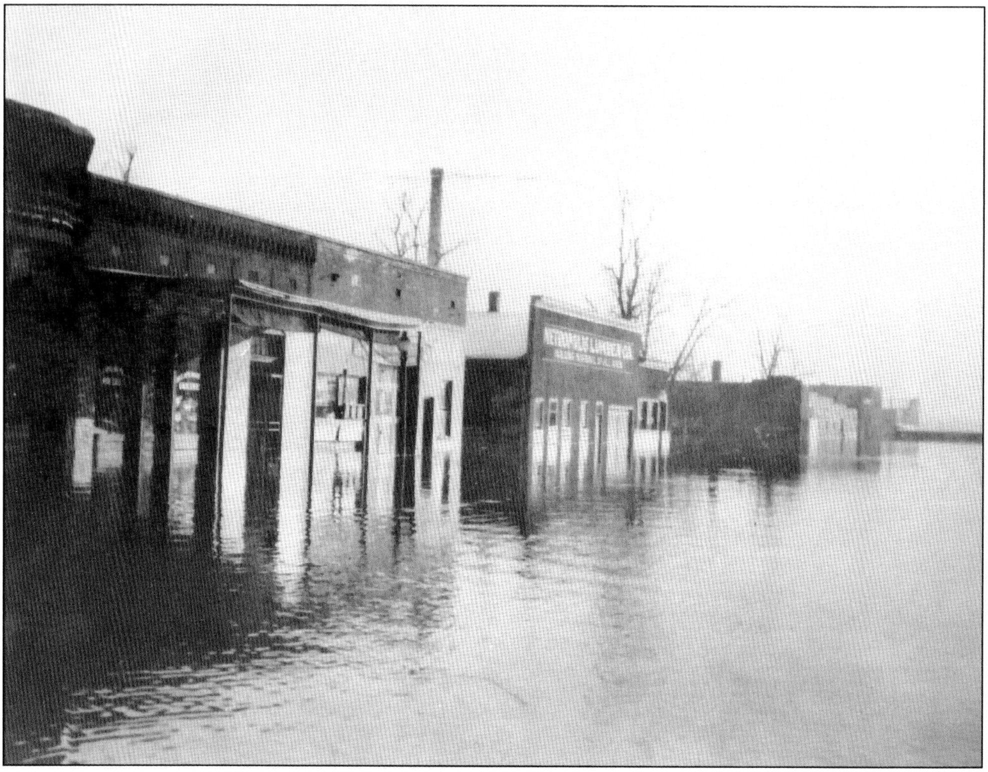

This view, looking southeast, shows the Metropolis Lumber Company in the 1937 flood on Ferry Street, south of Third Street. (Photograph by Cardinal Studios.)

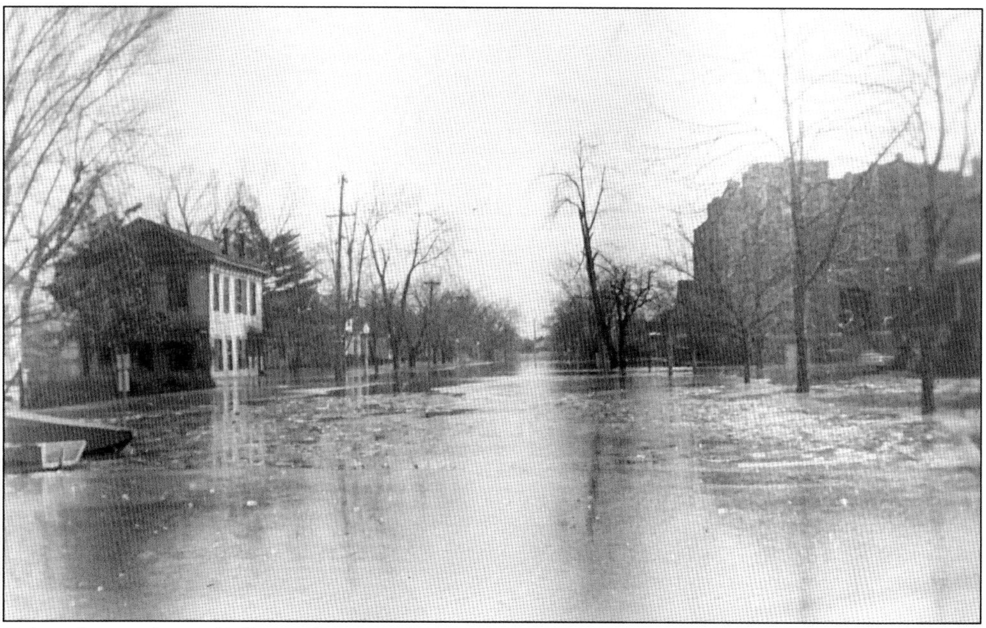

Taken during the 1937 flood, this view faces east from Fifth Street at Catherine Street, with the First Christian Church on the right. The old seminary is on the left; the site is home to a Dairy Queen in 2012.

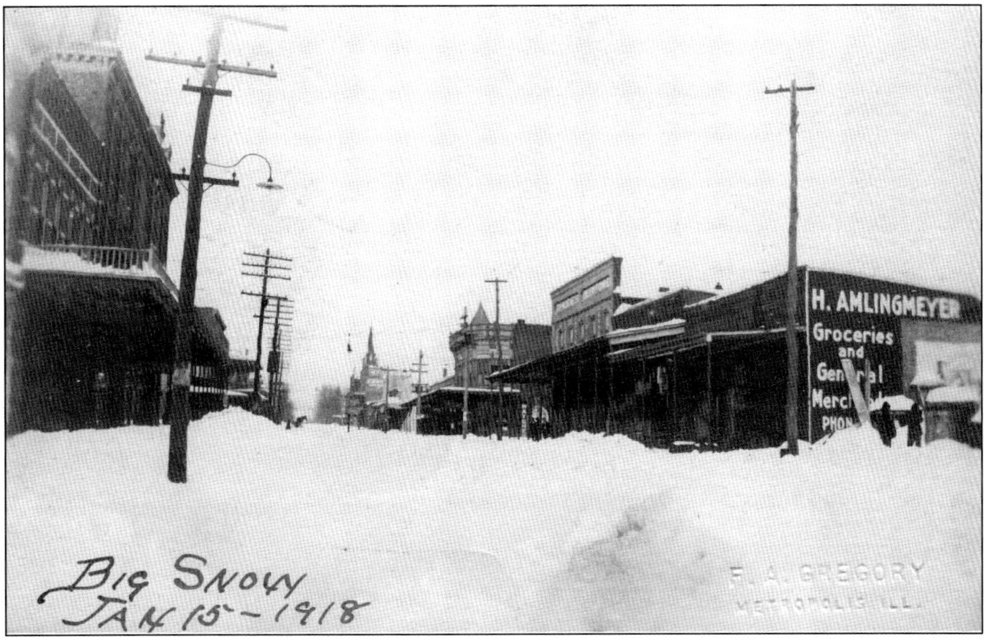

January 15, 1918 was long remembered as the "Big Snow," as stated on one of a series of postcards put out by F.A. Gregory's studio. The view looks north on Ferry Street from Second Street, with Amlingmeyer's Grocery and General Merchandise store in the foreground, followed by the Fritts Building, the New Central Hotel, and the spire of the First Methodist Church in the background.

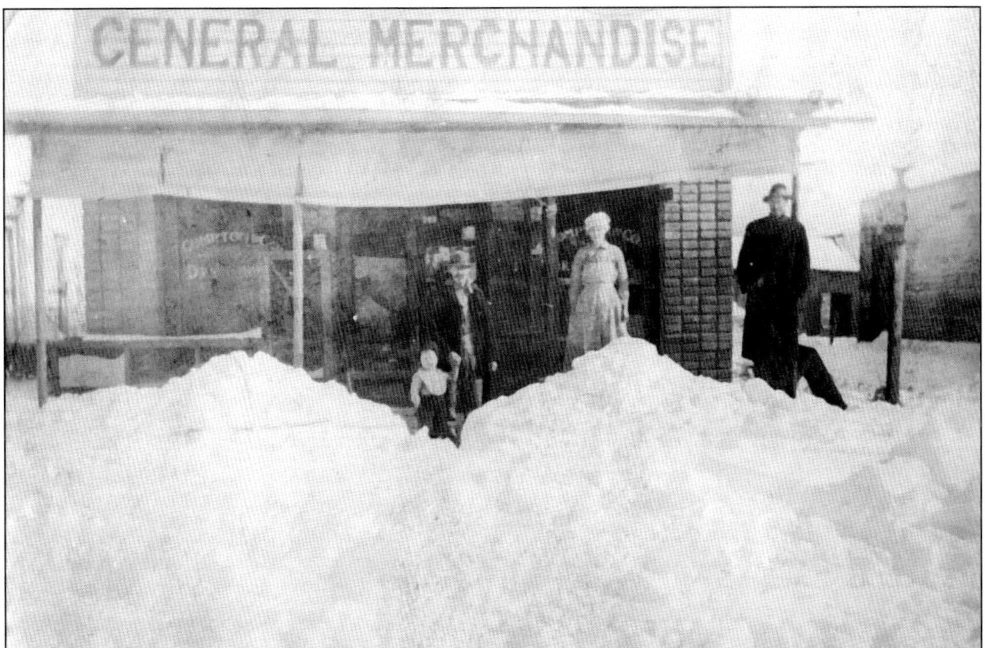

In 1918, teams of horses, rather than trucks, were used to plow snow from the streets, but in this picture it seems the job was completed just fine, as Compton's General Merchandise store appears open for business.

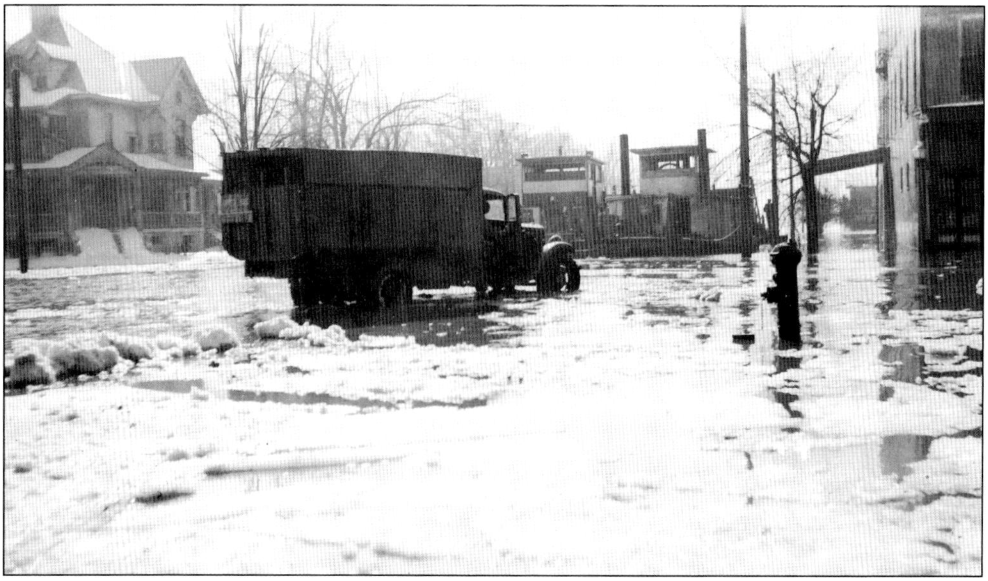

With boats already on Metropolis Street, the flood of 1937 is seen here before it reached its maximum height. The floodwaters rose another foot before they began to recede. One can see the C.C. Roberts house to the left at the southeast corner of Third and Metropolis Streets. (Photograph by Rosalie Whittman.)

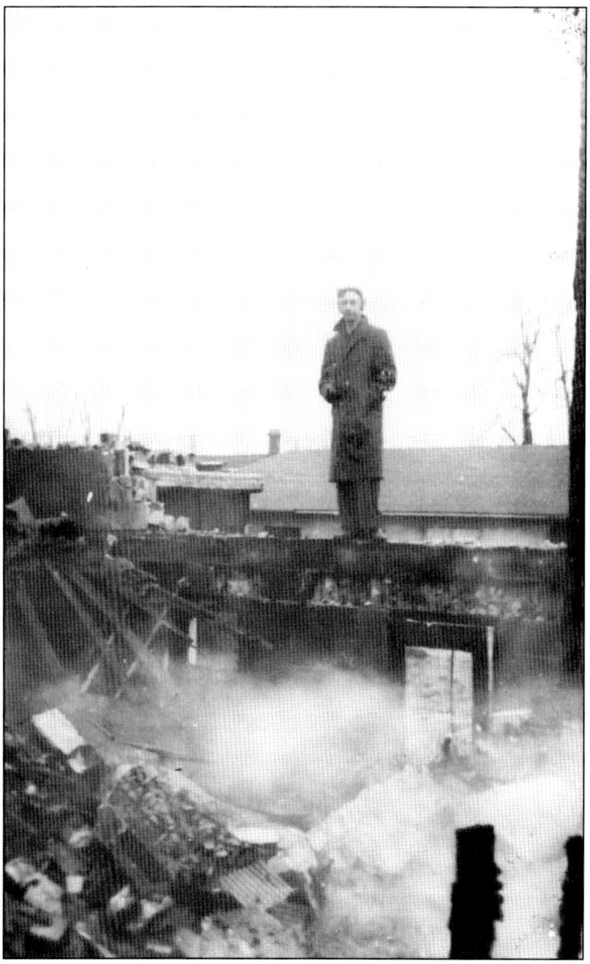

Mickey O'Brien is shown looking over the damage from the fire that destroyed the Illinois Theatre.

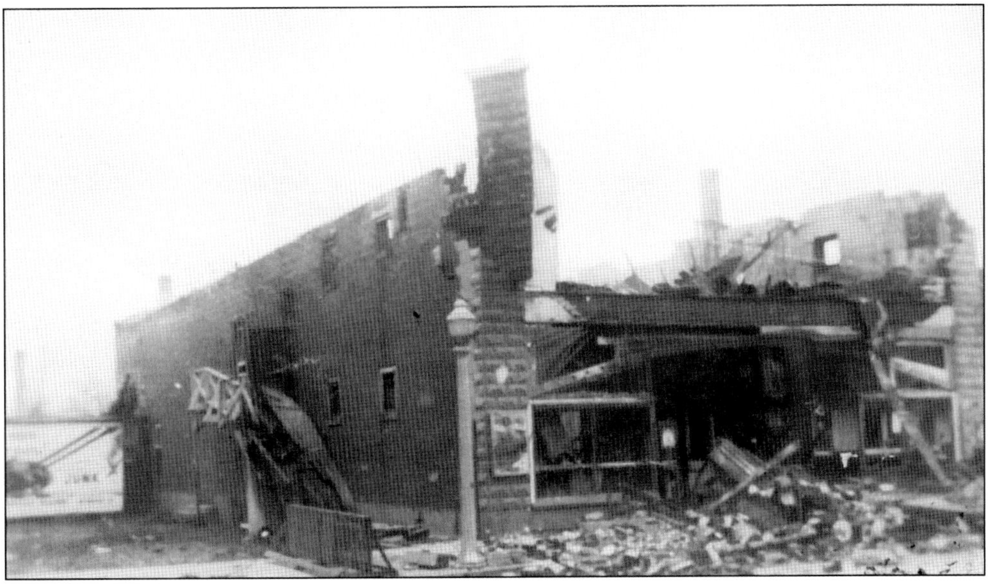

This building used to be the Illinois Theatre, before fire destroyed it. Metropolis has only one standing theater now, the Massac, and it has been closed for a number of years. The Illinois was next to the Metropolis Hotel on upper Market Street, and the fire occurred on the morning of December 20, 1942.

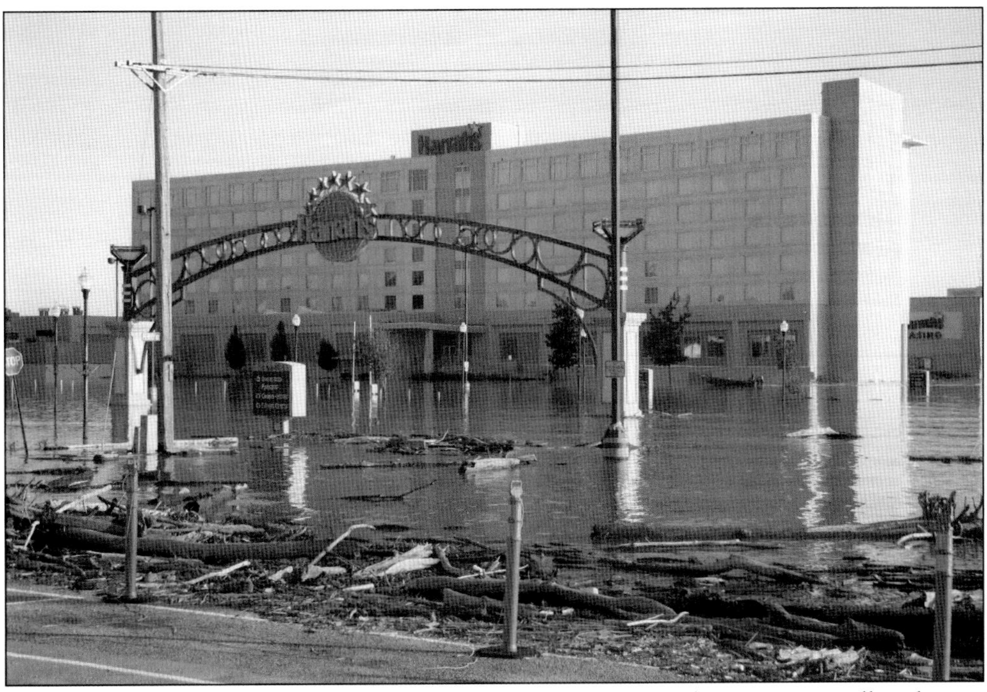

This photograph is of the flood of 2011. The hotel in front of Harrah's Casino, as well as the rest of the complex, was only accessible to essential employees by boat. One can be seen here against the right side of the building's facade.

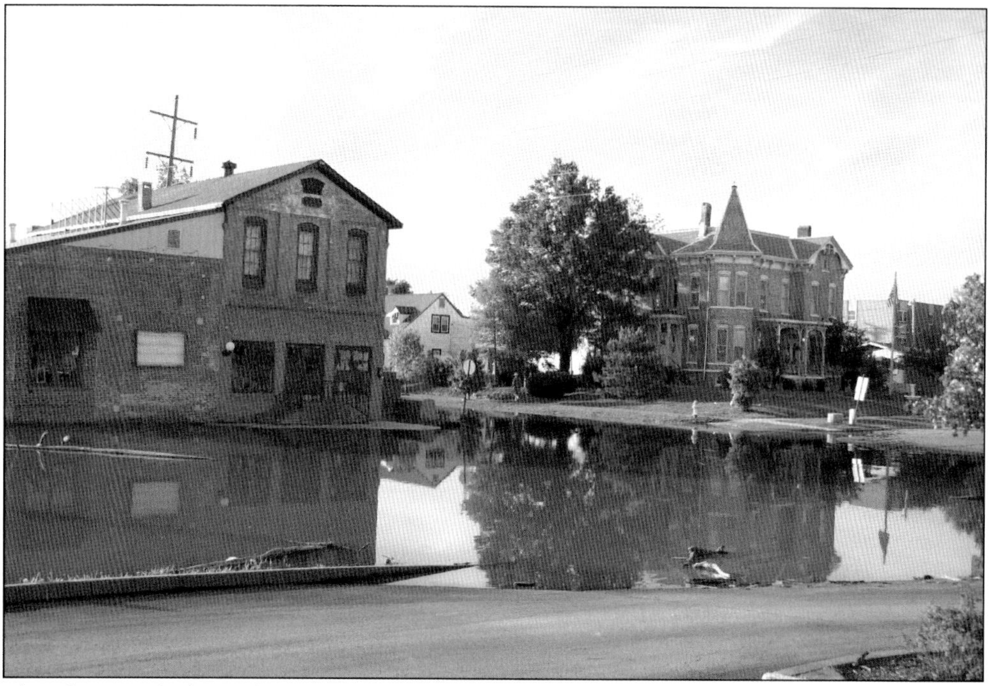

This photograph shows the former Miller's Dairy, later turned into a restaurant that is now closed, and the Quante house, which was renovated in 2008 and is now a bed-and-breakfast. The Miller Dairy Farm was located west of Metropolis.

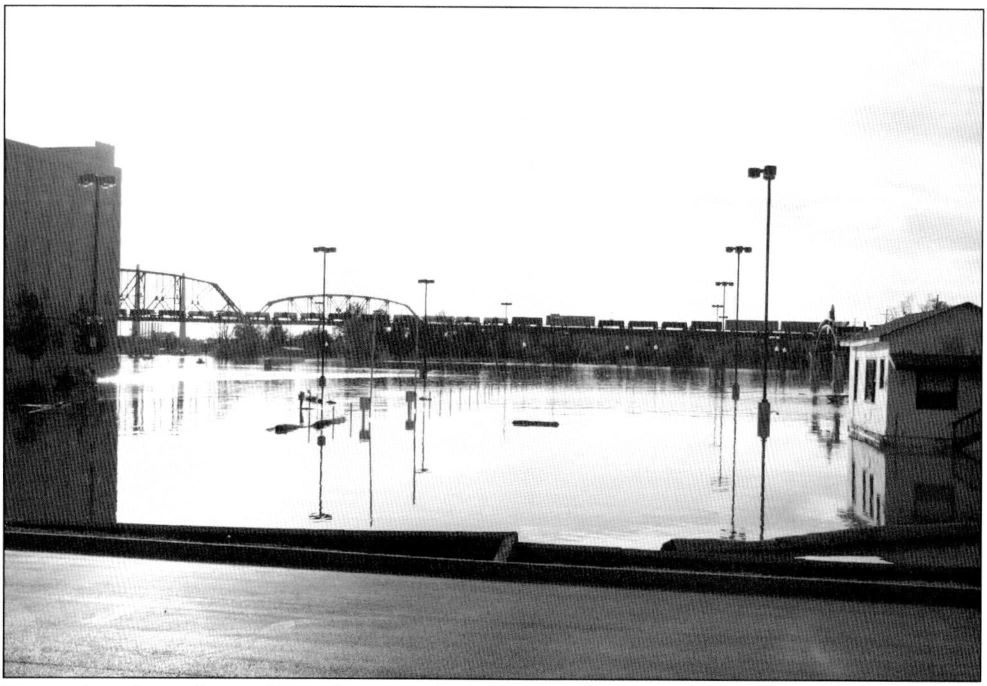

The parking lot in front of Harrah's casino looks almost like part of the river in this shot from the 2011 flood. An outlying building of the old Miller's Dairy is visible on the right, and the CB&Q Bridge is silhouetted in the distance.

Six

HOME AND FAMILY

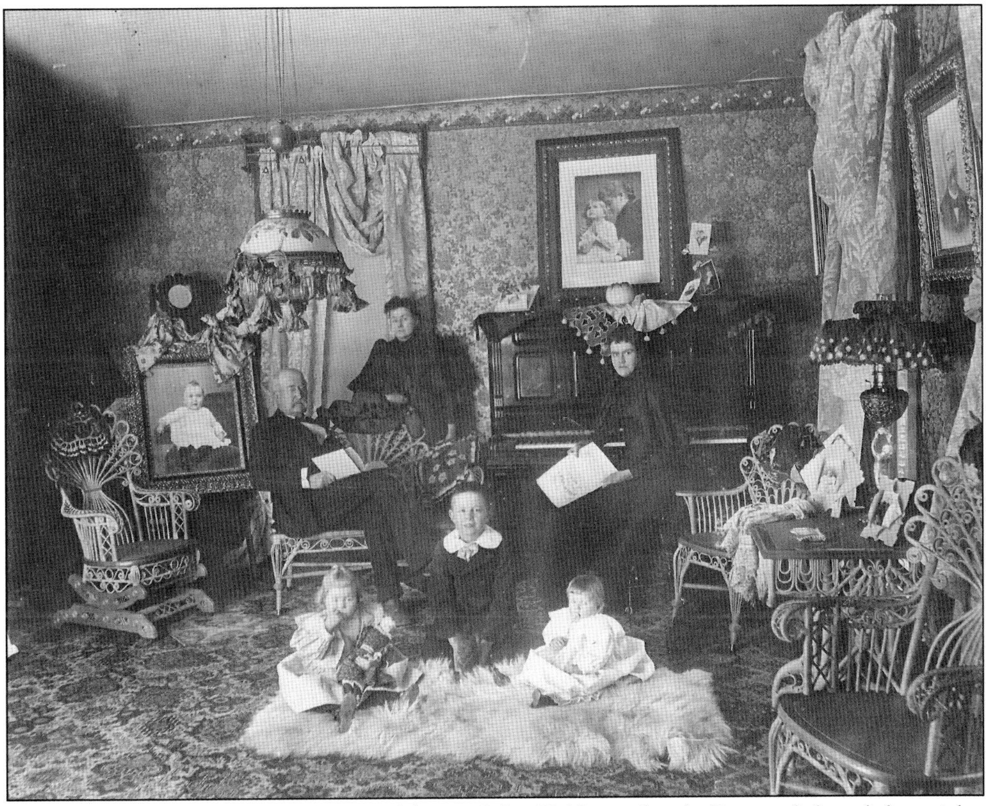

Here is the sitting room in the home of the Dr. John H. Norris family. Pictured, from left to right, are Dr. Norris, Mrs. Norris, and Isabel Jacobs (a daughter from a previous marriage) at the piano. On the rug, according to the back of the photograph, are "Celia with her dolly, John with his little dog, and Emma with her bottle." Emma is Emma Stewart, a cousin to the children who was adopted by the Norrises after her mother died. Emma went on to teach at Clark School.

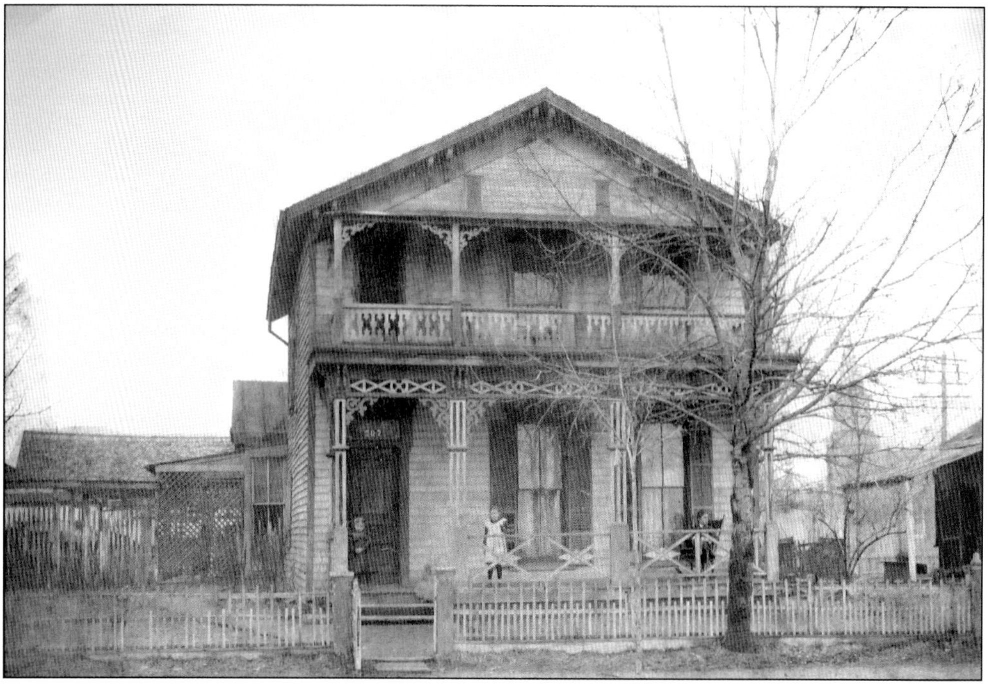

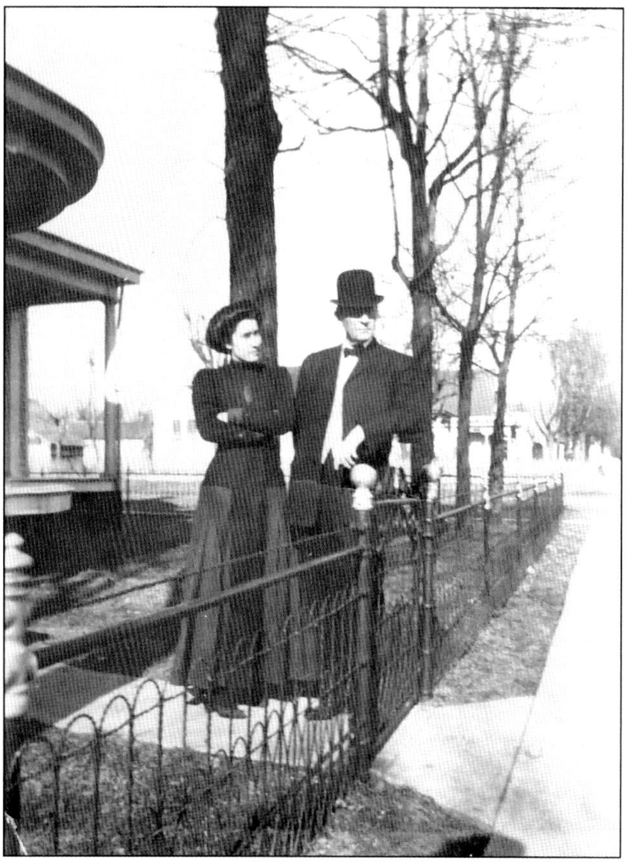

The Norris house stood at the northwest corner of Fifth and Ferry Streets. This is now the location of the Metropolis Post Office. Dr. John Norris had an office next to his house, in what is now an empty lot next to the Massac Theater. He moved to Metropolis in 1873, was married three times, and was the father of a total of seven children, the three youngest of whom can be seen on the porch here.

This couple standing in front of their Metropolis home around the turn of the century are unidentified.

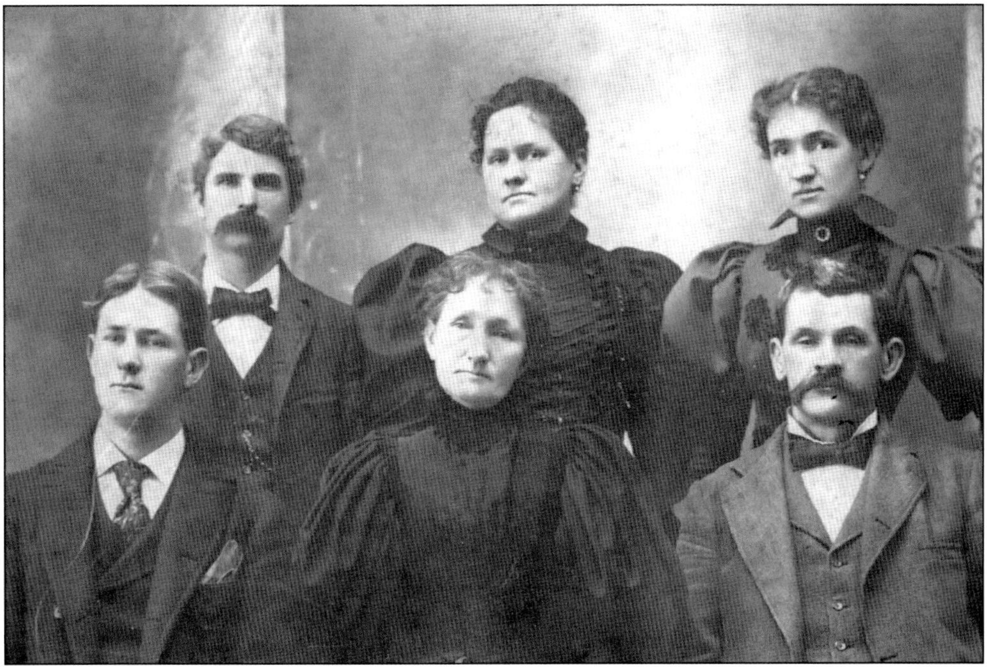

The family of former Metropolis mayor and prominent businessman August Quante includes, from left to right, (first row) probably W.H. Sielbeck, Hannah Quante, and August Quante; (second row) Walter McCauley, Addie McCauley, and Millie Sielbeck.

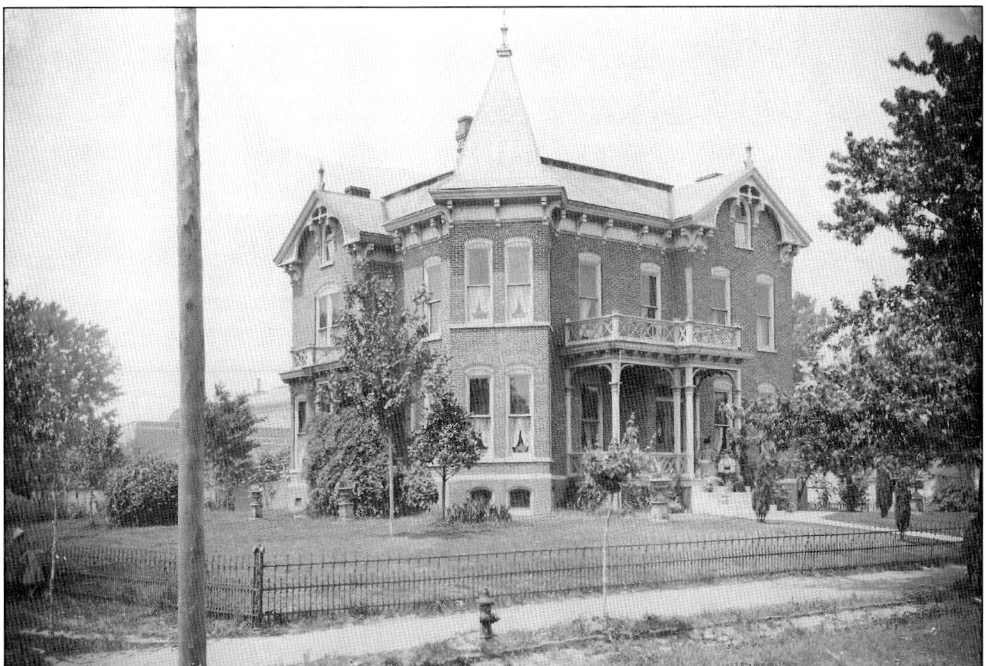

This photograph of the August Quante house was taken when it was still occupied by the Quante family. This scene is likely no more than a decade after its construction in 1889, and members of the family can be seen on the front porch.

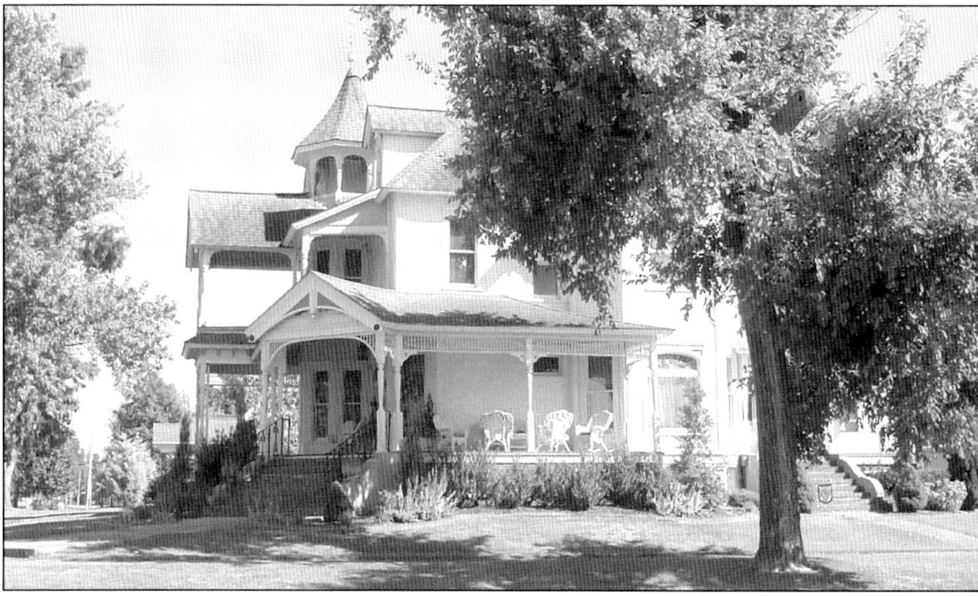

The C.C. Roberts house at the southeast corner of Metropolis and Third Streets was built around 1900.

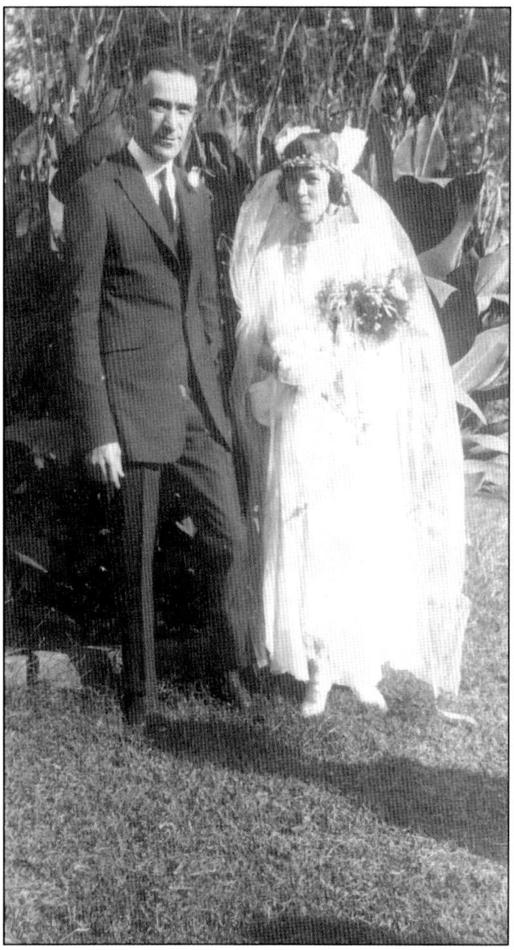

Jason Marberry and Edina Cowling are shown at her parents' home at Fourth and Girard Streets following their wedding. The only child of Capt. Edward Cowling and May Slimpert Cowling, Edina and her husband moved to Carbondale, Illinois, where he practiced dentistry and she taught piano into her 90s.

Two unidentified little girls dress up for their photograph to be taken in this early-1900s scene.

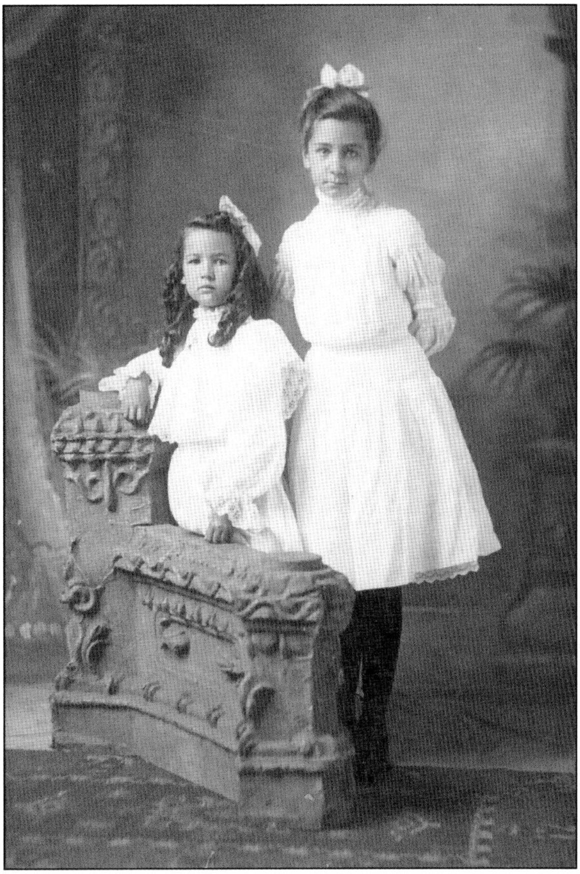

Curtis Edwin Miller is shown on his pony; the date is unknown. In town, a boy would have had to come from a well-off family to afford such a luxury.

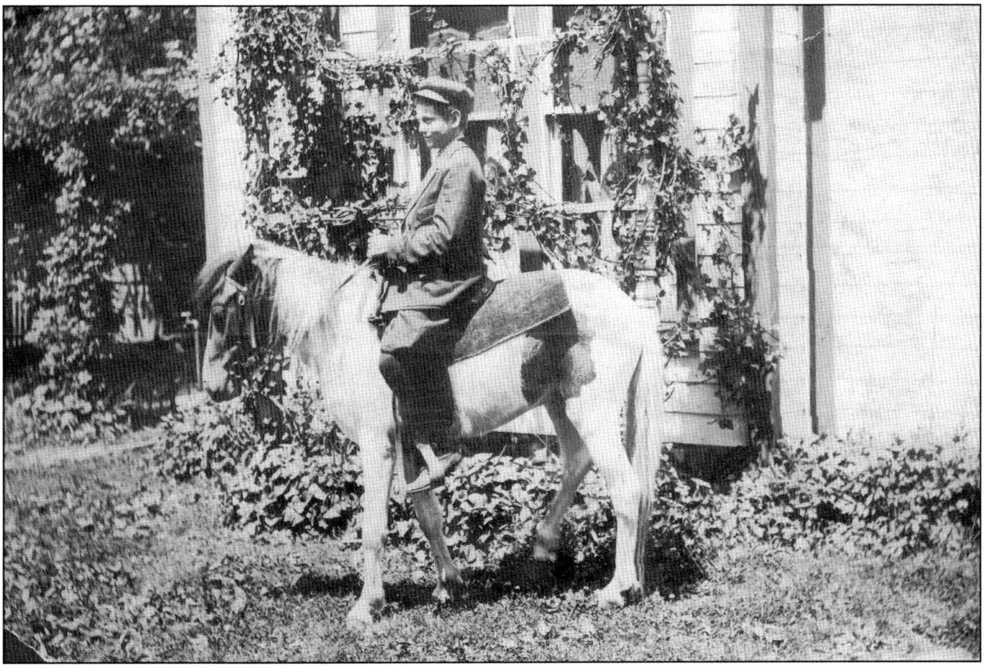

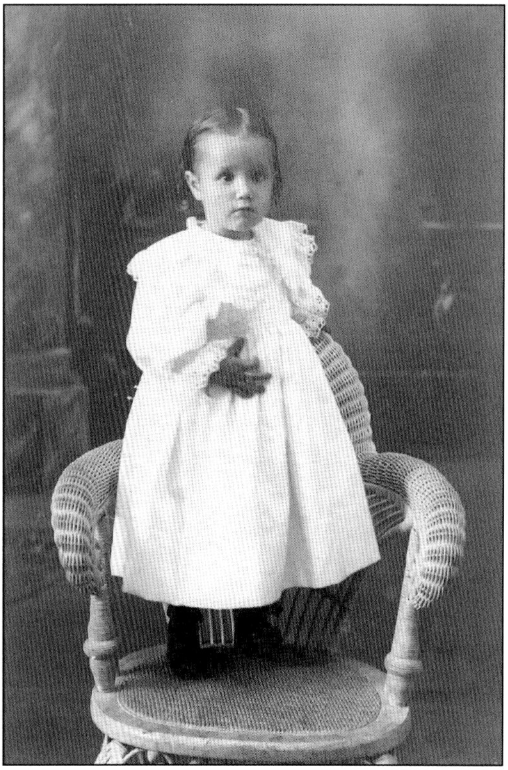

These two portraits show that in the late Victorian era, parents dressed their children identically, regardless of gender—no pink, no blue, just pure white, the color of innocence, and long, flowing dresses. Little Valeria Fitch, at left, is very cute here, as is Curtis Edwin Miller, below, seen here at 17 months old on March 2,1897, using a new invention—the telephone. His photograph is a platinotype—a photographic print made using platinum rather than silver— by Henderson Studios, at the corner of Ferry and Fourth Streets.

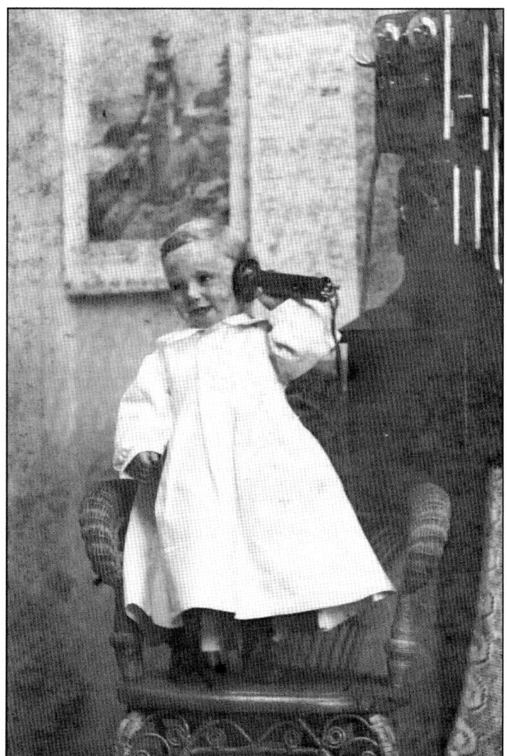

The family of city attorney Seward Bartlett "Bart" Kerr, shown here, was beset with tragedies. Their daughter, Adalaide (right), died at age three. Their son, Lloyd (seated in his mother's lap), drowned near Fort Massac at age 16. Bart and his wife, Eva, both died in separate incidents from complications arising from falls. Bart's sister and brother both died in fires— again, in separate incidents. Youngest son Edwin Virgil Kerr attended West Point, became a lieutenant colonel, and survived the Bataan Death March before dying in a POW camp in 1945. Happily, youngest daughter Harriett married, had children, and taught school for many years.

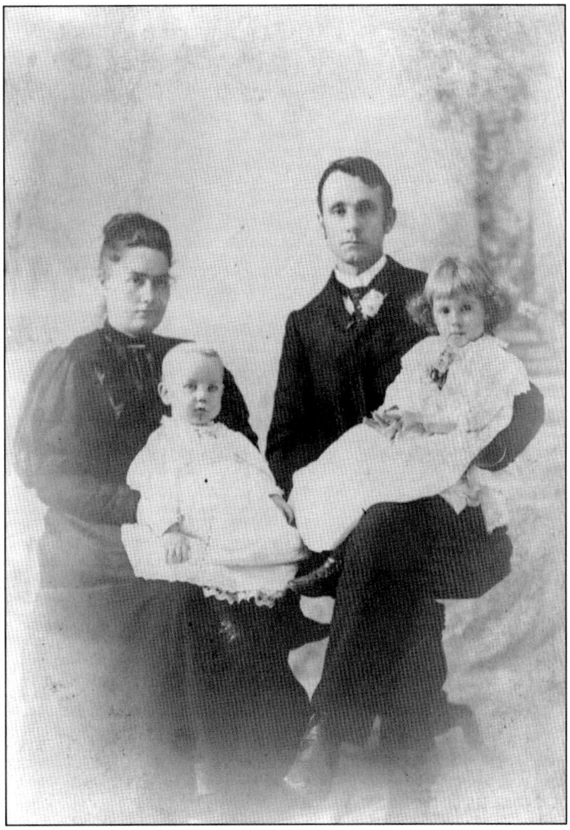

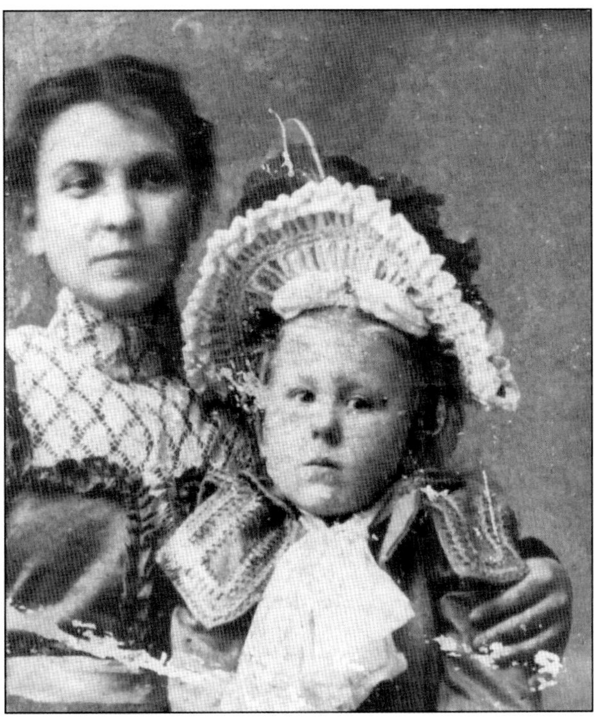

Mignon Amelia Curtis was the daughter of Elijah P. and Helen Curtis and was born in 1894 at their home at 405 Market Street. At the age of six, after losing her parents, Mignon went to live in St. Louis with her brother and his wife, Mae Johnson Curtis, who may be the woman in the photograph with her. Mignon later taught in St. Louis, married William Cooper Woodson in New York, and then taught there for 25 years after her husband's death. She died in 1985, survived by two sons and numerous grandchildren and great-grandchildren.

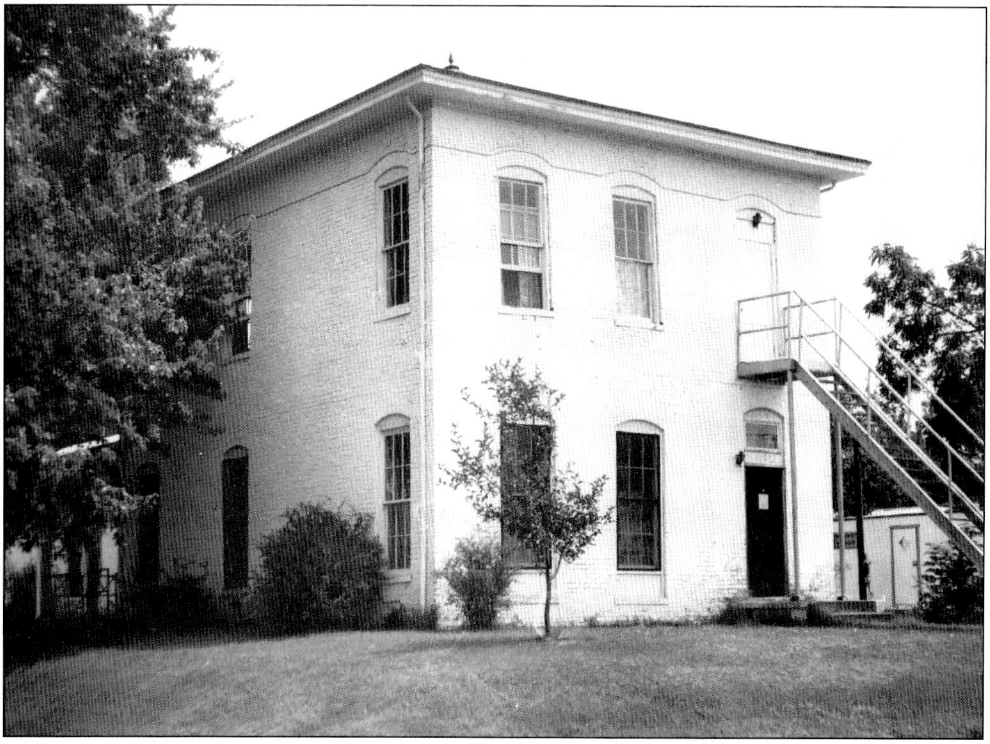

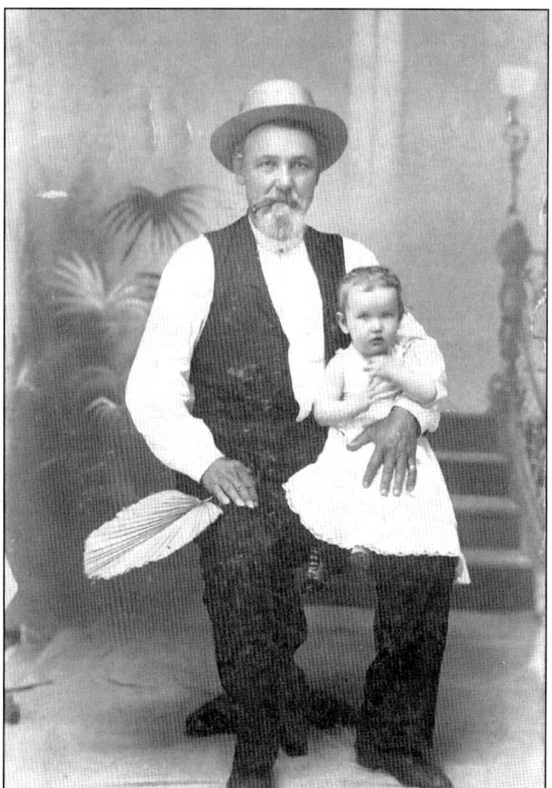

Here is a photograph of the Tom Smith house. Smith was the first man from Massac County killed early on in the Civil War. The Tom Smith Post of the Grand Army of the Republic, Post No. 456, was named for him. The GAR posts are all defunct now, as the veterans from that war are all deceased. This house was built by Smith in the late 1850s or early 1860s at the corner of Second and Metropolis Streets and is still standing.

Col. Richard Asberry Peters (1818–1905) poses with his grandson Raymond Peters. The colonel was a veteran of the Civil War.

Pictured are the children of Sam and Ellen Daly. Sam owned a large sawmill and lumber-processing plant in Metropolis. Pictured are (first row) twin girls Agnes and Anna; (second row) brothers Lester and Arch. Lester became an architect and designed city hall and Washington School in Metropolis and the Coca-Cola Building in Paducah, Kentucky. Brother Arch lived most of his life as a bachelor on a houseboat in St. Petersburg, Florida.

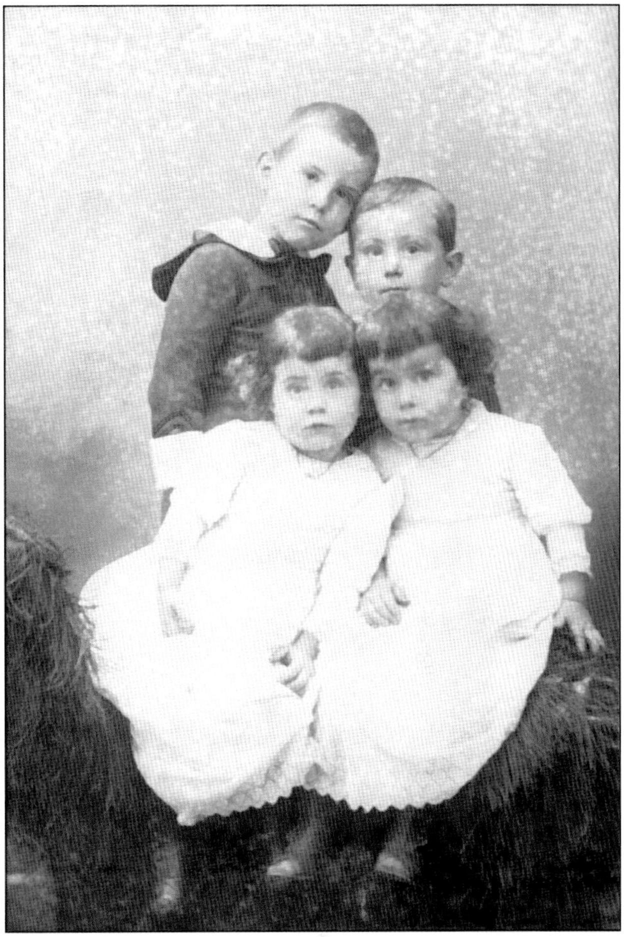

The Austin family poses on their front porch. They are, seated from left to right, Richard Sr., Richard II with doll, and Sylvia; eldest son Roy is standing. Numerous Austin family artifacts and photographs have been donated to the Massac County Historical Society, and a room at the Curtis House museum is named for them.

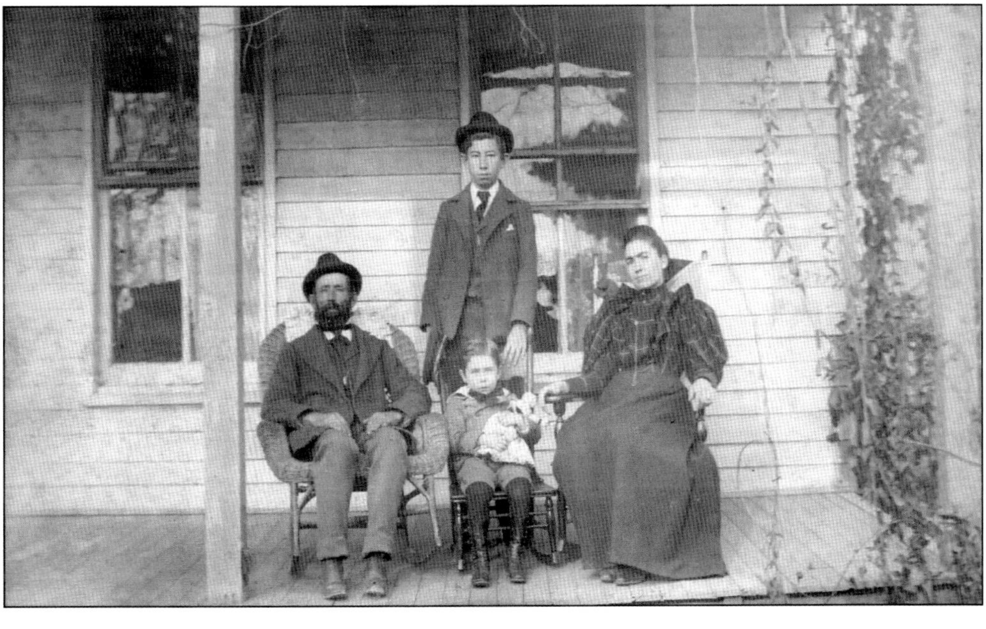

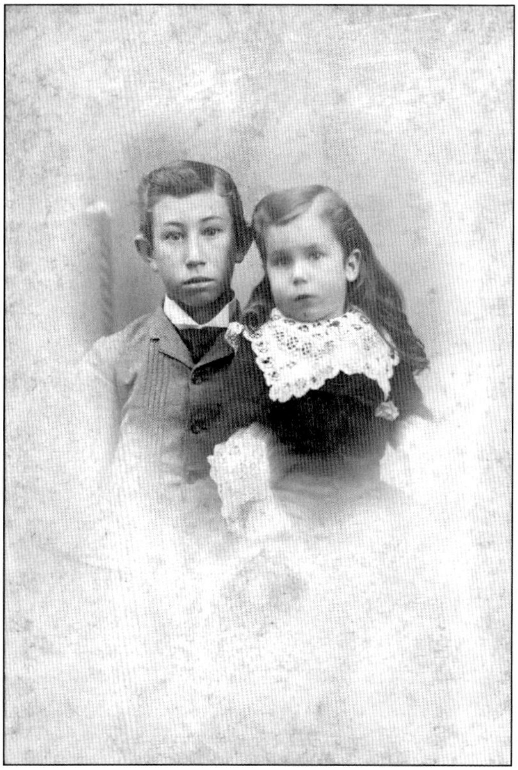

Roy Austin, on the left, is pictured with his little brother Howard, though one could be forgiven for mistaking Howard for Roy's sister. Not only were young boys typically dressed the same as girls at this time, but long, meticulously curled and styled hair was often favored by doting mothers.

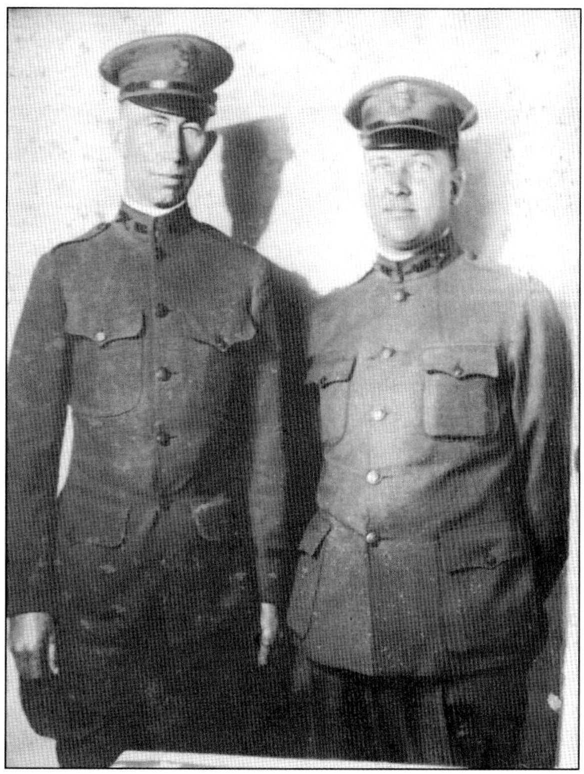

George LeRoy "Roy" Austin (left) is shown with an unidentified service mate. Austin's uniform, along with other photographs of Roy's life and family, is on display at the Massac County Historical Society in the Curtis House.

Richard Austin II followed his older brother Roy into military service. Though Roy served during World War I, judging by the age difference, Richard Jr., as he was known, likely served in peacetime. He later married Etta Krueger.

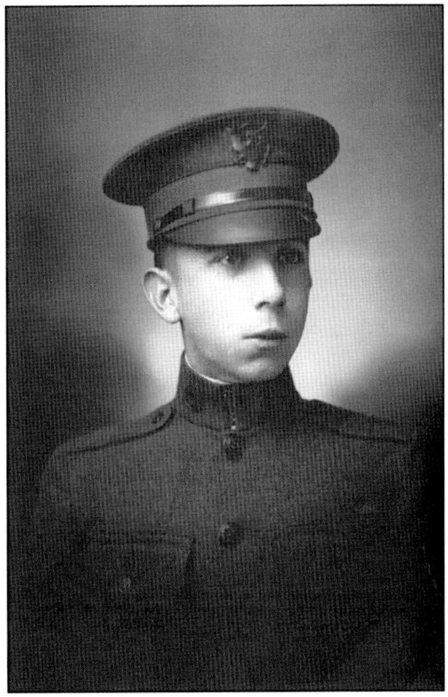

Locally, John Marvin Steele (left) was known in the Metropolis area as Marvin; his dad was John, or more often "Pops." Marvin was with the 82nd Airborne when they parachuted into France in 1944. His experience there was recounted in the 1962 movie *The Longest Day*, in which he was portrayed by Red Buttons. Marvin was the one hanging by his parachute from the steeple of the church in the town of Sainte Mère Eglise. He lived a long and fruitful life and is buried in Metropolis. Tragically, his brother Norman (right) was killed in Germany in the last days of the war.

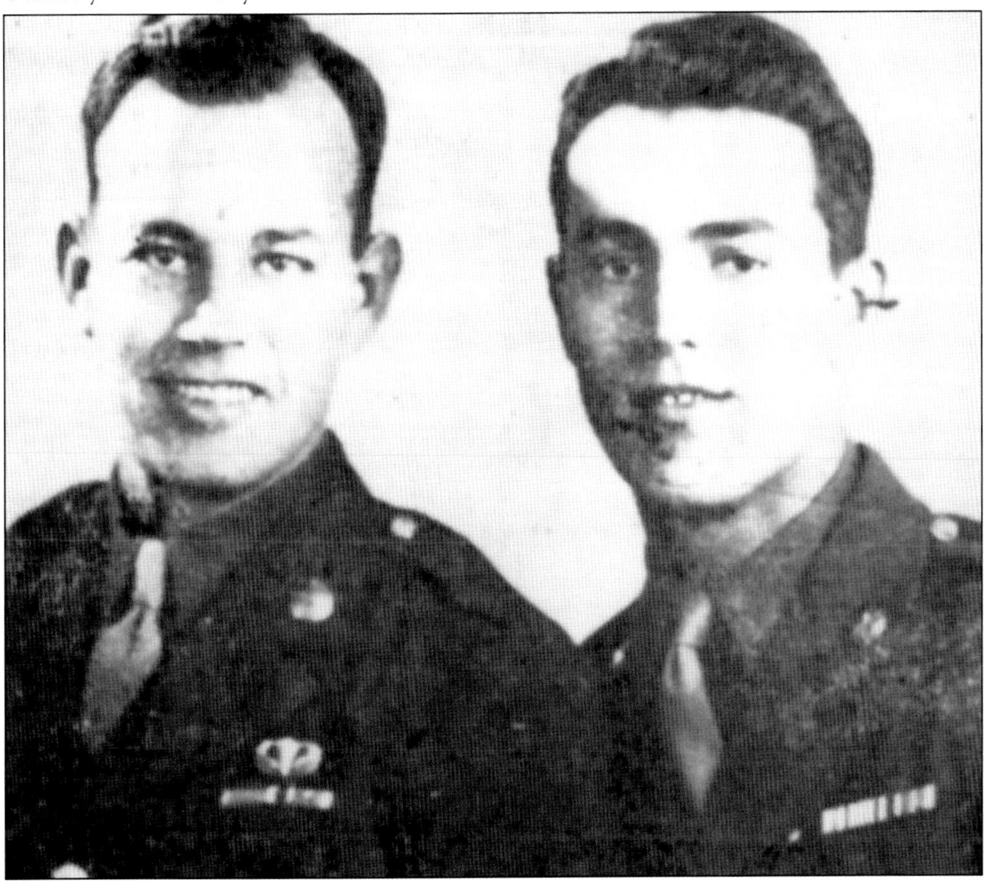

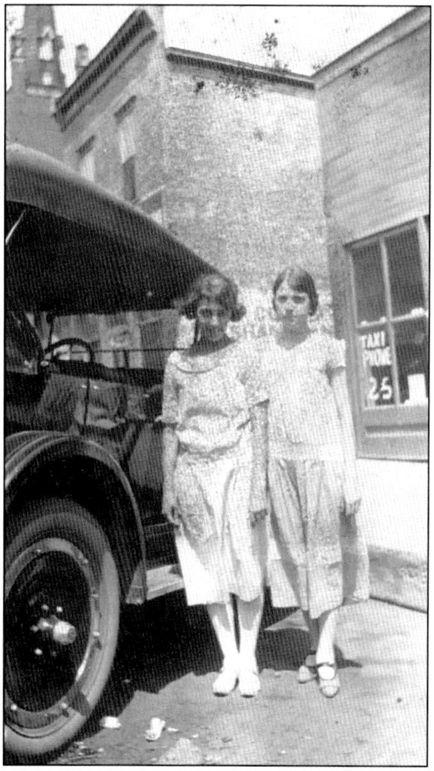

Alexandra and Hazel Lassiter are standing in front of their father's photography studio, which, presumably, is situated to the left of the taxi stand, near the intersection of Metropolis and Ferry Streets.

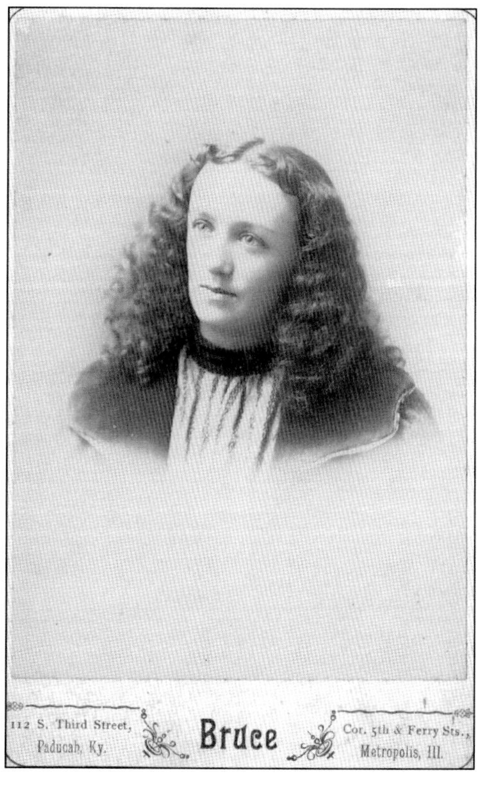

Pictured here on April 10, 1894, Julia Kincaid was a local elocutionist. Her family's farmhouse, built in 1876, stood on the largest of what came to be known as the Kincaid Mounds, a series of earthen mounds in eastern Massac County that comprised the cultural center of one of the largest Mississippian chiefdoms. The book that details the results of the University of Chicago's excavations there is titled *Kincaid: A Prehistoric Illinois Metropolis.*

Louis Vallee owned a bookstore and newsstand. His wife, Zackie Ann, operated a millinery shop. The Vallees lived at Fair Oakes, a house on Brookport Road.

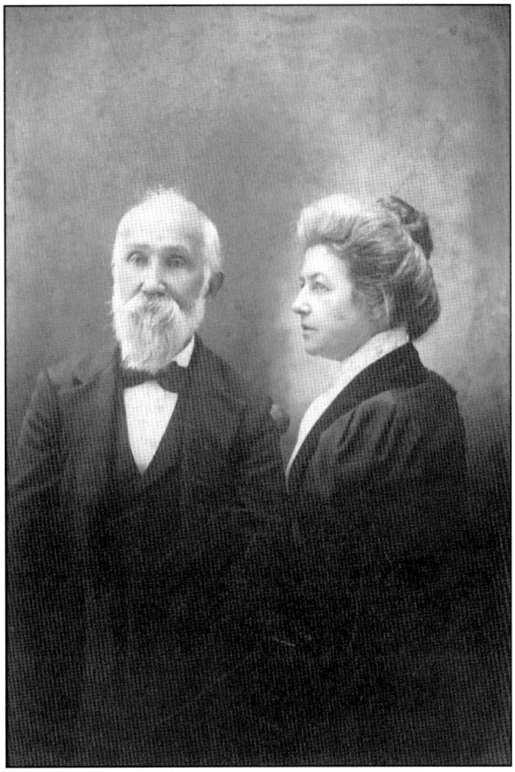

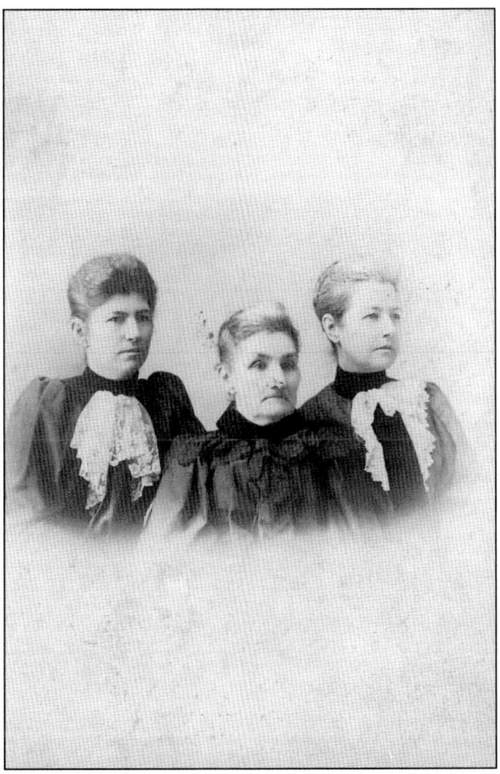

Zackie Ann Vallee (right) is shown with her mother, Mrs. Matheny (center), and sister Mrs. Briggman. When in her 80s, in the 1920s, Zackie Ann, then a widow, married Nathan Shick, a partner in the pottery firm of Slater & Shick. Not long after, still in the 1920s, the Shicks died within a few weeks of each other.

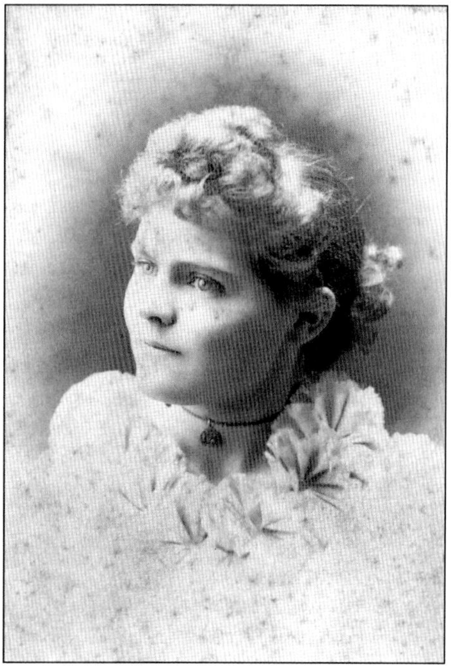

Kate Neftzger Humma, wife of Henry Humma, was the mother of three other prominent Massac County druggists—Harry and J.B. Humma, and Mary Humma Smith.

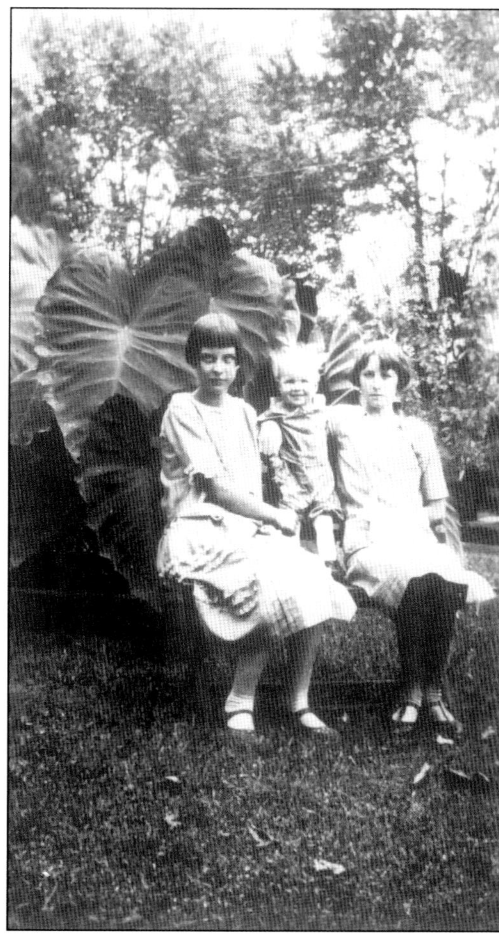

Cristina Clayton (left), later Christina Faulkner, sits with two unidentified children, probably at the Fort Massac Pavilion. Christina was a member of the first fourth-grade class to attend the new Central Elementary School, completed in 1922 at Eleventh and Ferry Streets.

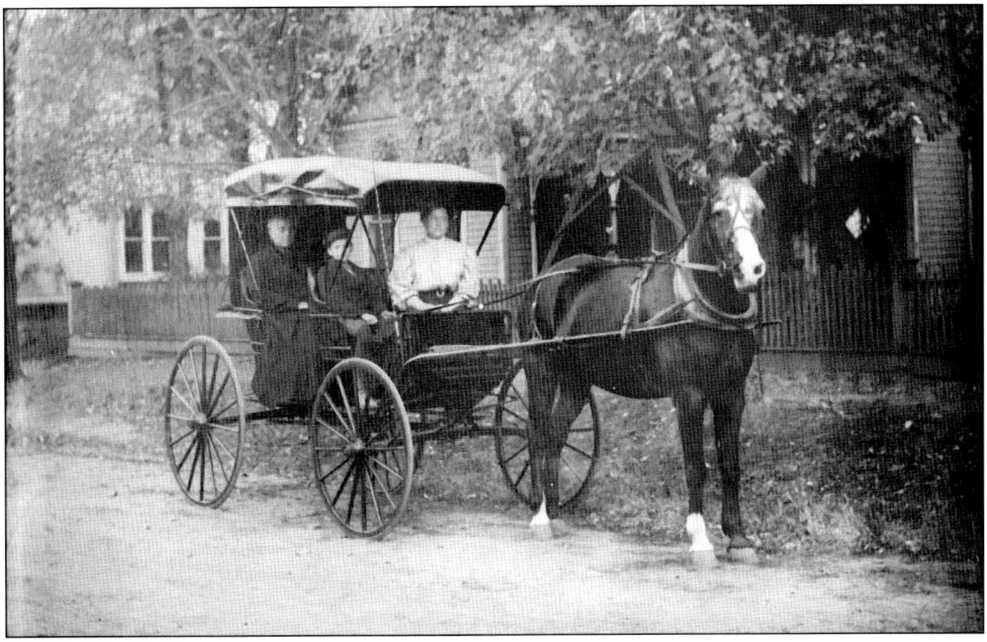

The Curtis family is out for a ride around 1900. From left to right are Mary Sidener Curtis, Curtis Edwin Miller, and Nora Curtis Miller.

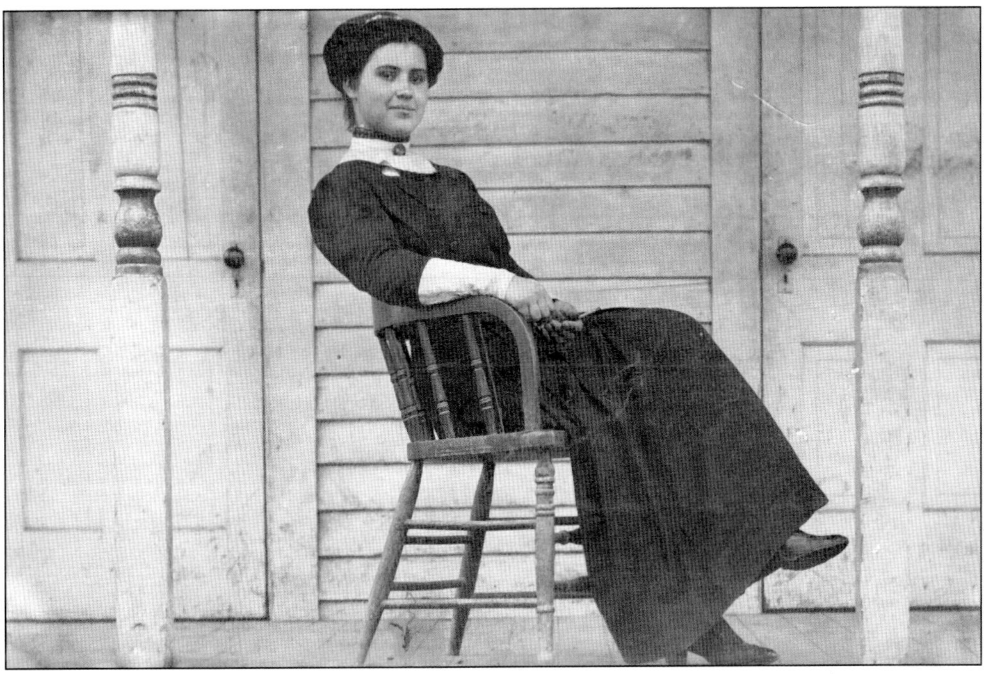

This prim young woman sitting on the porch giving a serene smile is a young Sylvia Austin.

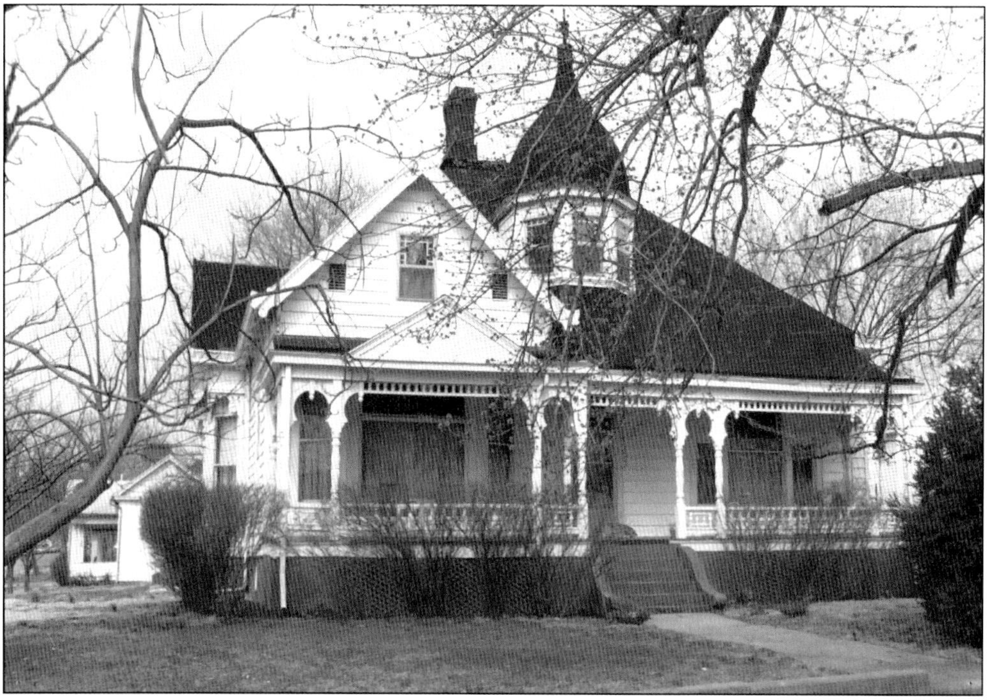

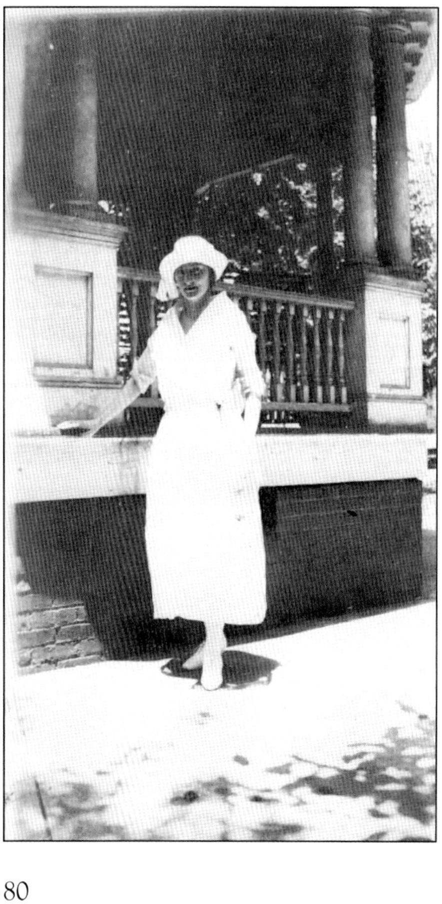

The house of William A. McBane II is pictured at 605 Girard Street. William II was a nephew of the founder of Metropolis. The founder left no direct descendants. Louis and Mary Horman restored the house in the 1970s.

Virginia Trousdale was the daughter of F.A. Trousdale, cofounder of the *Metropolis Herald* and a key person in the effort to rebuild the Washington Square Park gazebo.

Seven

SCHOOLS

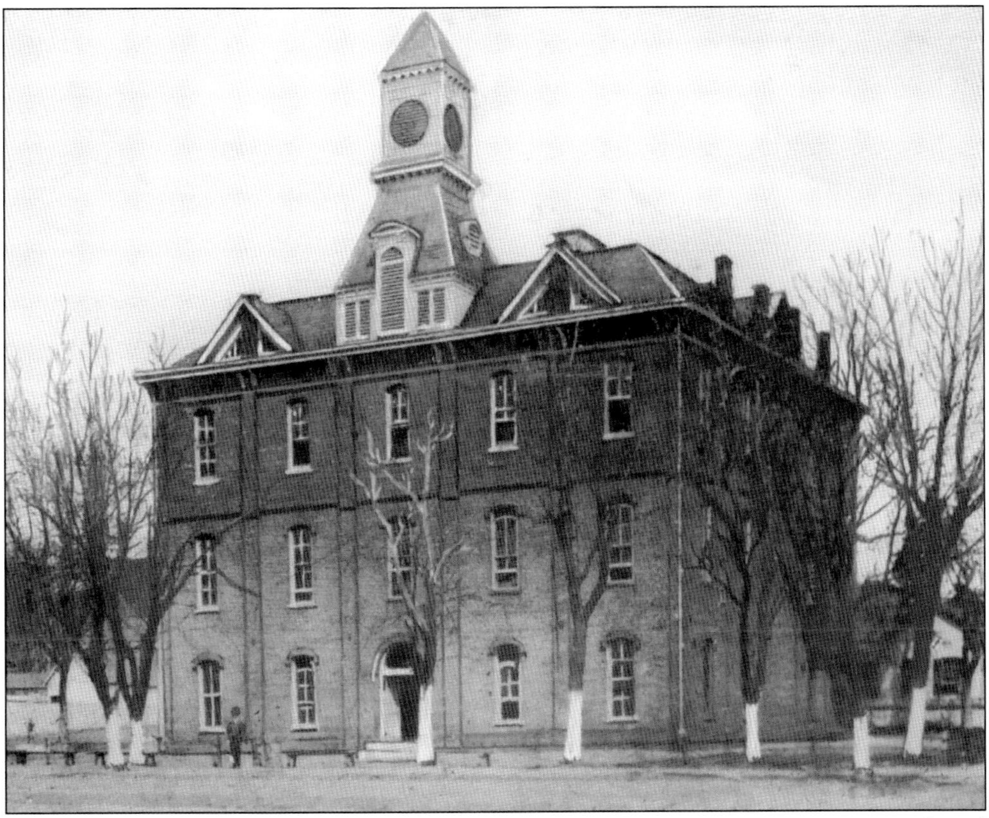

The building known as the Old Central School was built in 1875 as a two-story combined elementary and high school at the corner of Fourth and Metropolis Streets. In 1883, a third floor was added to accommodate population growth. The location of Central School was changed in 1922, but the old building remained in place until 1935, used first to house a business college, then a lingerie factory.

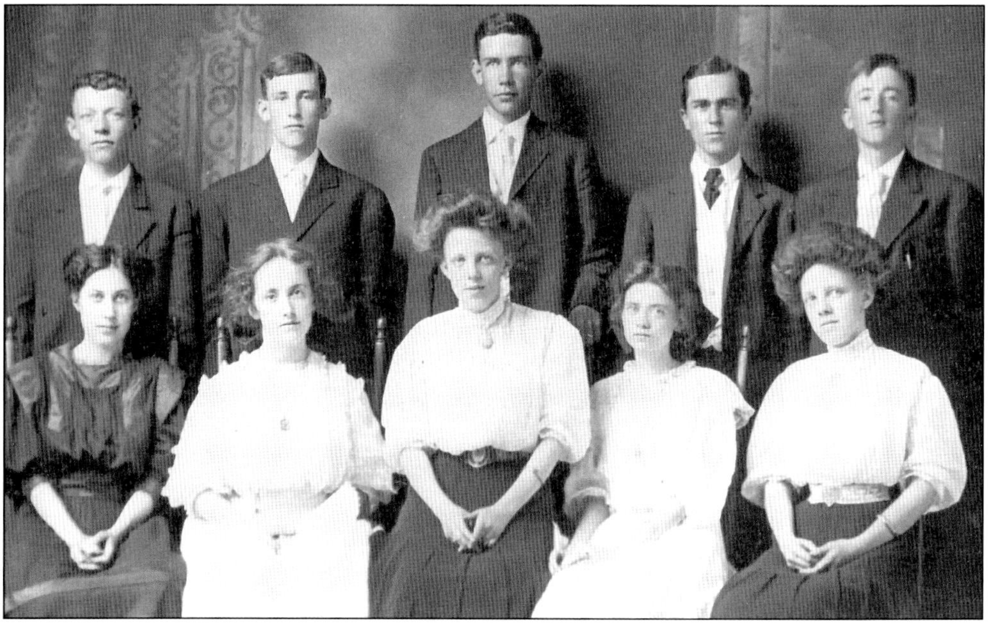

Here is the 1908 graduating class of Metropolis High School. Pictured are, from left to right, (first row) Ruth Brown, Hattie Mann, Hazel Stewart, Nelle Elliott, and Hattie Stewart; (second row) Raymond Davis, Lloyd Helm, Frank Randolph, Bonner Leonard, and Leslie Rush. Mann was a longtime newspaperwoman in Metropolis.

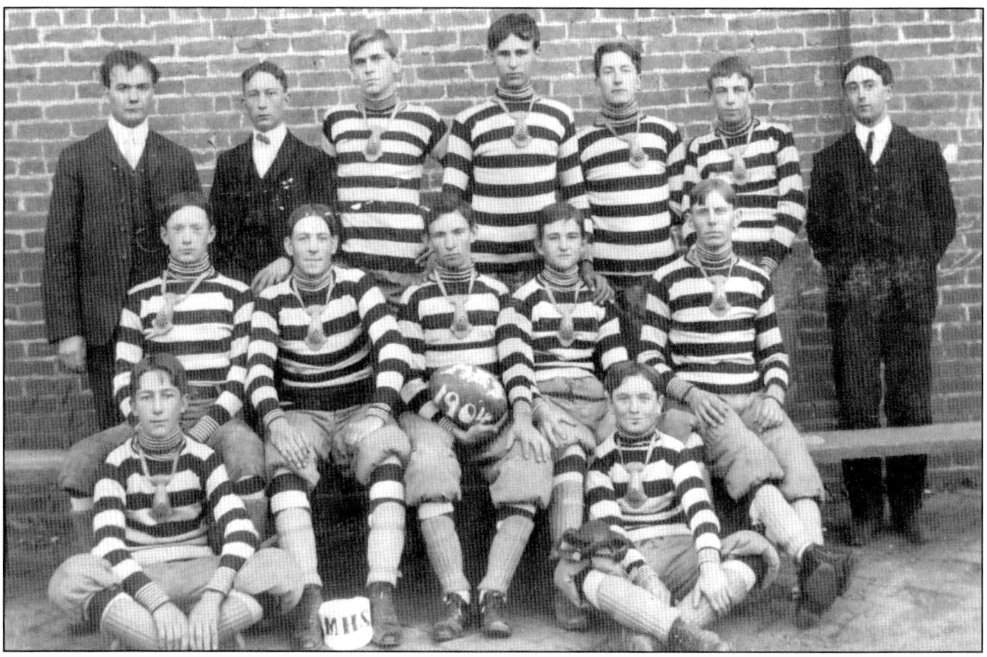

This picture of the Metropolis High School football team in 1904 shows the team wearing what look like odd medallions but are, in fact, nose guards, held in place by the strap while clenching a rubber bit with one's teeth. Before the advent of helmets, pads, and forward passes, football was becoming so dangerous that numerous deaths occurred across the country (18 in 1905 alone), stirring public outrage that prompted then president and football fan Theodore Roosevelt to demand rules changes.

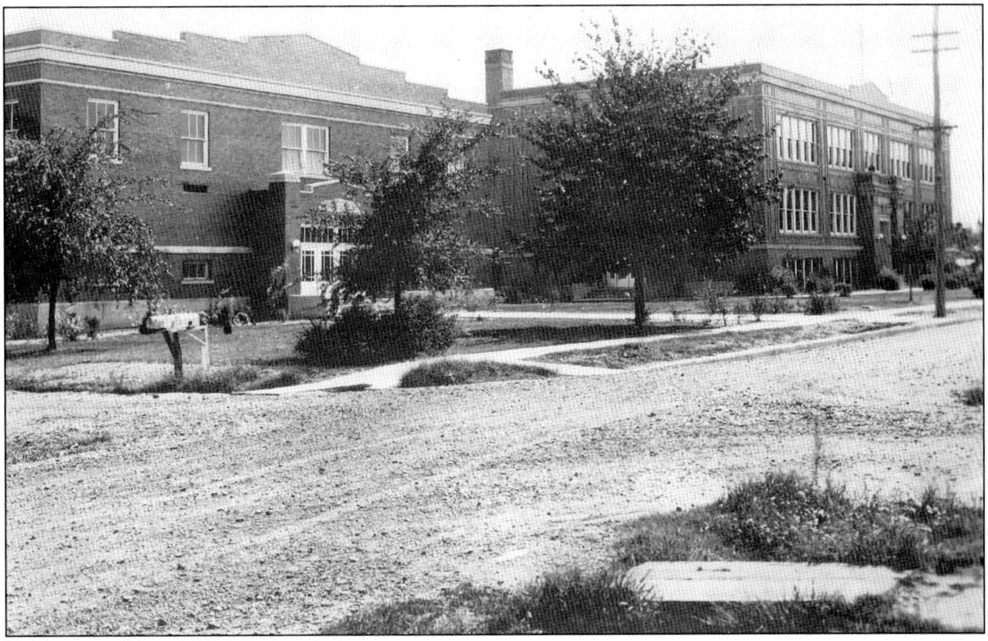

Here is Metropolis High School shortly after the gymnasium was added. Note that Catherine Street is still a dirt road. The school was built in 1912, with the gym being constructed in 1927 and dedicated as the Rose E. Cutting Gymnasium 10 years later.

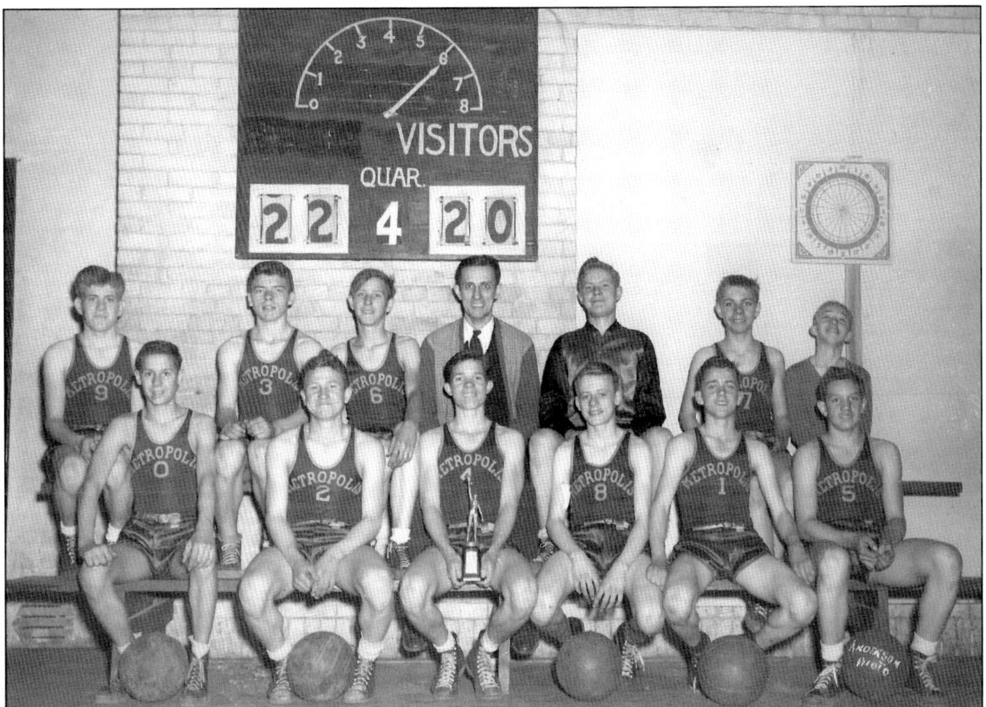

The Metropolis High School basketball players and their coach pose with their trophy, perhaps having just won it, with the scoreboard in back reflecting the game's result. The year and opposing team are unidentified.

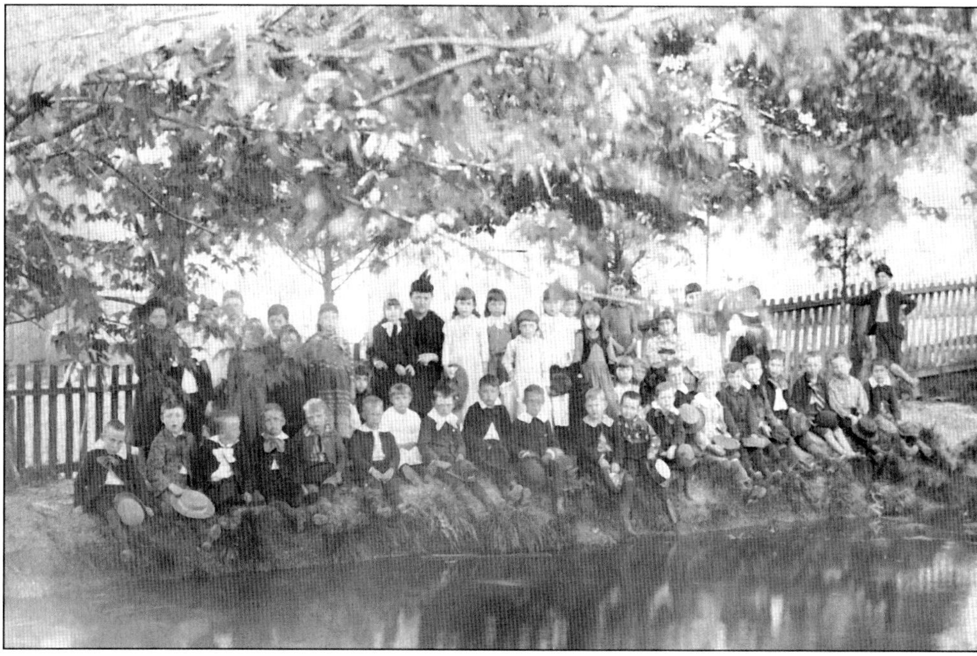

This photograph shows primary students in the Metropolis City School system in 1892. Grace McCartney Smith is the teacher wearing the feathered hat to the left of center.

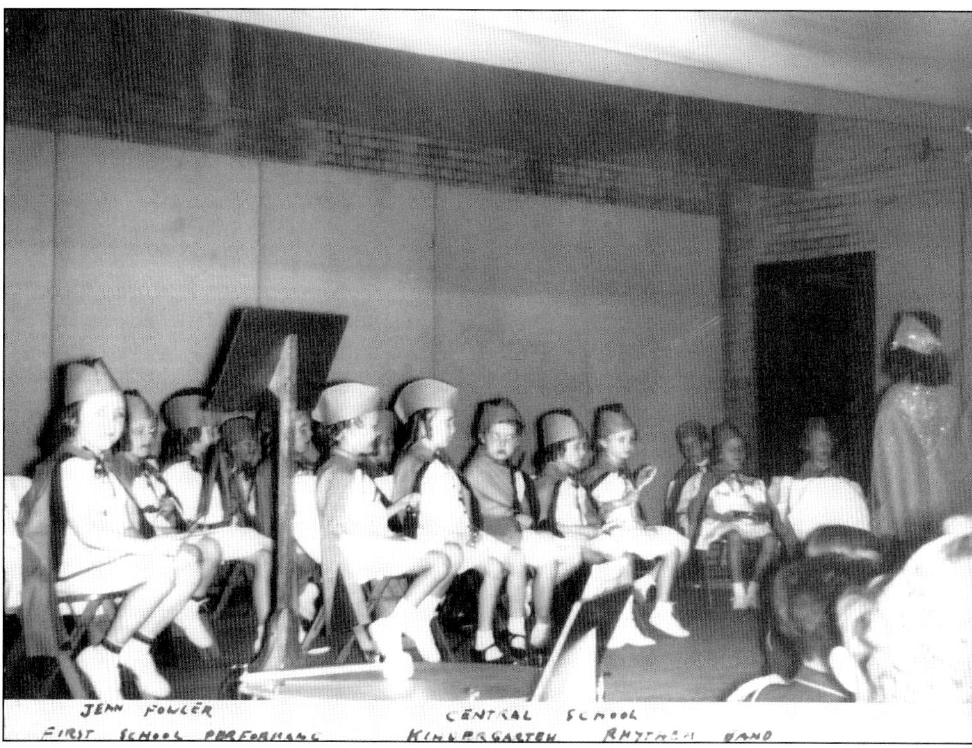

The kindergarten rhythm band at Central School is quite adorable in this undated photograph.

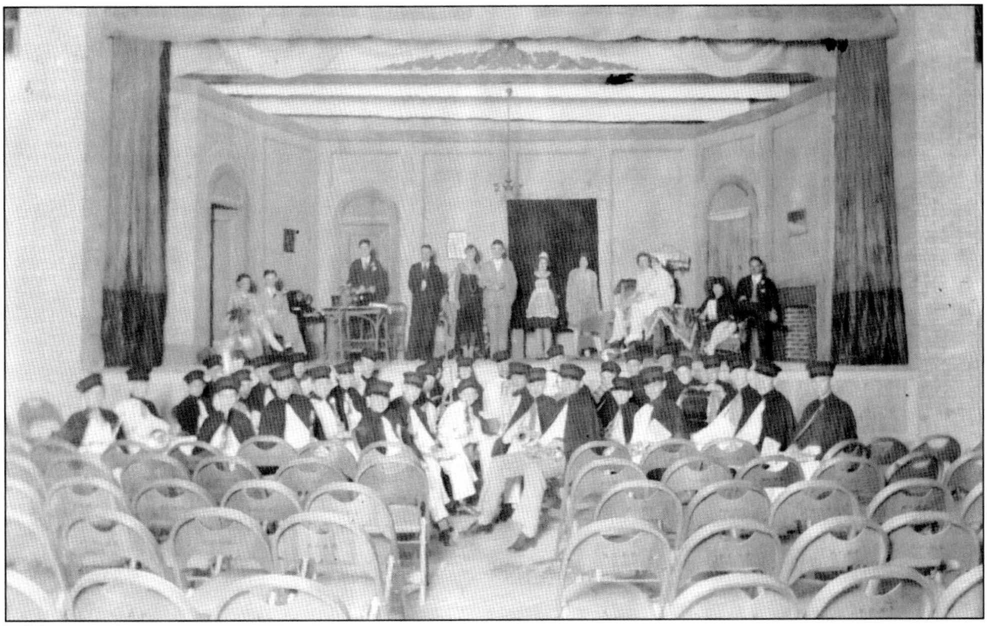

This production of *The Whole Town's Talking*, billed as "A Farce in Three Acts," was put on by the Metropolis Community High School Booster Club in the school's gymnasium on April 22, 1930. The play by Anita Loos and John Emerson was made into a silent film in 1926, with Edward Everett Horton and Delores Del Rio. It bears no connection to the 1935 film of the same title with Edward G. Robinson.

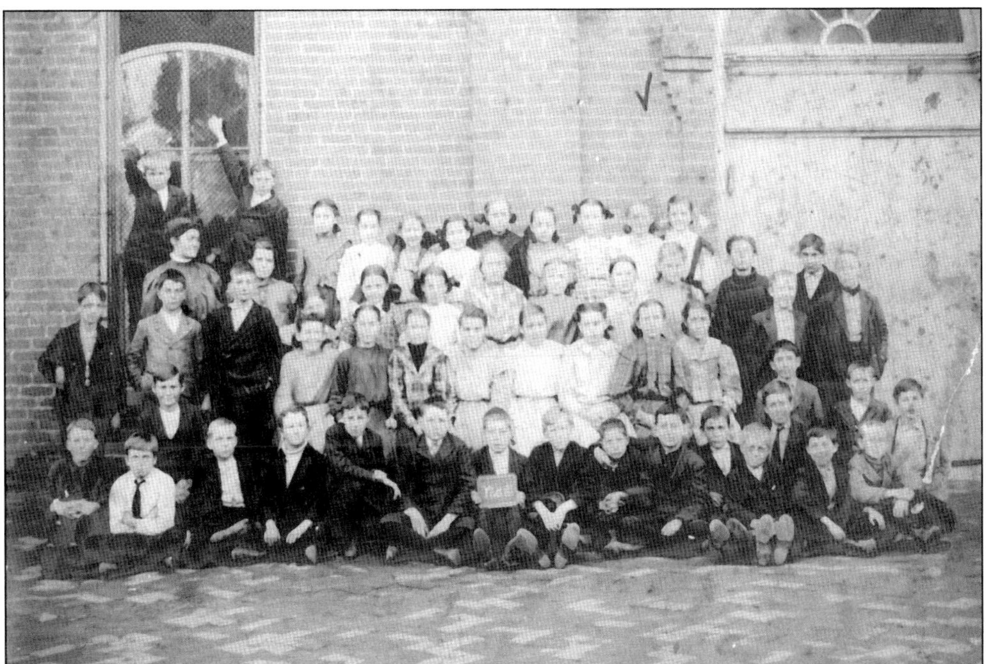

The two fifth-grade boys standing in front of the window to the left behind teacher Maude Dean Haverkamp almost appear to be testing the strength of the wire on the window. This Central School class photograph is from about 1905.

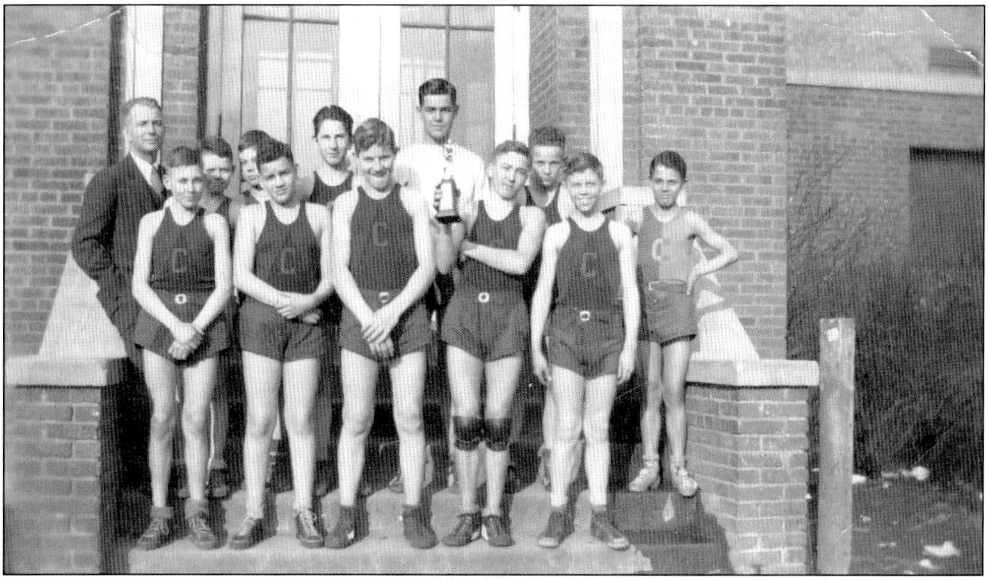

The seventh- and eighth-grade basketball team from Central School poses with its trophy in 1935. From left to right are (first row) Jim Pierce, Bill Humma, Bud Lasley, Charles Alliston, and Bobby-Joe Smith. In the back, coach Charles Gabbart is seen on the left, and Joe Zaricor is at right. The others in the middle are not identified.

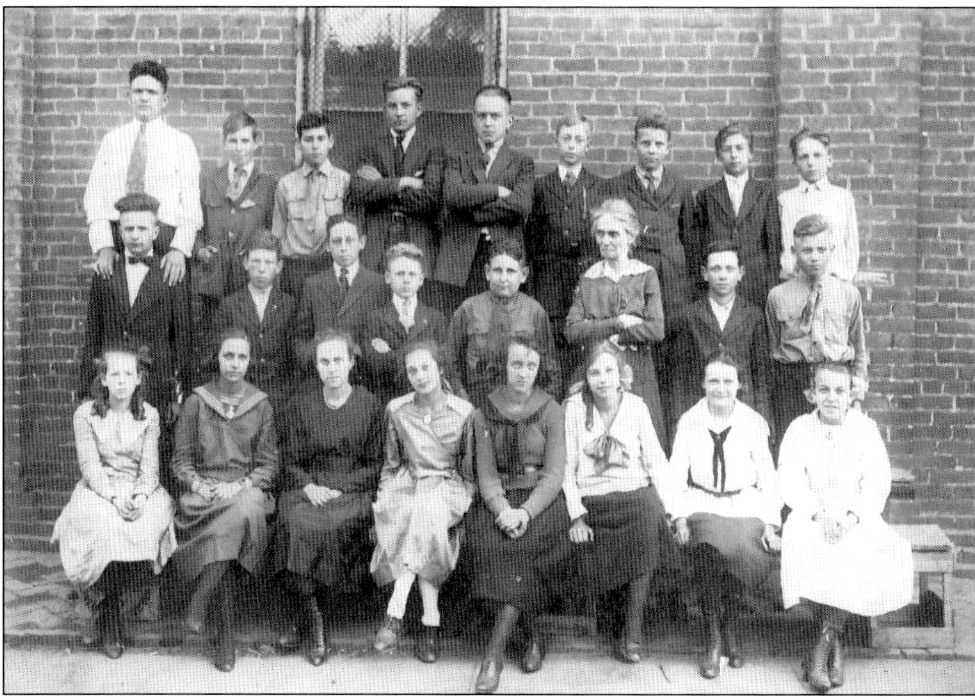

This amusing photograph is of the Central School eighth-grade class in the 1919–1920 school year. The teacher, Emma Brainard, is third from the right in the second row, with arms crossed and apparently looking disapprovingly at either the two students to her right in the third row (Othel Pryor, left, and Edwin Sutherland), or the boy second to her right (future Metropolis mayor Kenneth Jones). All three boys seem to be mocking their teacher's posture.

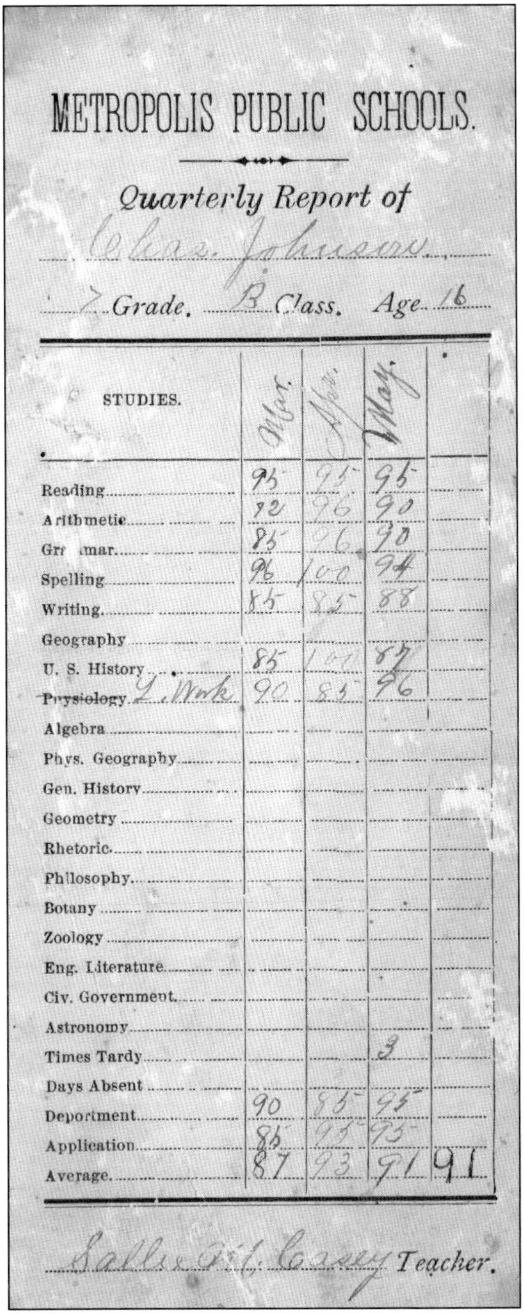

METROPOLIS PUBLIC SCHOOLS.

Quarterly Report of Chas. Johnson

7 *Grade.* B *Class.* *Age* 16

STUDIES.	Mar.	Apr.	May	
Reading	95	95	95	
Arithmetic	92	96	90	
Grammar	85	96	90	
Spelling	96	100	94	
Writing	85	85	88	
Geography				
U. S. History	85	100	87	
~~Physiology~~ L. Work	90	85	96	
Algebra				
Phys. Geography				
Gen. History				
Geometry				
Rhetoric				
Philosophy				
Botany				
Zoology				
Eng. Literature				
Civ. Government				
Astronomy				
Times Tardy			3	
Days Absent				
Deportment	90	85	95	
Application	85	95	95	
Average	87	93	97	91

Sallie G. Casey *Teacher.*

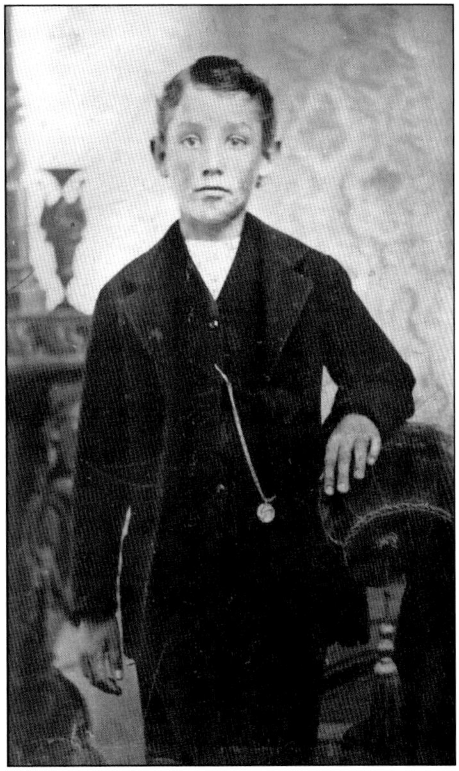

Student Charles G. Johnson is pictured at age 11 in 1880. This report card indicates that he is 16 and in the seventh grade. His average score was 91 for the March, April, and May (spring) term in 1886. Students at that time frequently did not follow an age-dependent pattern regarding grade levels. Johnson's progression in school was likely hindered by work—whether on the family farm or in a local factory. The card is signed on the reverse by his father, James H. Johnson.

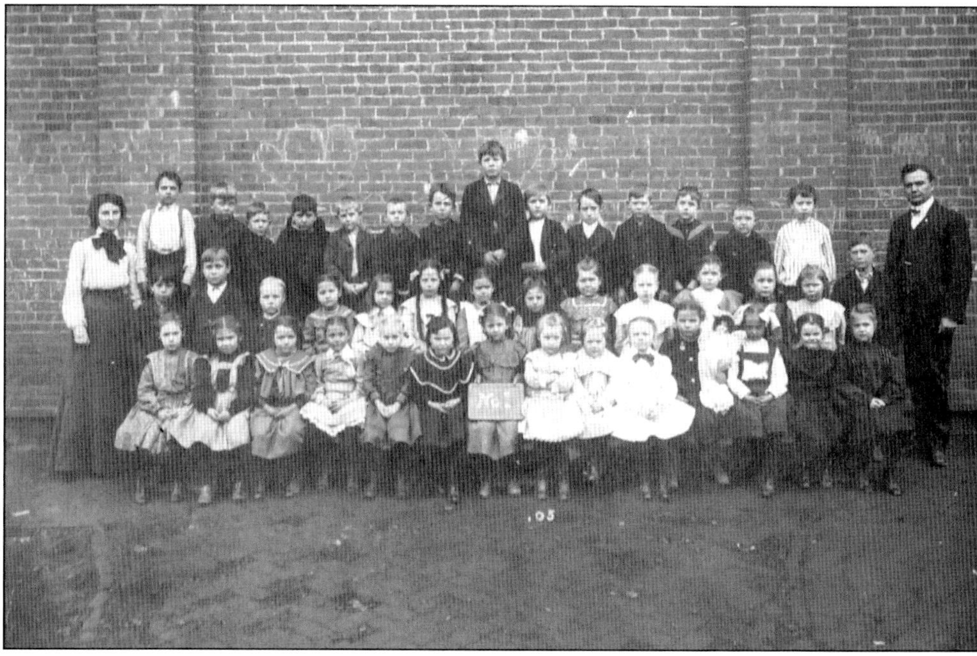

In 1917, this first-grade class, taught by Clara Wells at the old Central School in the 1904–1905 school year, would become the first graduating class from the new Metropolis Community High School, built in 1912.

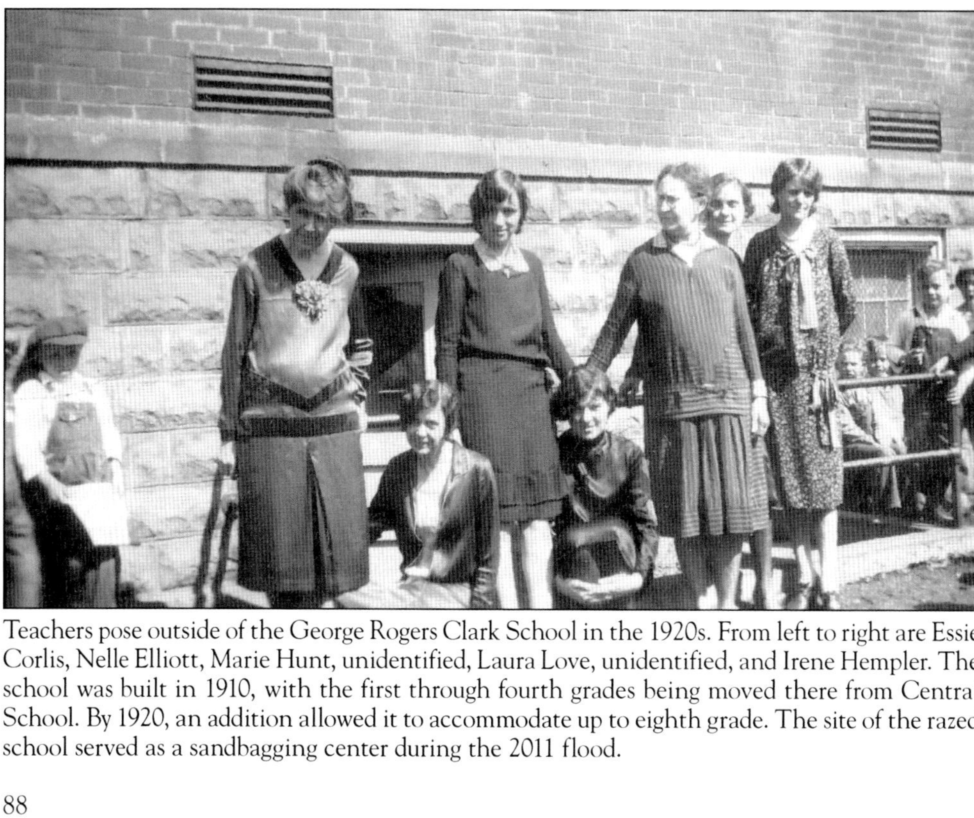

Teachers pose outside of the George Rogers Clark School in the 1920s. From left to right are Essie Corlis, Nelle Elliott, Marie Hunt, unidentified, Laura Love, unidentified, and Irene Hempler. The school was built in 1910, with the first through fourth grades being moved there from Central School. By 1920, an addition allowed it to accommodate up to eighth grade. The site of the razed school served as a sandbagging center during the 2011 flood.

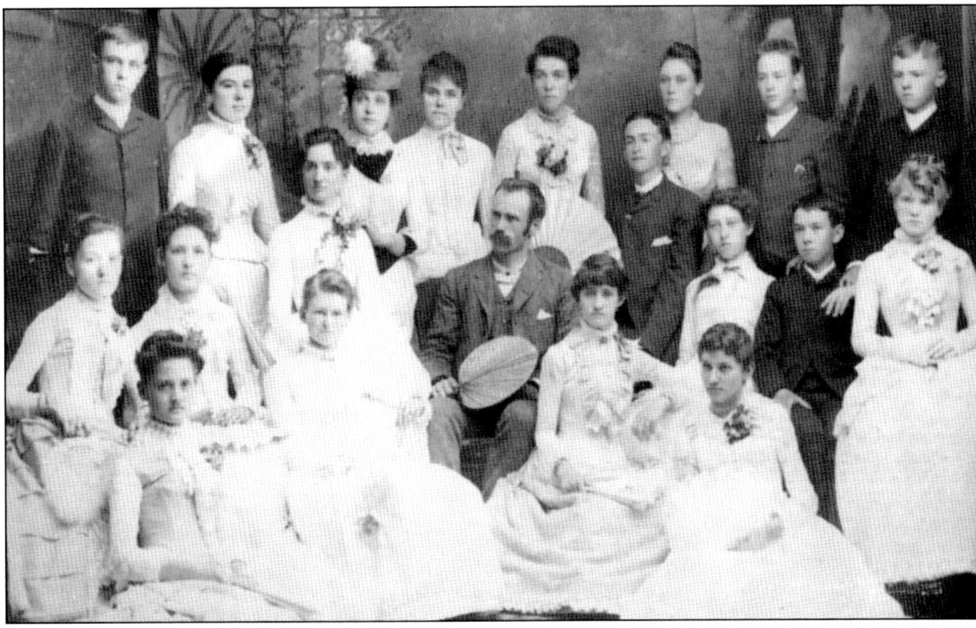

This unusual photograph of the high school graduating class of 1887 is the oldest of a local graduating class known to exist. In the center, in the midst of the largely female student body and holding a fan, is principal Joel Bowlby. On the right in the third row is Edward J. Cowling, who would go on the take over his father's steamboat operation and name two boats after him.

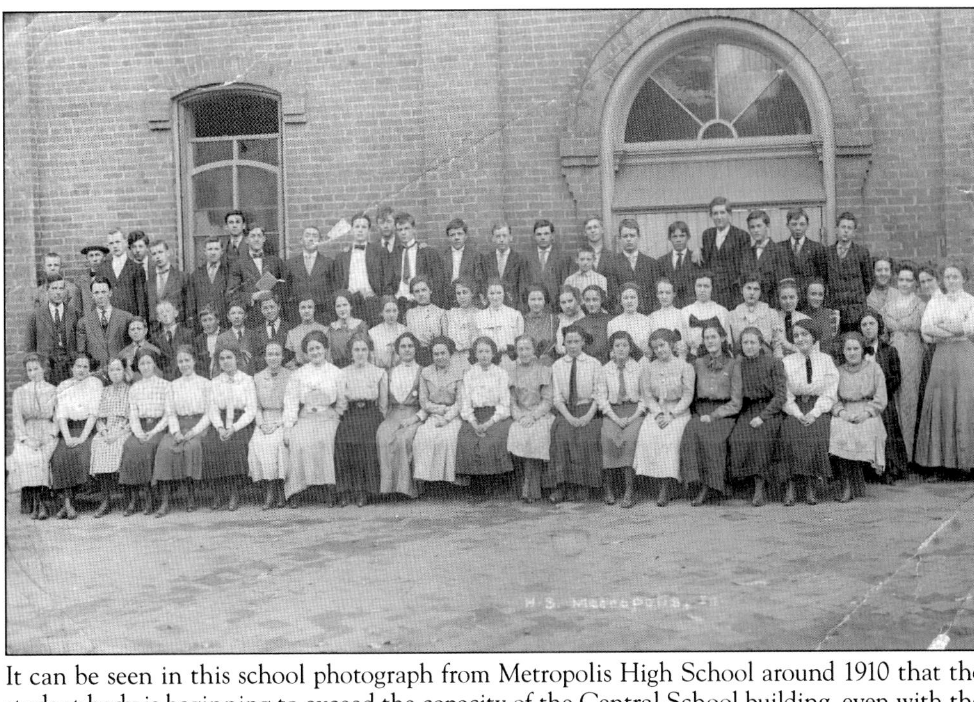

It can be seen in this school photograph from Metropolis High School around 1910 that the student body is beginning to exceed the capacity of the Central School building, even with the grades up through the fourth being moved to Clark School that year. A new high school building would not be finished for two more years.

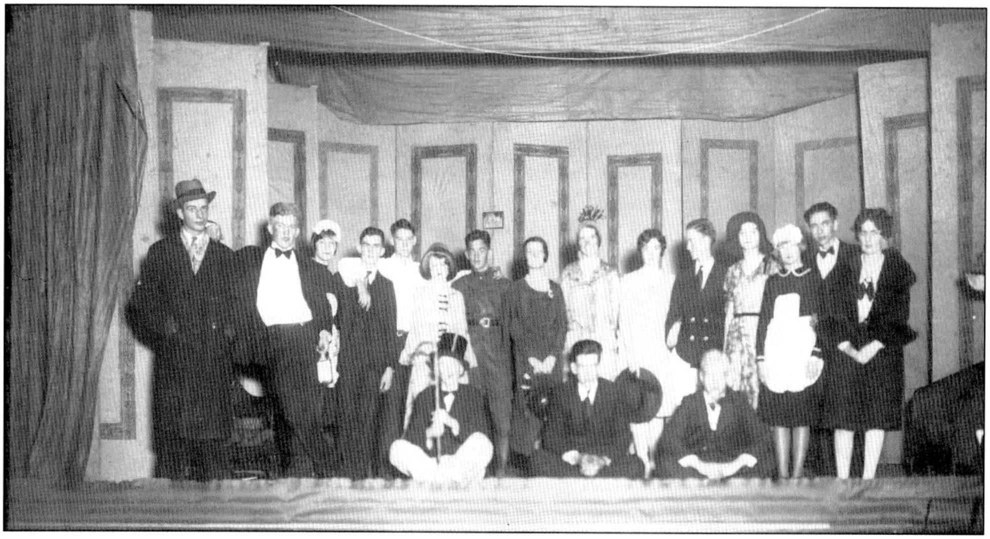

The play being performed here at Metropolis High School is *Our American Cousin*, written by English playwright Tom Taylor and notable for being the play Abraham Lincoln attended the night he was assassinated. Standing seventh from the left is Marvin Steele, whose part is unknown, though he appears to be wearing some type of military uniform, an interesting coincidence considering his later experiences detailed in chapter six.

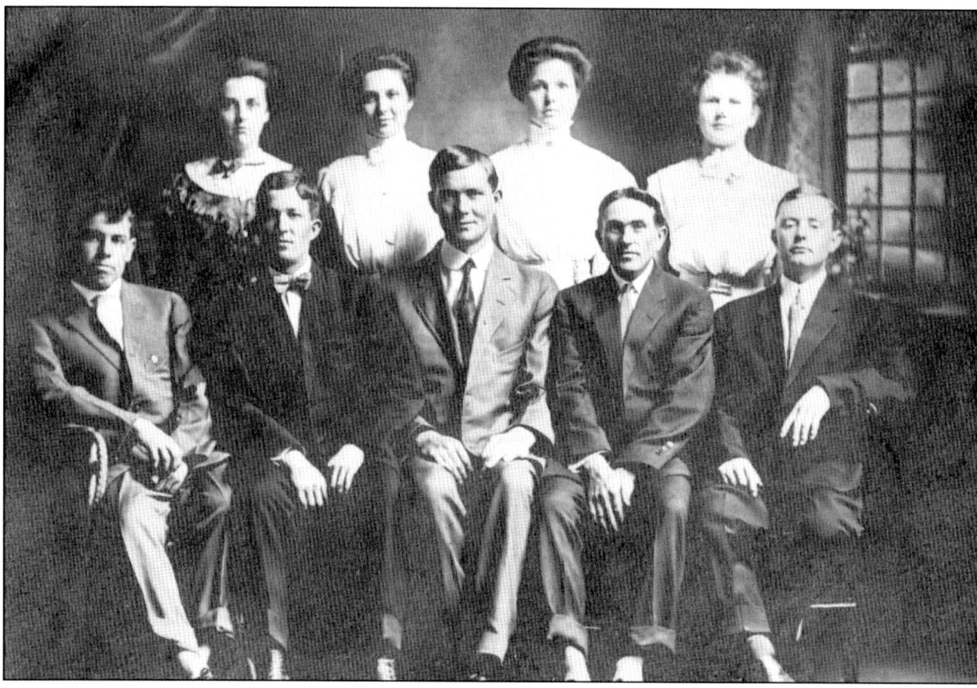

As mentioned before, age was not the primary factor in determining grade level at a time when very few people attended high school. This photograph shows Massac County eighth-grade graduates who have just completed the six-week spring term at Southern Illinois Normal University in Carbondale and are now ready to teach in county schools. Pictured, from left to right, are (first row) unidentified, Ward Dunn, William Bremer, Hiram Mescher, Ray Morse; (second row) Fleeta Roundtree, Edna Adkins, Mary Bremer, and Lottie Pergande.

Eight

Civic Life

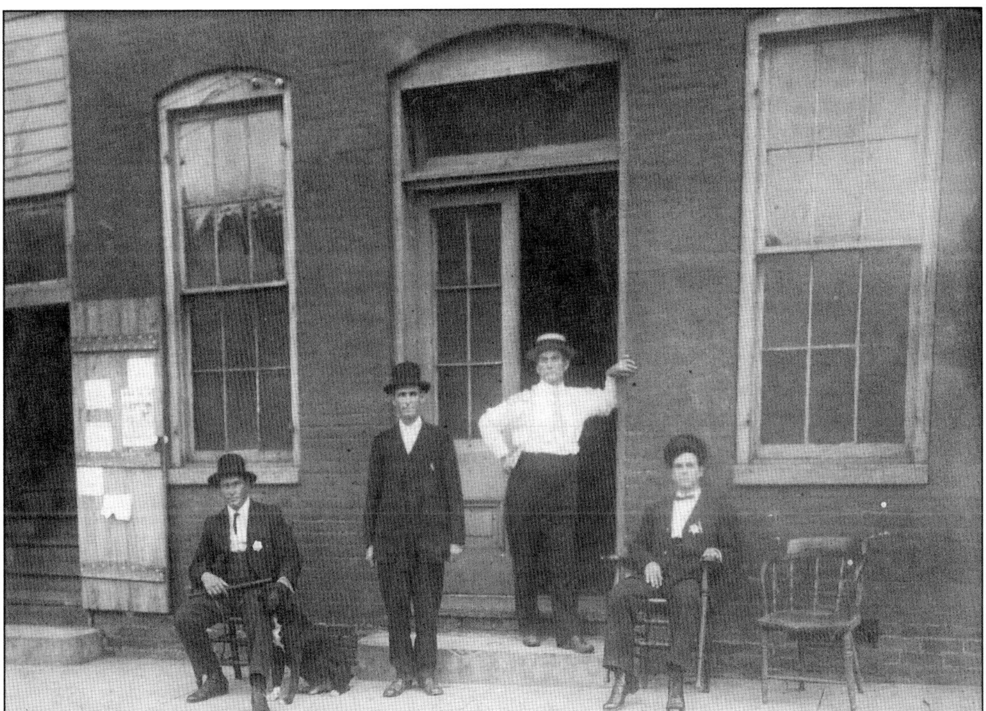

This photograph shows police officials from 1910 in front of old city hall. From left to right are Lannes Davis, marshal; Robert N. Smith, police magistrate; Harvey A Evans, city attorney; and Ike Brannon, deputy. The marshal, on the left, has on his lap a baton or "the badge of office," as it was called.

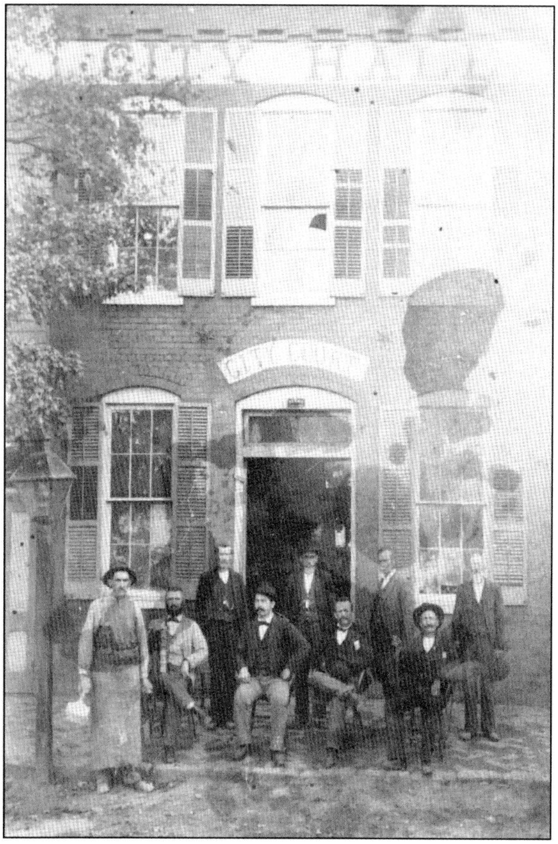

The city leaders in 1890 pose in front of old city hall. Pictured are, from left to right, Conrad Hursh, Judge ? Liggett, Squire ? Hutchison, Charles Cox, Sheriff Rob Barham, Judge ? Sawyers, Squire ? Wright, Night Chief Thomas Hunt, and Squire Thomas J. Austin

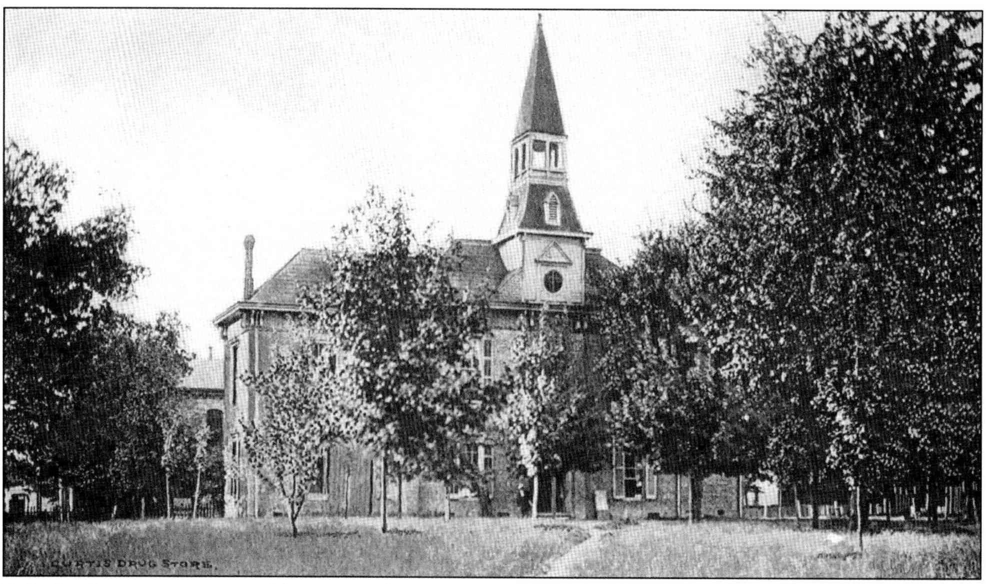

Bids for the construction of the original Massac County Courthouse, shown here, were taken in the spring of 1860, and the project was completed by the end of 1862. According to court records, the total cost of the project was $2,166.65. County offices were on the ground floor, with a courtroom and jury rooms upstairs. Plans to install a clock in the base of the spire never materialized.

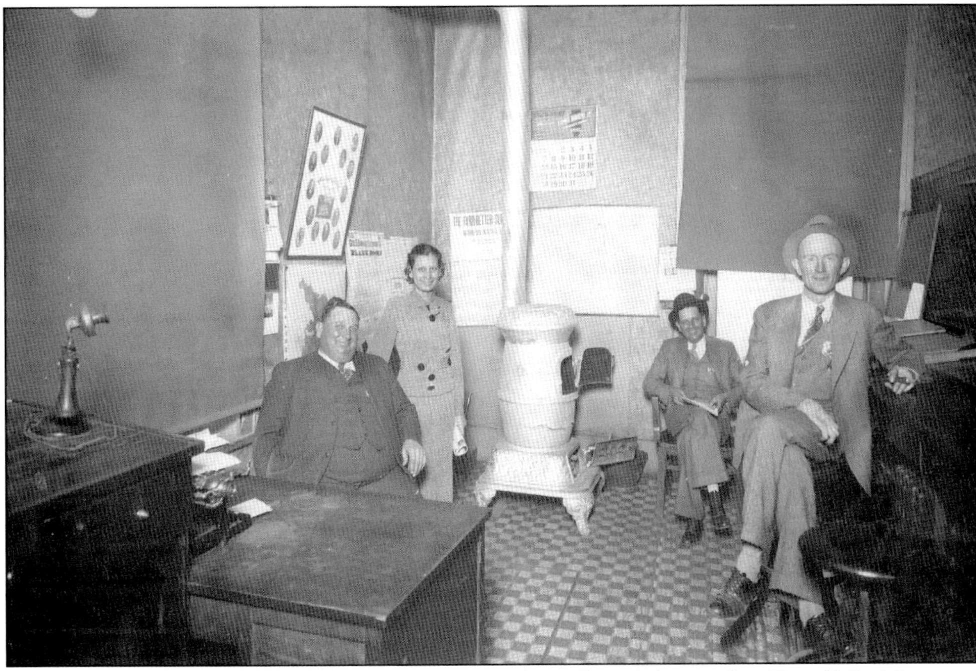

The sheriff's office is shown around 1935. Pictured are, from left to right, Sheriff Fred Risinger, his daughter Alice, Deputy Melvin O'Brien, and Deputy Herbert Goyert. Fred's wife, Florence, was named Massac County sheriff in 1937 to finish out her husband's term after he died in office. She was the first female sheriff in Illinois.

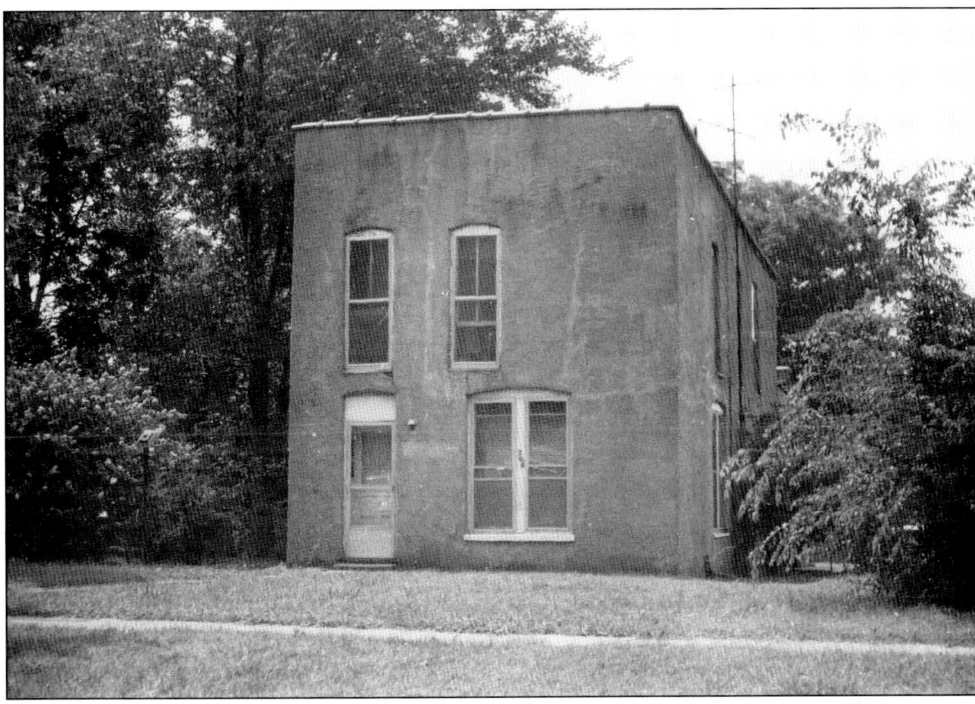

County jails were sometimes placed on the upper floor of a courthouse, often alongside the residence of the sheriff. This one sit separately.

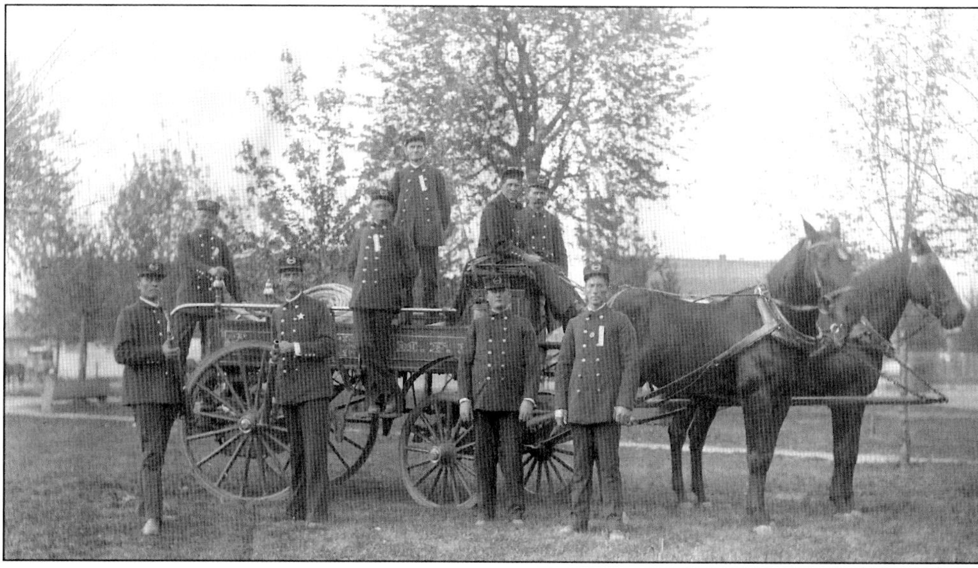

The earliest fire wagons in Metropolis were pulled by hand with volunteers and were purchased after a disastrous fire in the area of Third and Ferry Streets in April 1876. Prior to that time, there was no organized fire department in the city, and the destruction wrought by that conflagration drove home the need for specialized equipment. The horse-drawn wagon shown was purchased sometime around 1905 and is displayed here shortly after that on the Courthouse Square. By the 1920s, motorized fires engines were making their appearance.

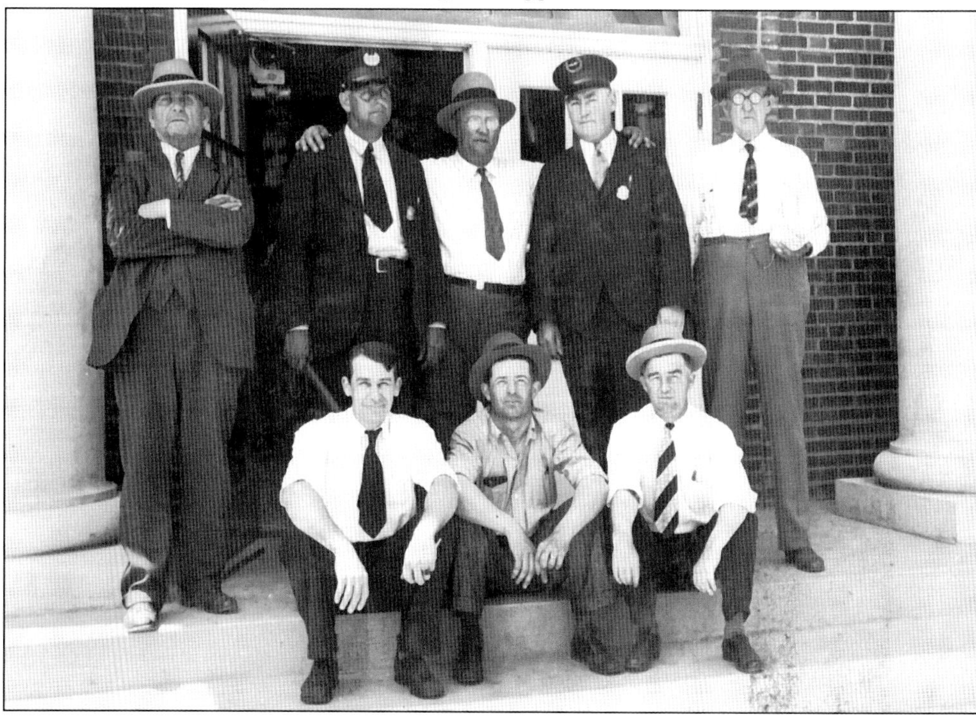

City police and associates in front of the new City Hall are, from left to right (first row) Bob Palmer; unidentified; and Mitch Rutledge; (second row) unidentified; Lloyd Rice, chief of police; Doc Simpson; Charles Techenbrock; and unidentified.

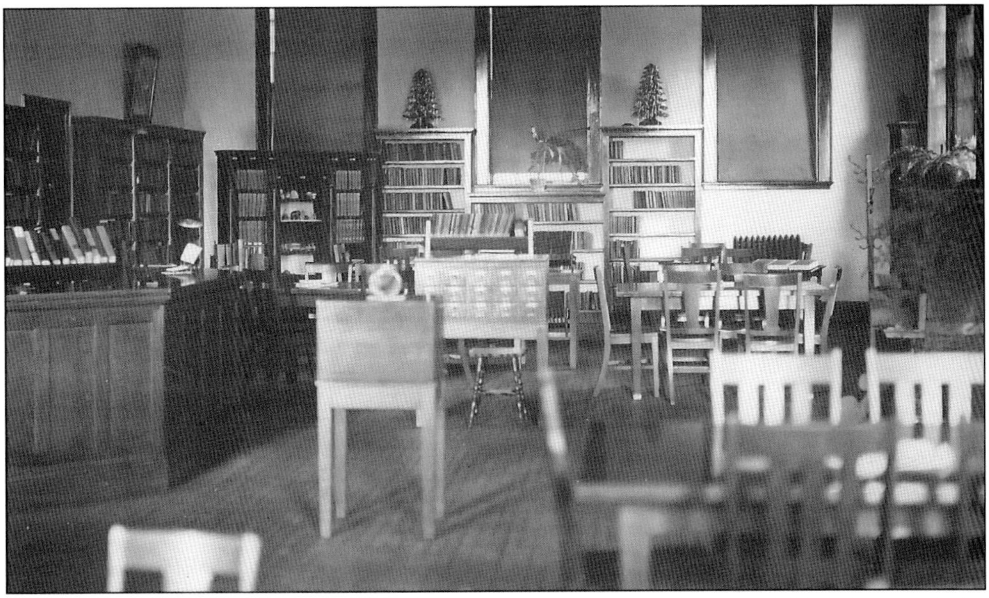

Construction began on the Carnegie library in Metropolis on June 8, 1913. After nearly 20 years in a section of the McCartney Music Hall, the library moved to land donated to the city by Metropolis founder William McBane. Shown is the interior of the library in the 1950s. The item in the middle is a card catalog.

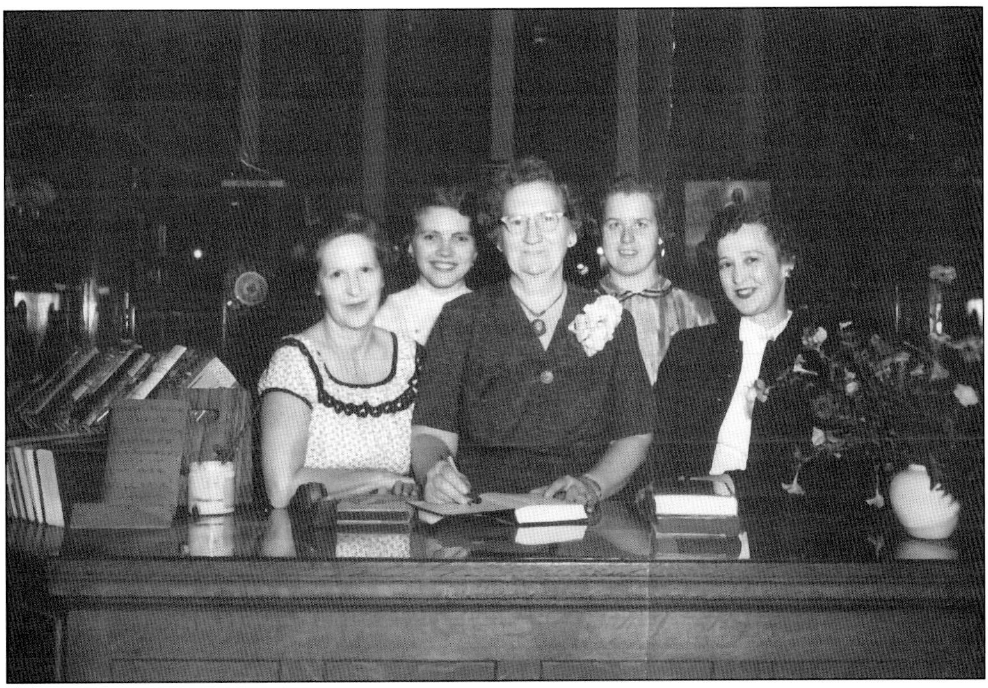

In 1953, the Metropolis Public Library staff includes, from left to right, (first row) Inez Davis, head librarian Carolla Ruggles, and assistant librarian Ruth Middagh; (second row) Alfrieda Horman and unidentified.

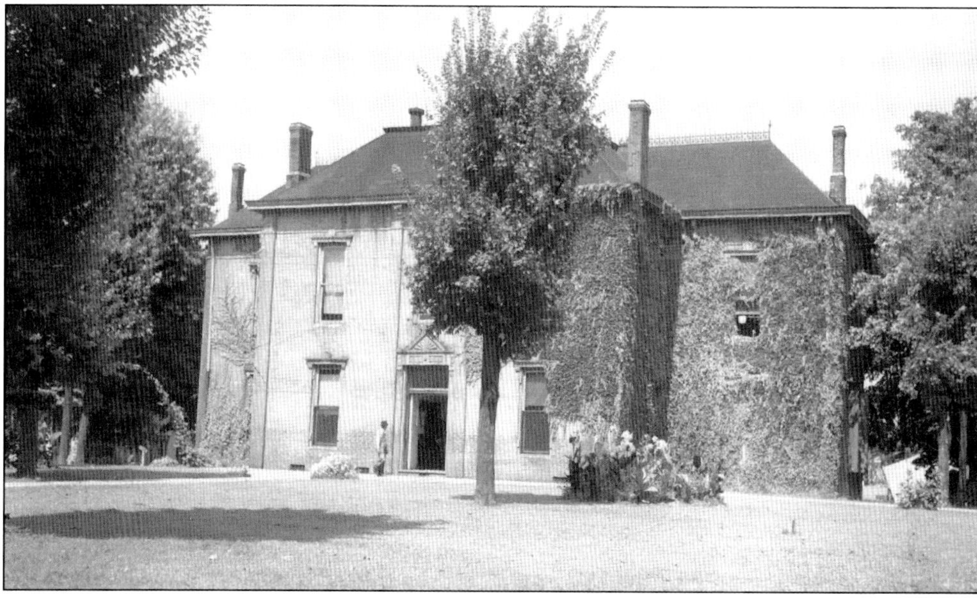

After additions were made to the north and south sides of the building in 1891, a fire caused major damage to the old courthouse sometime shortly after 1900. Repairs cost approximately $2,000, very near the original construction price. Accounts differ as to whether the removal of the spire happened at this time or after a 1910 windstorm.

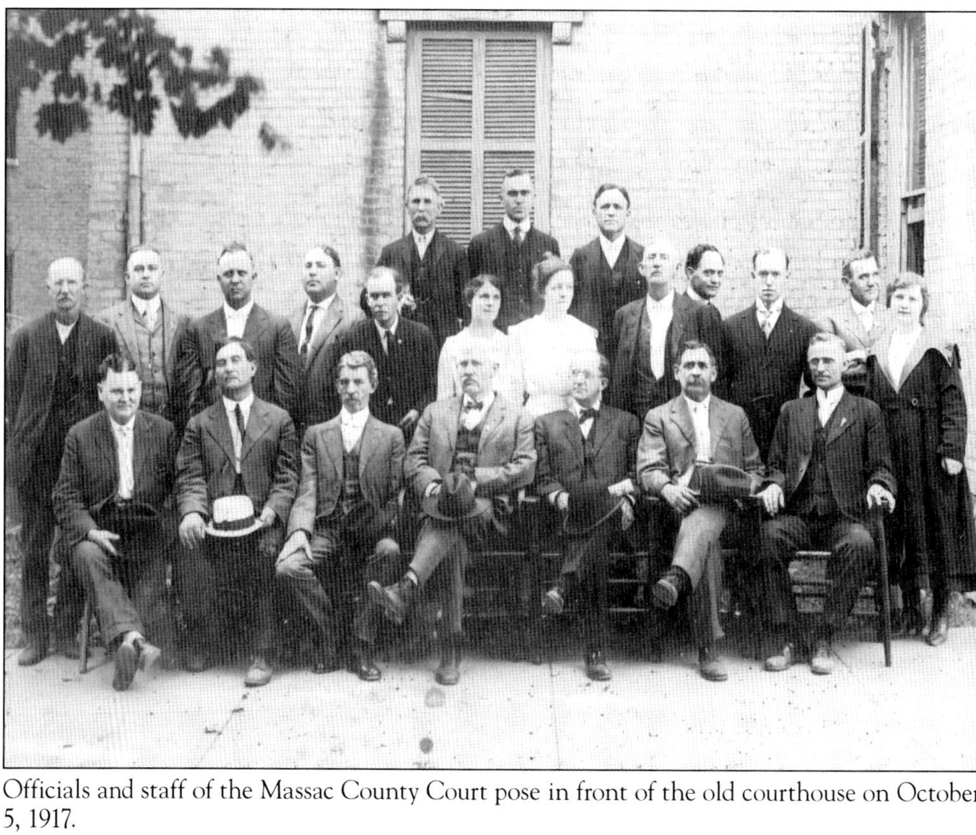

Officials and staff of the Massac County Court pose in front of the old courthouse on October 5, 1917.

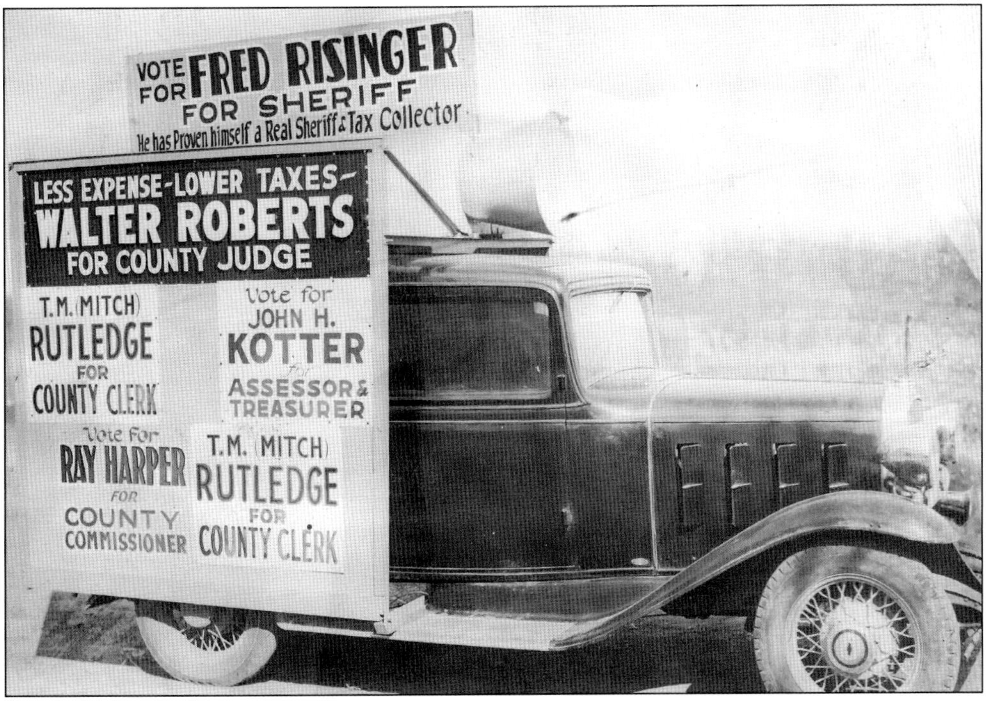

A truck, owned by Harold Gowins, is bedecked with campaign posters from an election. The vehicle is a 1931 Chevrolet; the posters are for 1932 Republican candidates. It should be noted that a county judge in older county government systems was a county administrative position, akin to a county commissioner or county supervisor.

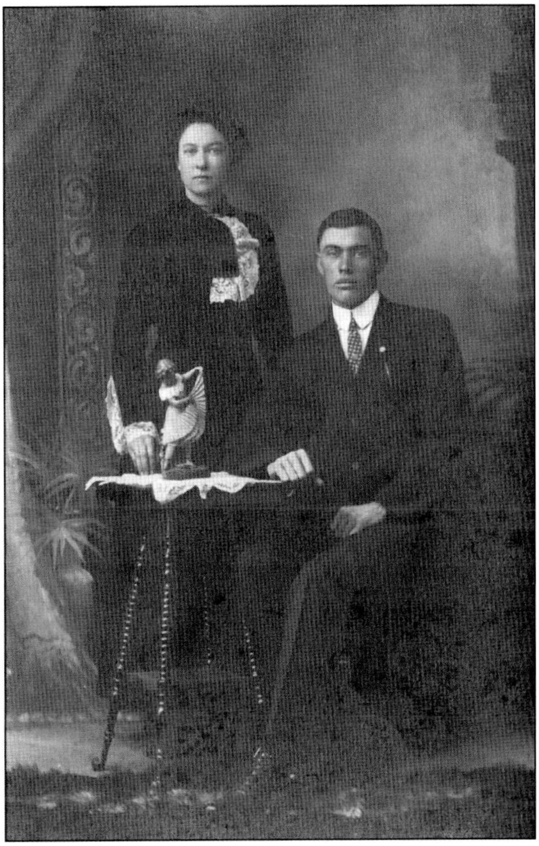

Longtime county clerk Henry Morrow and his wife, Emma, pose for the camera; the date is unknown.

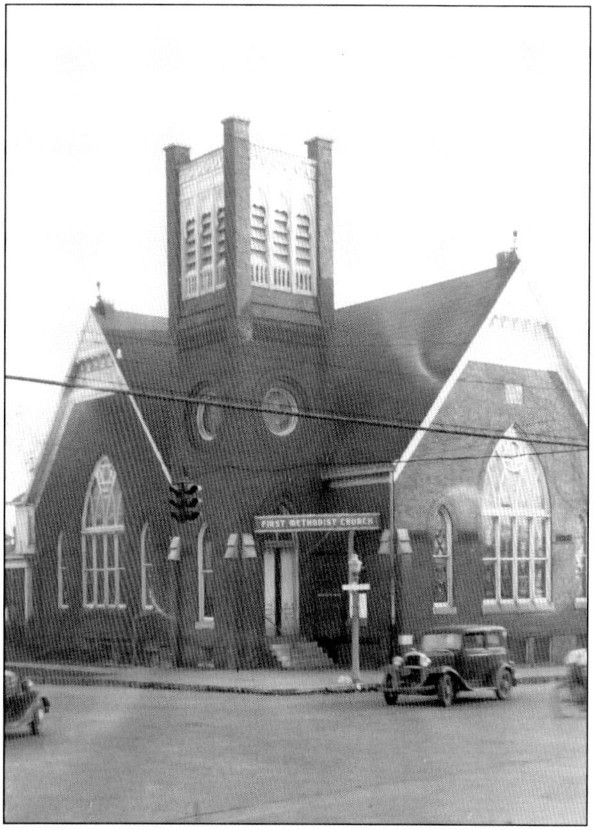

The First Methodist Church was built between 1889 and 1892. It is seen here during the 1930s, after the first steeple was damaged in a storm. A new steeple was added and the sanctuary remodeled in 1969, only to be destroyed in a fire with the rest of the main church building on January 11, 1970. The newer, more modern present-day church was begun on December 13, 1970, and completed in January 1972.

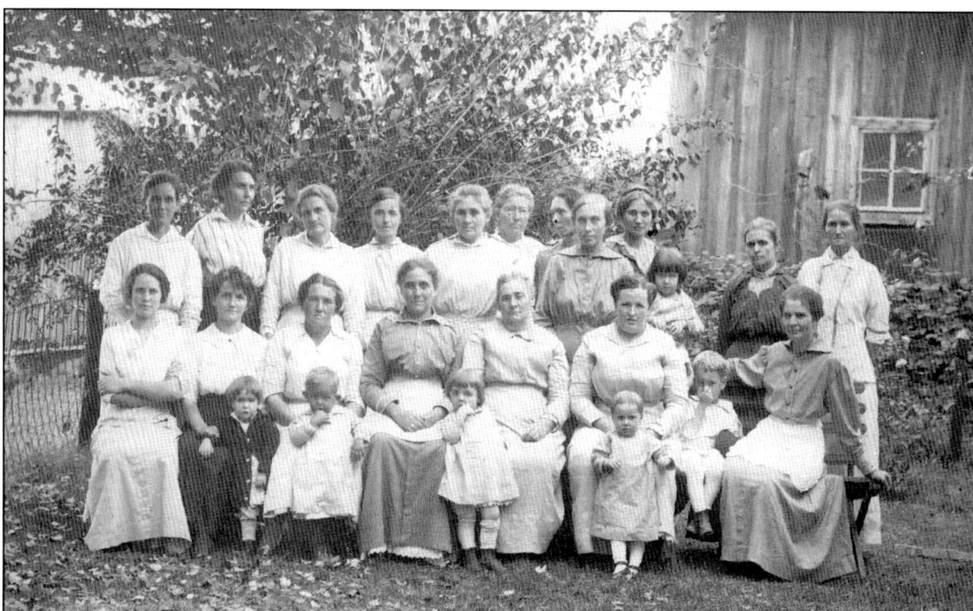

Members of the First Methodist Ladies Aid Society are pictured here with some of their children in 1916. In 1914, a new organ was placed in the church, made possible by an endowment from Andrew Carnegie and, of course, the work of the women of the church.

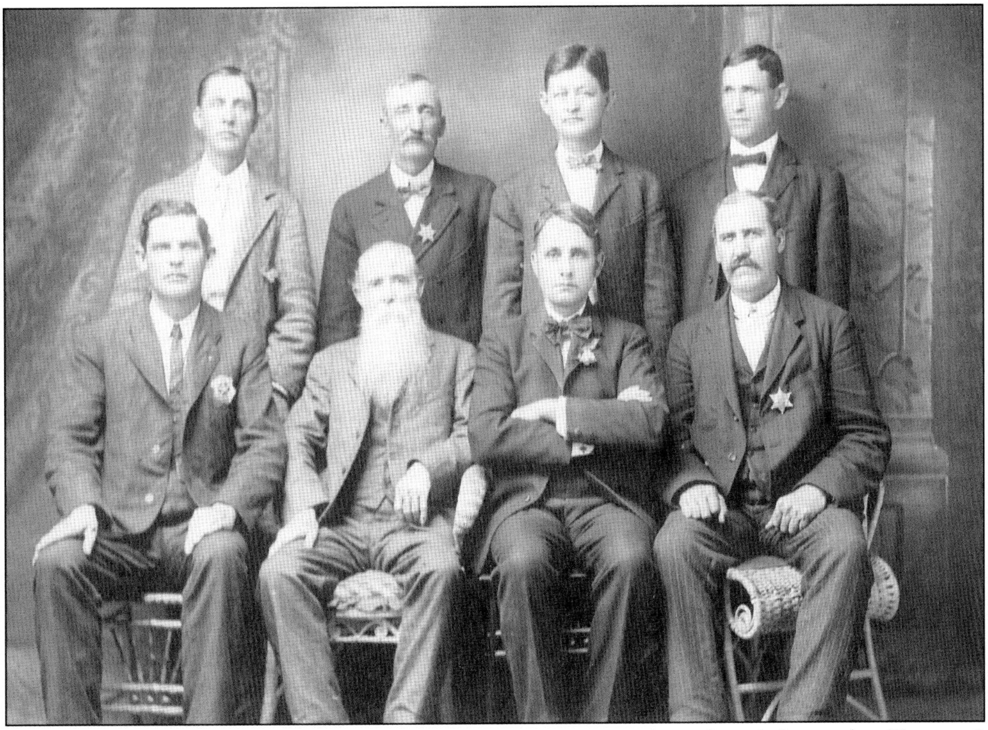

Here are Metropolis city officials in the 1905–1908 era. Pictured are, from left to right, (first row) James L. Munal, marshal; John M. Elliott, mayor; Bart Kerr, attorney; and William Wiant, deputy; (second row) Ed Compton, clerk; Tom Hunt, deputy; Louis Quante, treasurer; and Robert Smith, police magistrate. Elliott was the founder of Elliott's Furniture as well as being an undertaker.

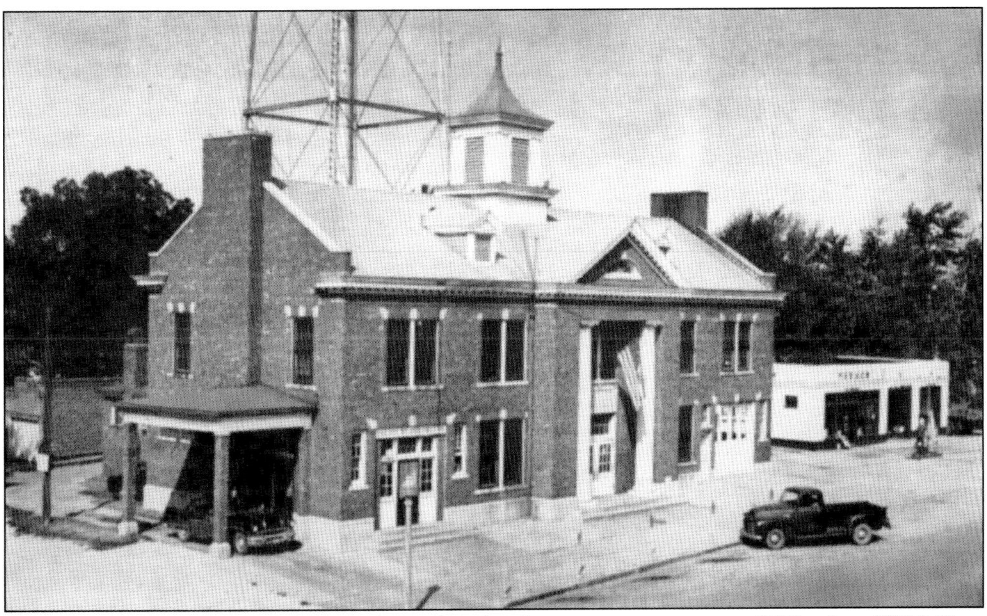

The new city hall building is shown here shortly after its construction in 1930, when W.H. Karr was mayor. The fire and police departments were located in the same building until 1986.

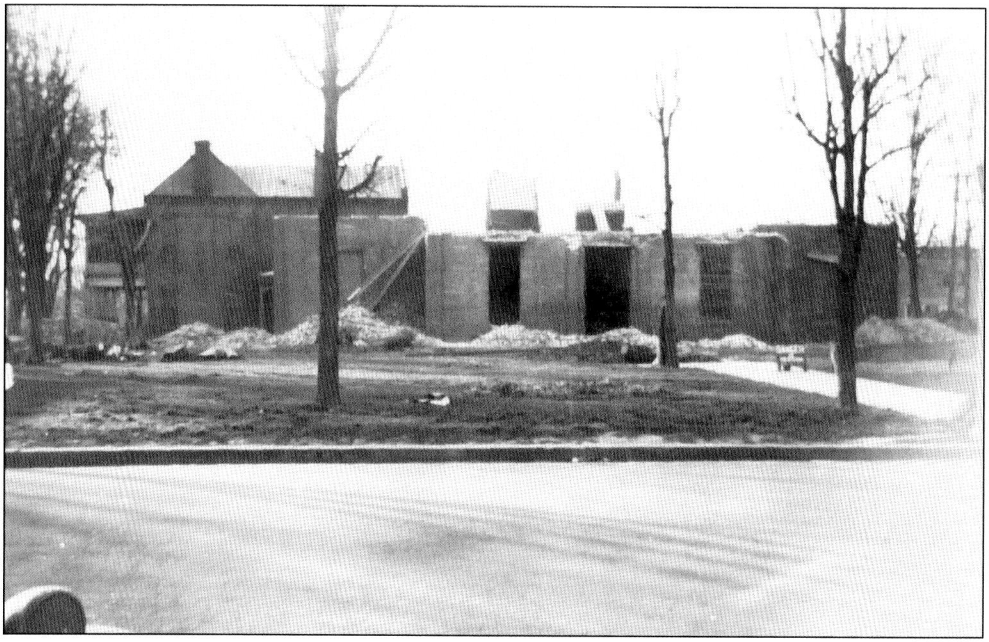

In the spring of 1940, almost 80 years to the day after the committee to oversee its construction was formed, demolition began on the old Massac County Courthouse. The sheriff's residence and jail is still standing at this time.

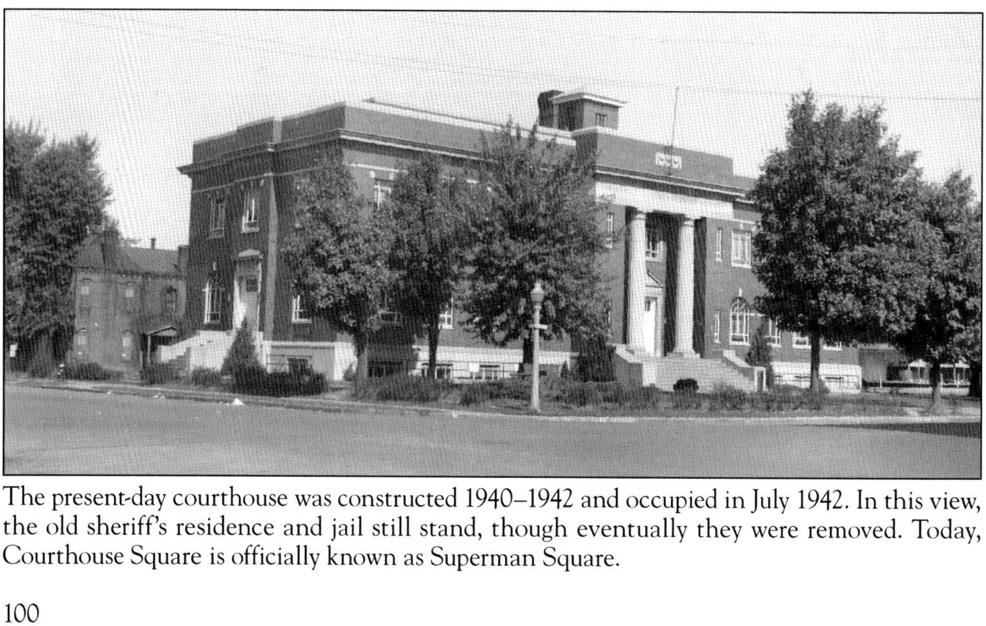

The present-day courthouse was constructed 1940–1942 and occupied in July 1942. In this view, the old sheriff's residence and jail still stand, though eventually they were removed. Today, Courthouse Square is officially known as Superman Square.

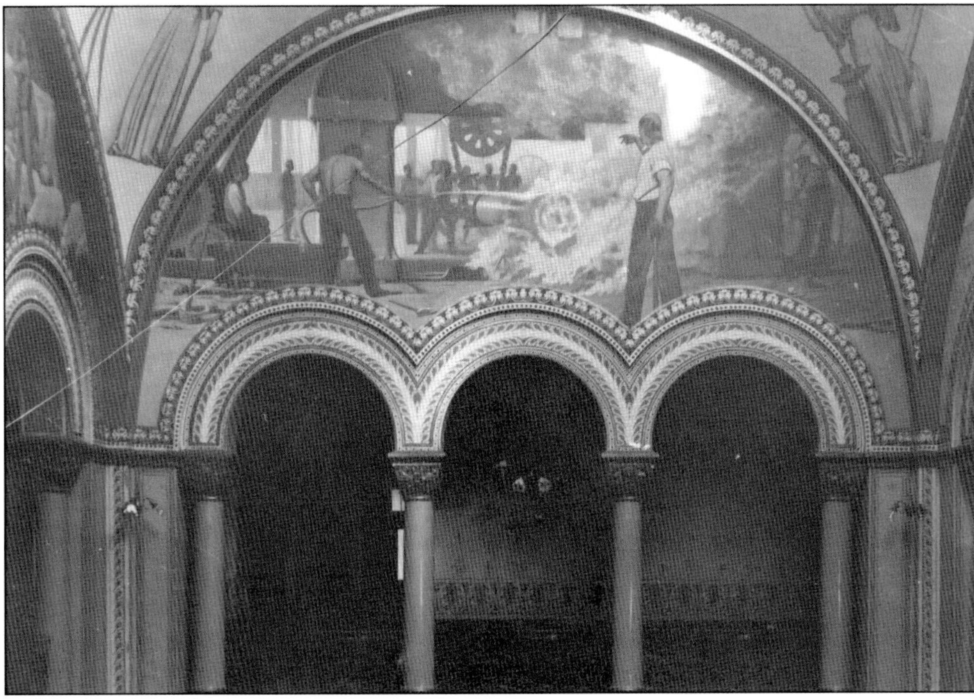

This is purportedly the interior of the McCartney Music Hall, with a mural that appears to date from the New Deal era.

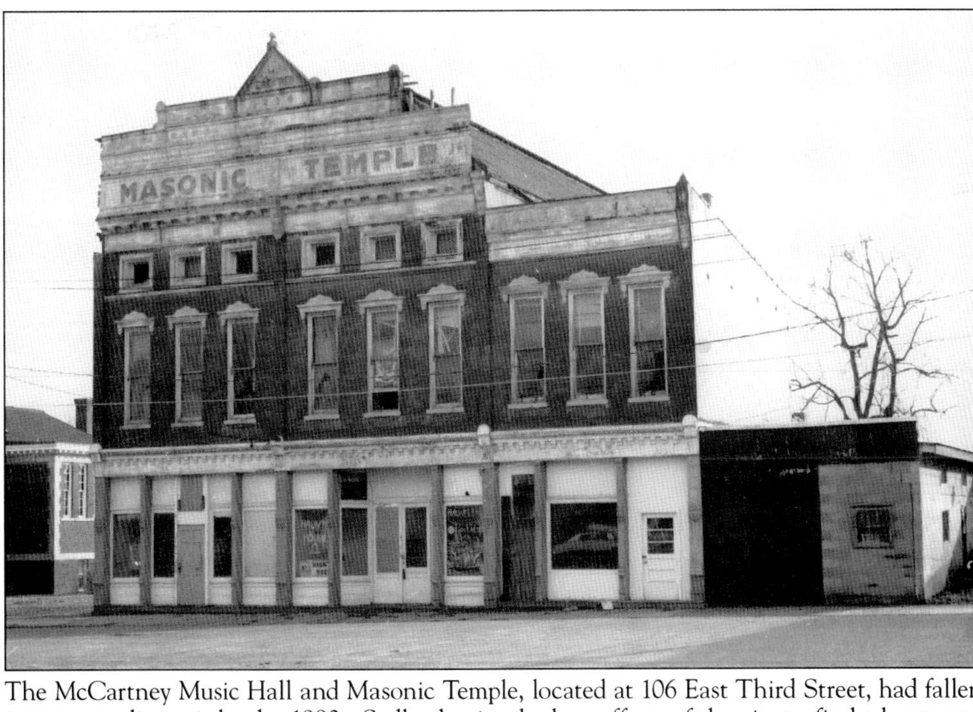

The McCartney Music Hall and Masonic Temple, located at 106 East Third Street, had fallen into severe disrepair by the 1980s. Sadly, despite the best efforts of the city to find a buyer and those of the Massac County Historical Society, who helped get the nearly 100-year-old structure named to the National Register of Historic Places, the building was eventually demolished.

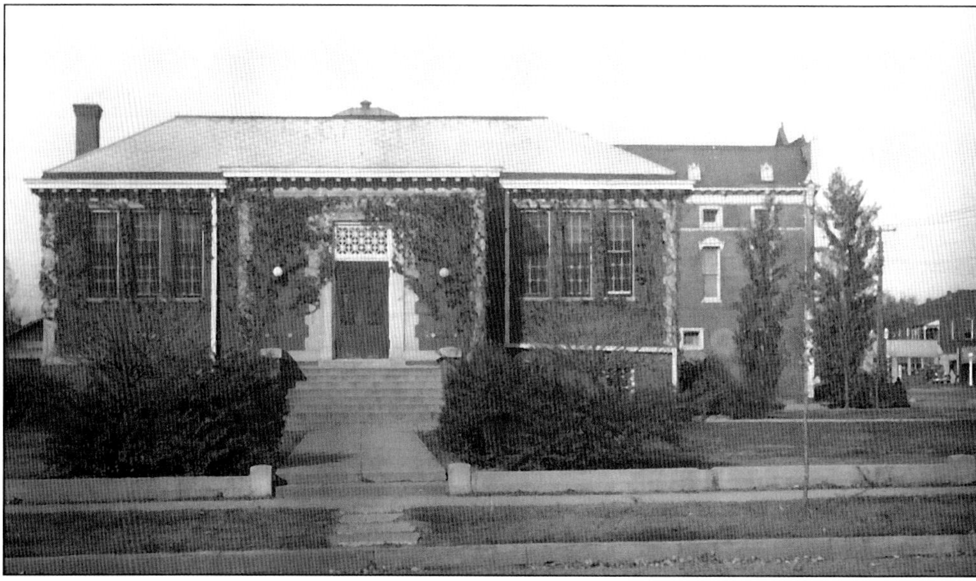

Built with assistance from the Carnegie Corporation, the Metropolis Library was dedicated on November 27, 1915. Prior to that, the library had been housed in a section of the McCartney Music Hall (visible on the right, behind the new library) for over 20 years. The library now has two new wings and a great collection for a small town.

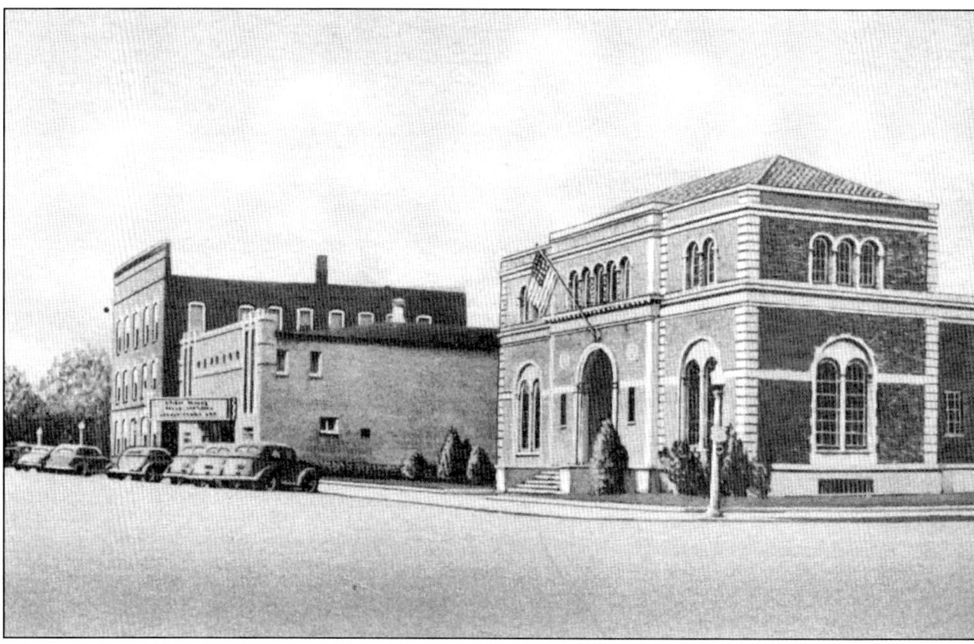

The US post office, built in 1928 on the former site of the Norris house, is located next to the last remaining movie house in Metropolis, the Massac Theater, built in 1938. Efforts are underway to save the theater, now unused for over 30 years and in need of a new roof. A nonprofit organization was formed to help preserve the property, and a buyer, who hopes to restore the property, was finally found in January 2012.

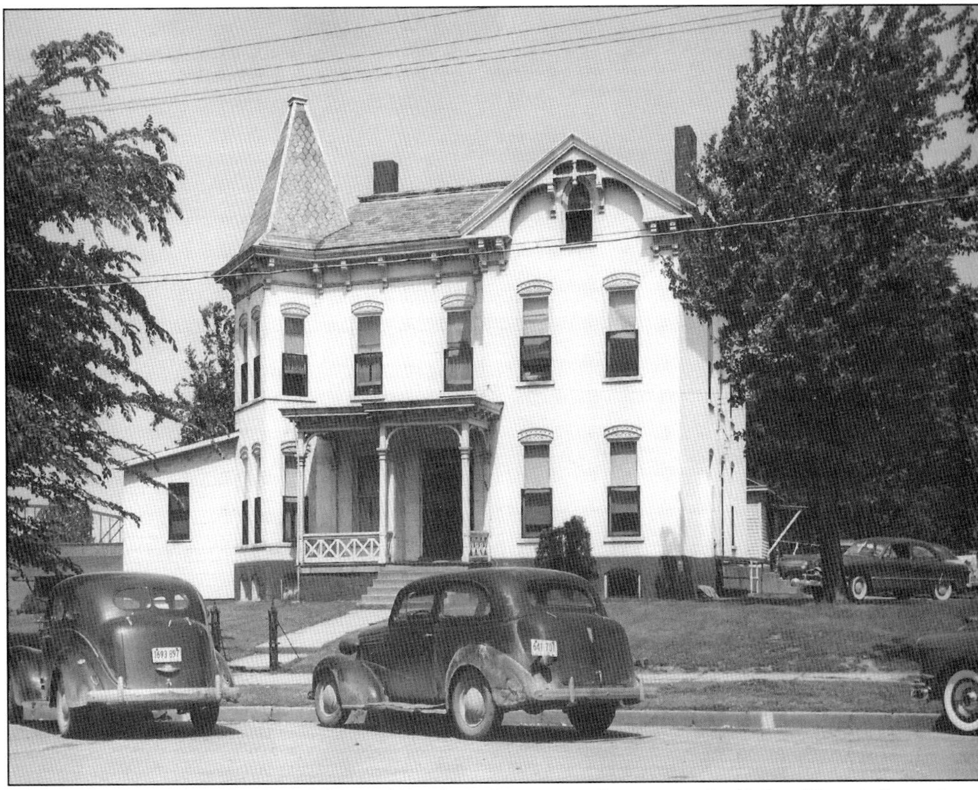

The Quante house is shown in the early 1950s, when it was known as the Fisher Hospital, a private facility founded by Dr. Joseph Allen Fisher. For approximately 20 years prior to the opening of Massac Memorial Hospital in 1956, it served as the primary health care facility for Metropolis and much of the surrounding area.

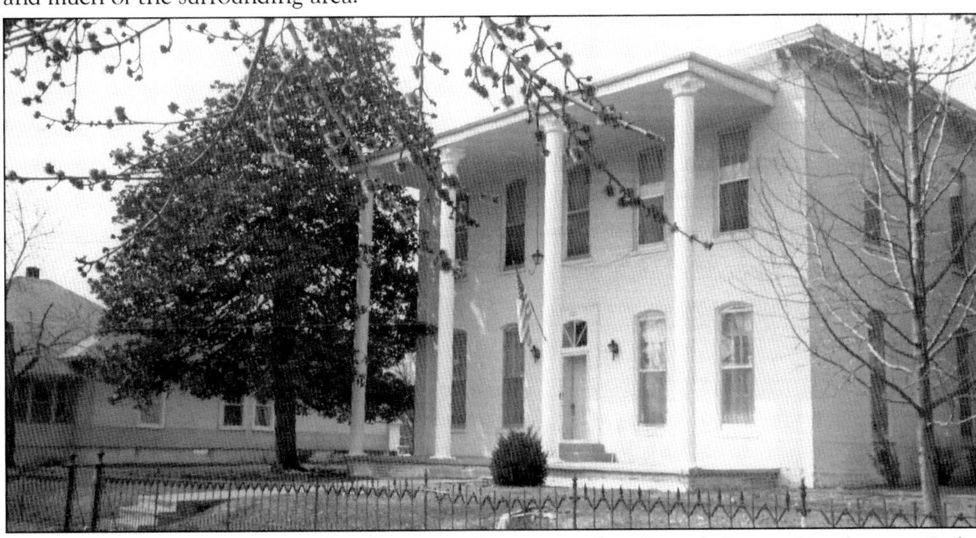

Before the Fisher Hospital, another former residence served as the only hospital in the area. Judge John Mulkey had been elected to the Illinois Supreme Court in 1879, and when he decided not to stand for reelection in 1888, he bought the house at 721 Metropolis Street, later dying there in 1905. After his death, the house was converted into the Walbright Hospital.

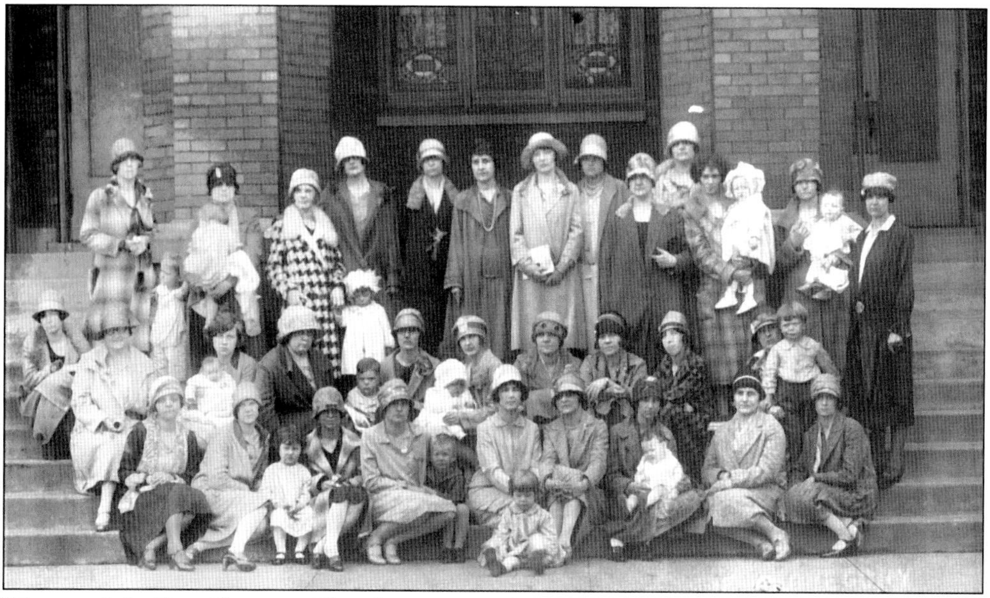

Women of the First Christian Church are pictured in 1927. The church was built on land deeded by William McBane, the founder of Metropolis, for the sole purpose of erecting and utilizing a house of worship—for the sum of $1 and despite McBane's professed agnosticism. The present sanctuary was constructed in 1914.

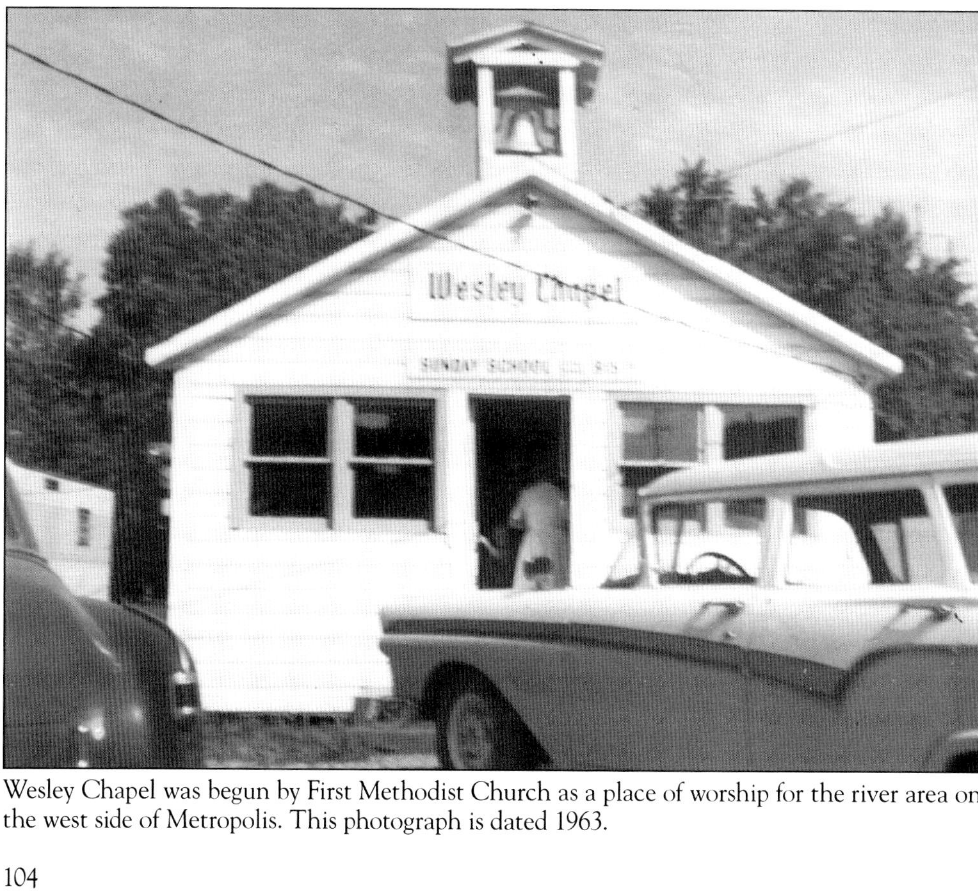

Wesley Chapel was begun by First Methodist Church as a place of worship for the river area on the west side of Metropolis. This photograph is dated 1963.

Nine

Social Life

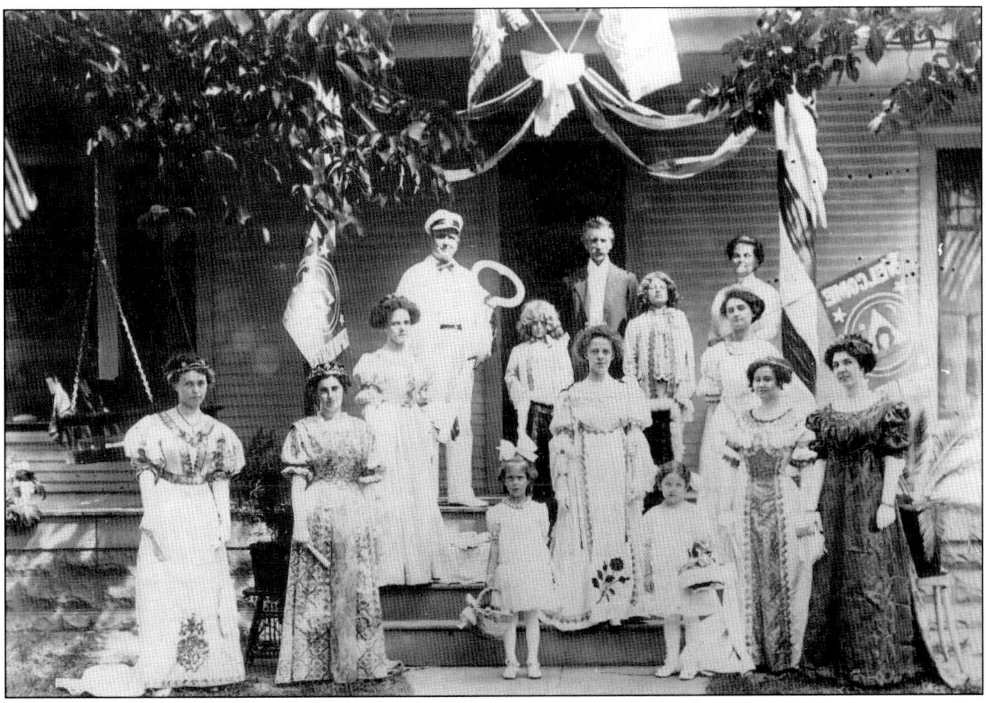

In June 1911, the Hustlers' Convention, a gathering of traveling salesmen, held a big parade in town, which even had a queen and court. Hazel Stewart (center) was crowned queen, while Hattie, her twin sister (third from left), looks on as a maid of honor. Mayor Willis Ward, dressed in white and holding the key to the city, and state senator Douglas Helm stand at the rear.

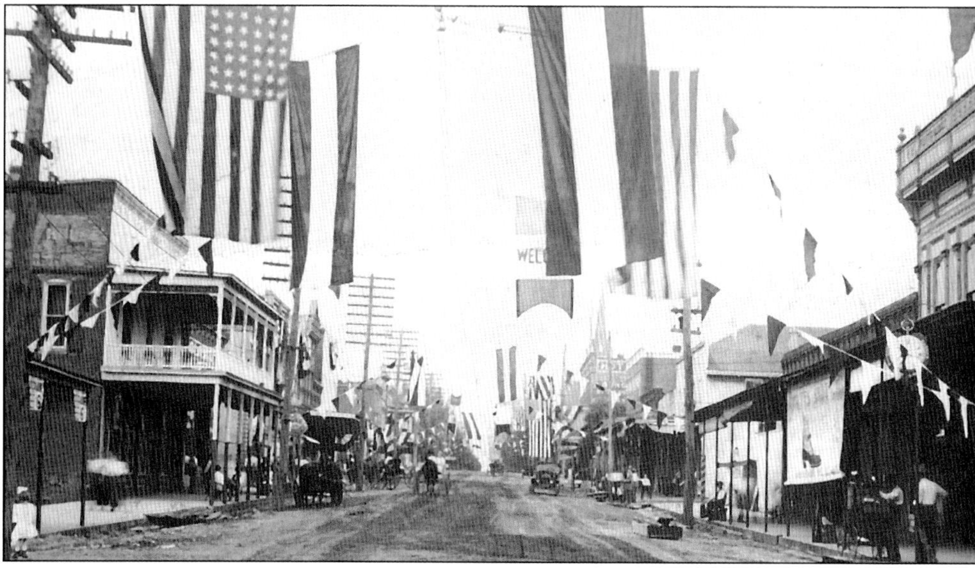

On lower Ferry Street, looking north from Third Street, decorations festoon every available spot in preparation for the Hustler's Parade in June 1911. A roll-down cloth sign in the lower right of the photograph is advertising Fritts' Shoe Store, and a popcorn wagon is next to the sign.

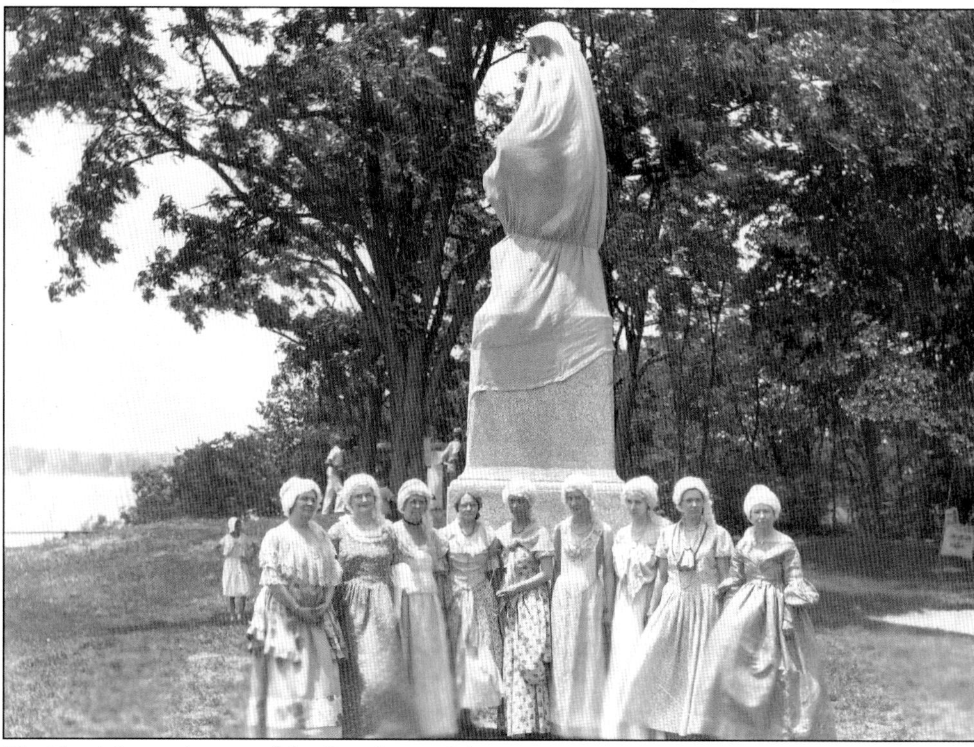

The Fort Massac chapter of the Daughters of the American Revolution prepares for the unveiling of the statue of George Rogers Clark in 1932. The state chapters of the group were instrumental in getting Fort Massac declared as Illinois's first state park in 1903, as well as erecting the original monument honoring Clark five years later. The chapters even shared responsibility for the park's management until 1917, when the Illinois's Department of Parks was established.

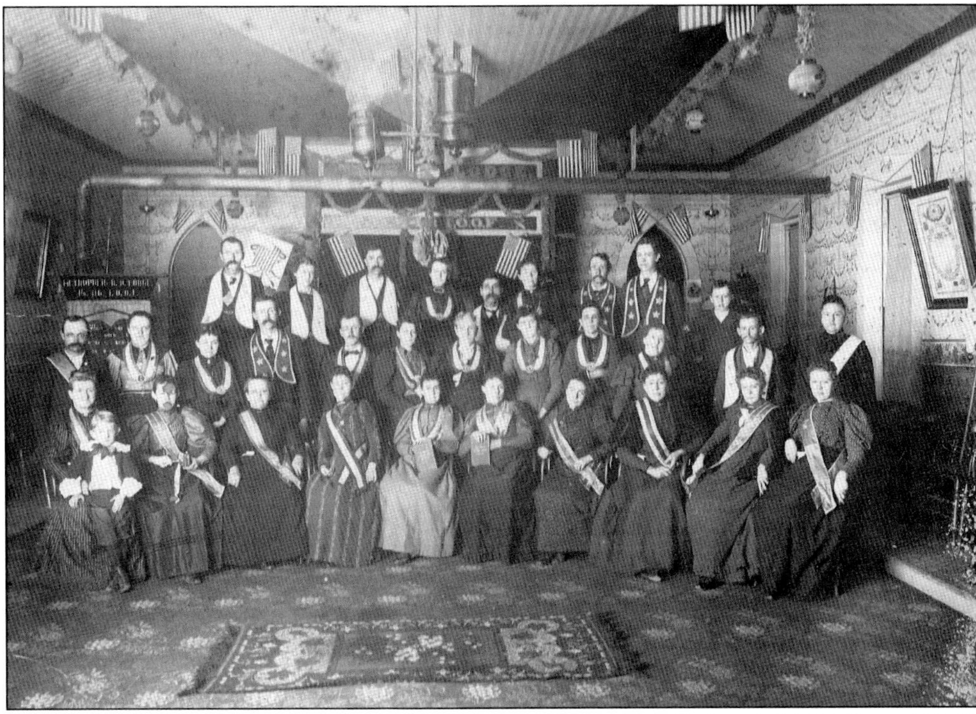

Members of the Rebekah Lodge No. 116 and the Independent Order of Odd Fellows (IOOF) Lodge No. 86 are shown around 1890.

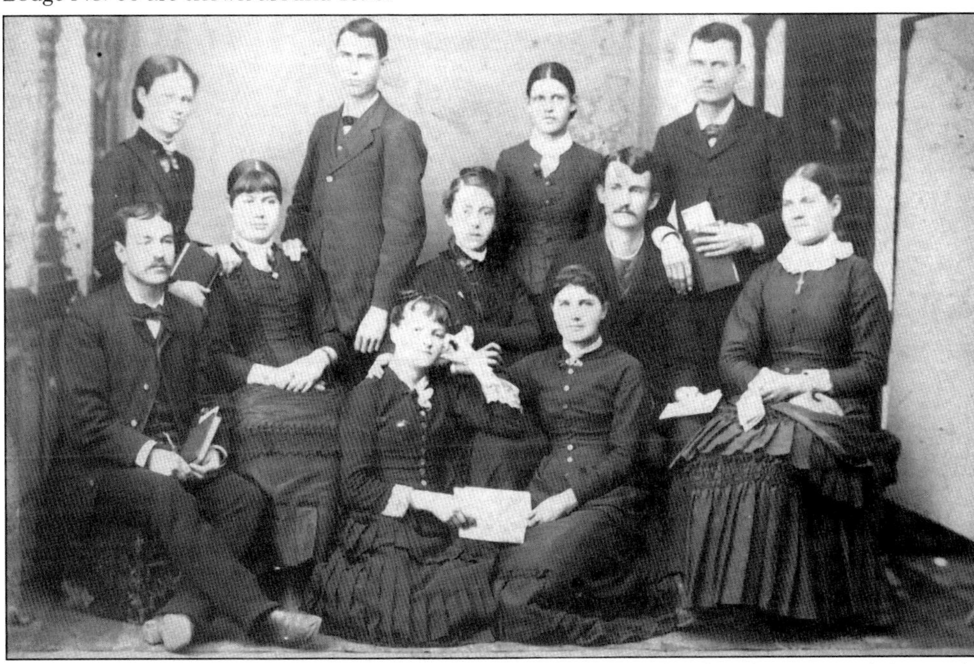

Most, if not all, members of this late-1880s literary society are schoolteachers. From left to right are (on the floor) Grace McCartney (later Trousdale) and Dora Riggs; (sitting in chairs) J.C. Leggitt, Eva Gowan, Ellen Daly, David? Smith, and Lulu Bartleson; (standing) unidentified, Jno. Williamson, Ida Neer, and Marcus McCartney. (Photograph by Henderson's Studio.)

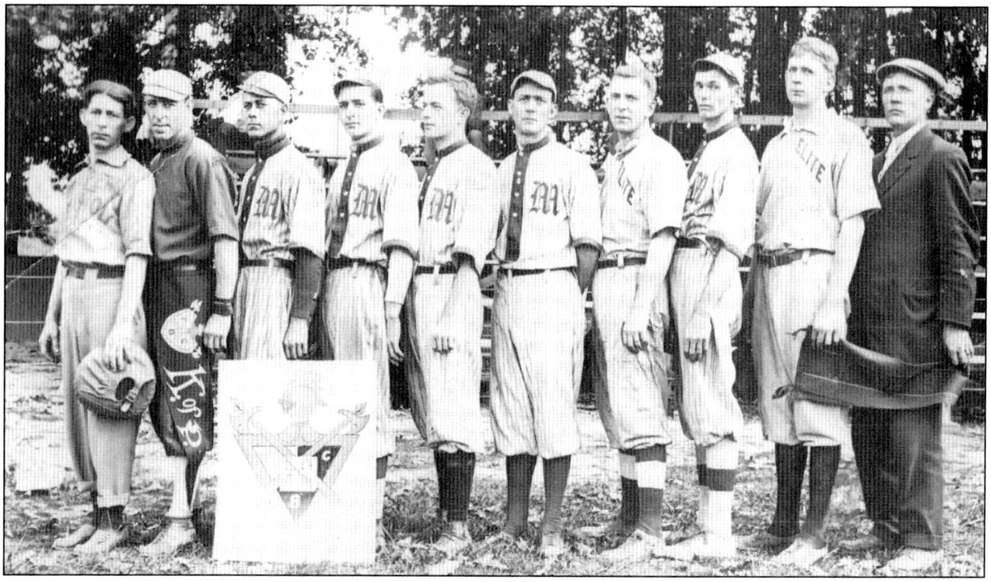

The Knights of Pythias sponsored a baseball team for years in the 19th and 20th centuries. This photograph from 1913 shows, from left to right, Eddie Mizell, H. Lester "Peggy" Craig, Simon Korte, Louis LaVeau, Frank Winters, Charlie Reider, Earl Armstrong, "Scrapper" Doyle, Charlie Amlingmeyer, and former Metropolis mayor Bill Karr.

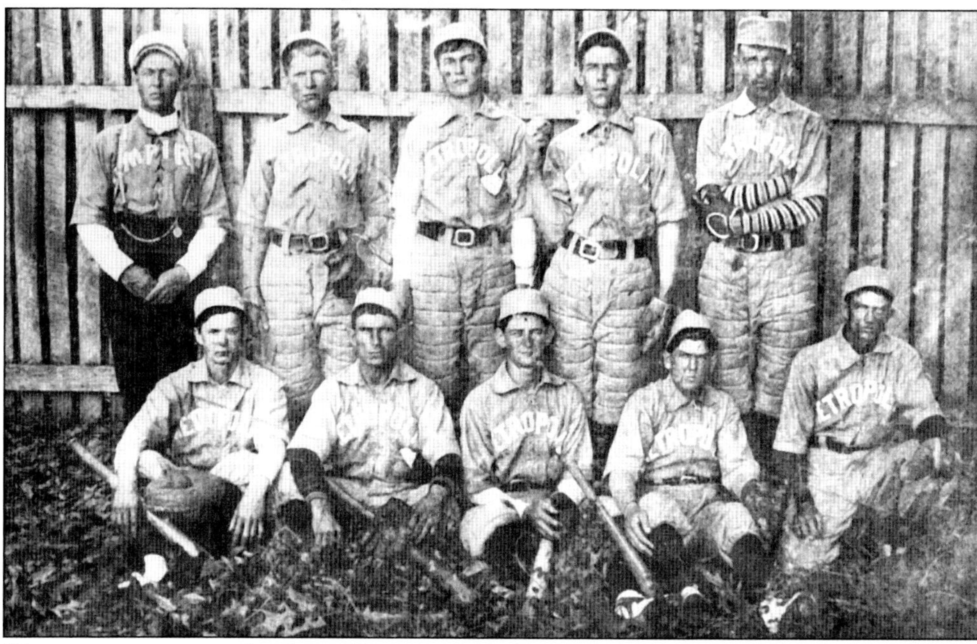

Winning games across Southern Illinois and Northern Kentucky, the Metropolis Blues baseball team was a force in regional sports during the early 1900s. The 1904 team is shown here, in new uniforms, at the Golconda Fairgrounds on May 24. The men arrived via the steamer *Dick Fowler* to play the hometown team, but not before getting stuck on a sandbar and delaying the game. Shown here are, from left to right, (first row) Louis Doyle, E. Ward, John McCorkle, Jesse Gregory, and John Martin; (second row), grocery store owner and team manager Ed Compton, Tom Spencer, Fred Rehlmeyer, Hal Munal, and Norris Shaw.

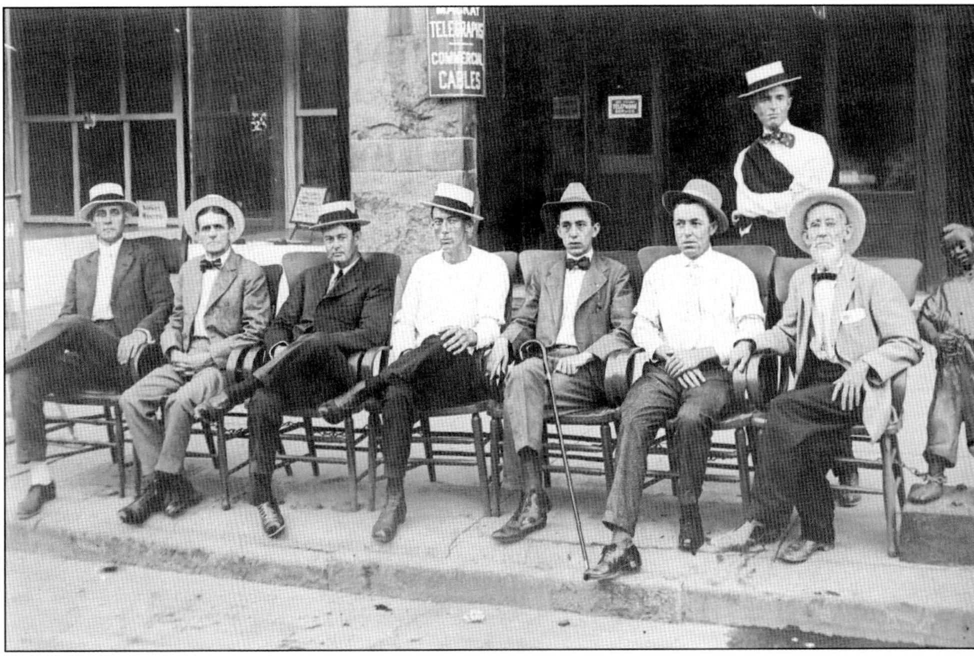

A group of gentlemen gathers on the curb in front of Mackay Telegraph offices in Metropolis. Judging by the largely identical hats and the arrangement of chairs, they may be attending one of the political parades common at the time. Richard Austin Sr. is seated on the right. Mackay was a national company at the turn of the 20th century, as common as Western Union is today.

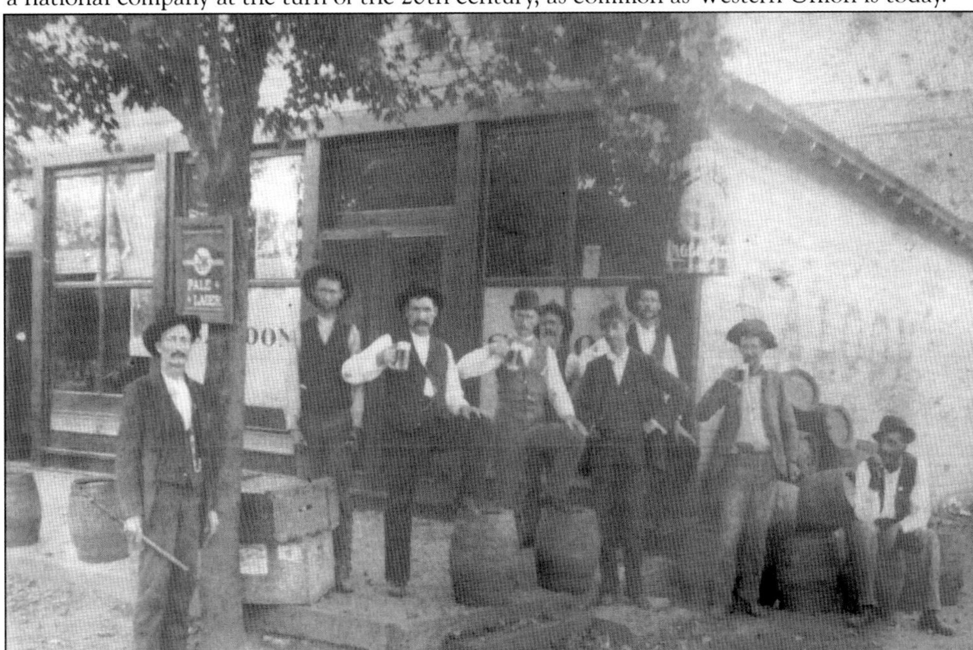

An unidentified saloon was located next to Carter's Livery Stable at Market and Sixth Streets near the turn of the century. The present building is now the location of the Super Museum. Pictured are, from left to right, Thomas Hunt, ? Benton, Jim Fisher, Monroe "Mun" Simmons, unidentified, Mike McFarland, unidentified, unidentified, and Manuel Waters

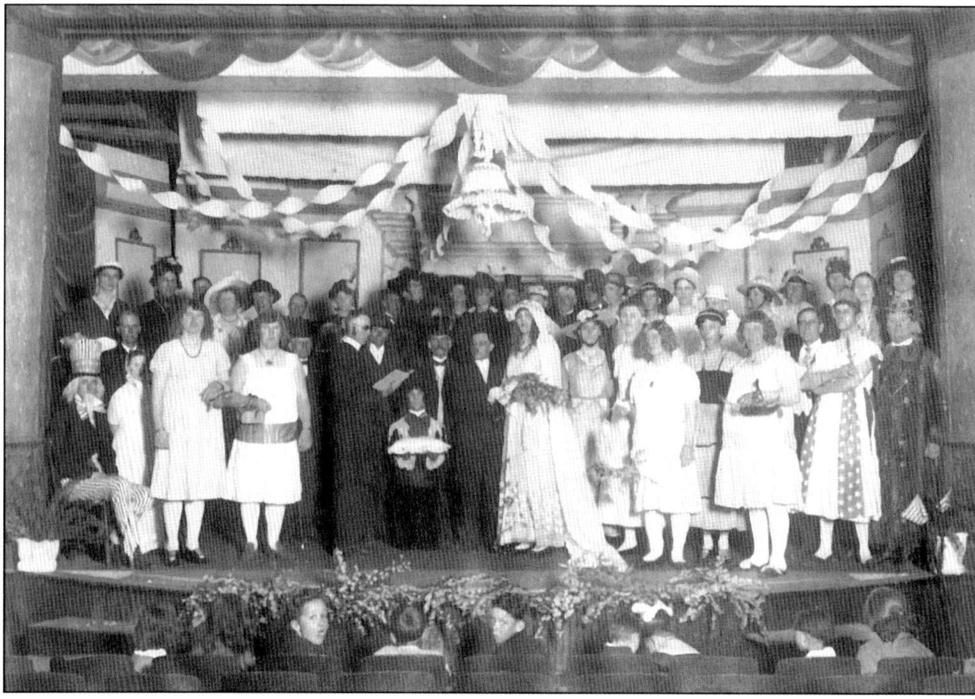

On first glance, this October 1917 photograph appears to be of a normal wedding, albeit with some quite homely ladies in attendance. On closer inspection, these celebrants are townsmen in drag, many of them quite prominent citizens, including Henry Humma, Sheriff Risinger (first row, fourth from right), and even "Uncle Sam" (seated, far left). The group appears to be putting on a show for children, who seem to be enjoying it, judging by their expressions.

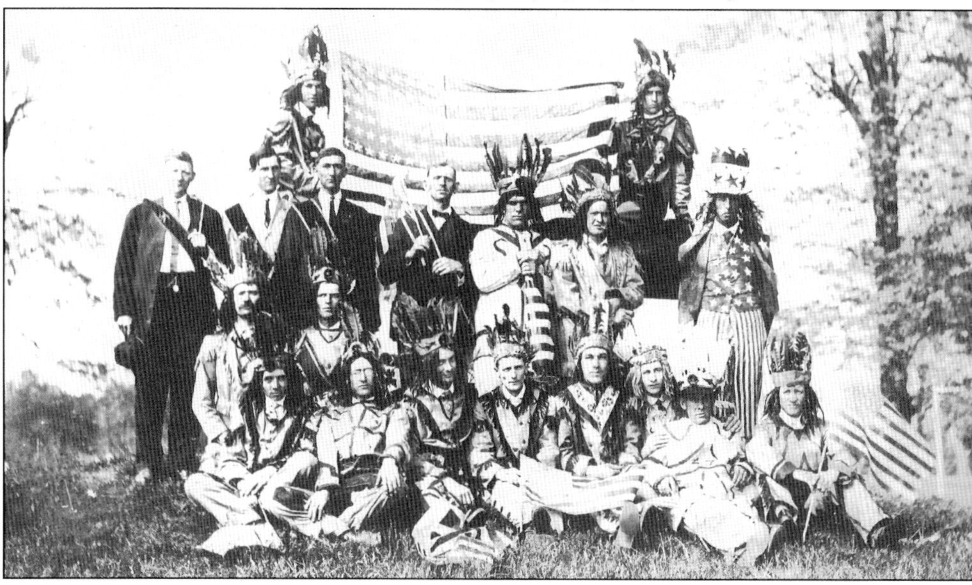

This photograph, taken at the entrance to Fort Massac, is supposed to show the Metropolis Indian ball team around 1915; however, no equipment of any sort is visible. There were baseball teams associated with various lodges in town, so perhaps, judging by the sashes on the noncostumed men, this is one of them.

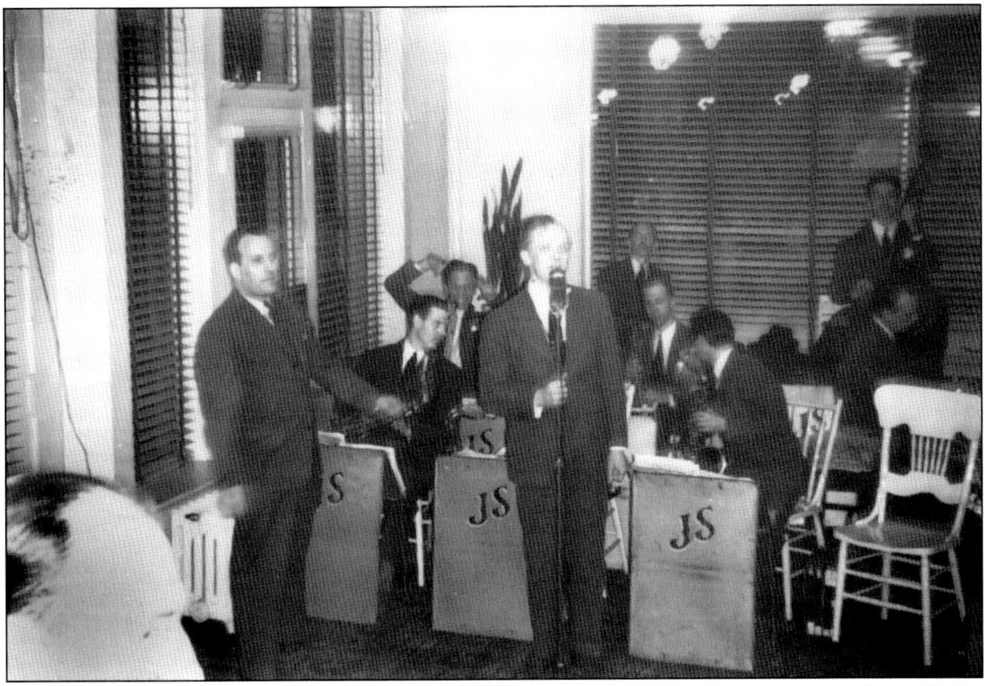

Jack Stalcup was Metropolis bred and a very popular bandleader from the 1940s through the 1960s. He is seen here, on the left, at the formal opening of the Hotel Metropolis in the 1940s.

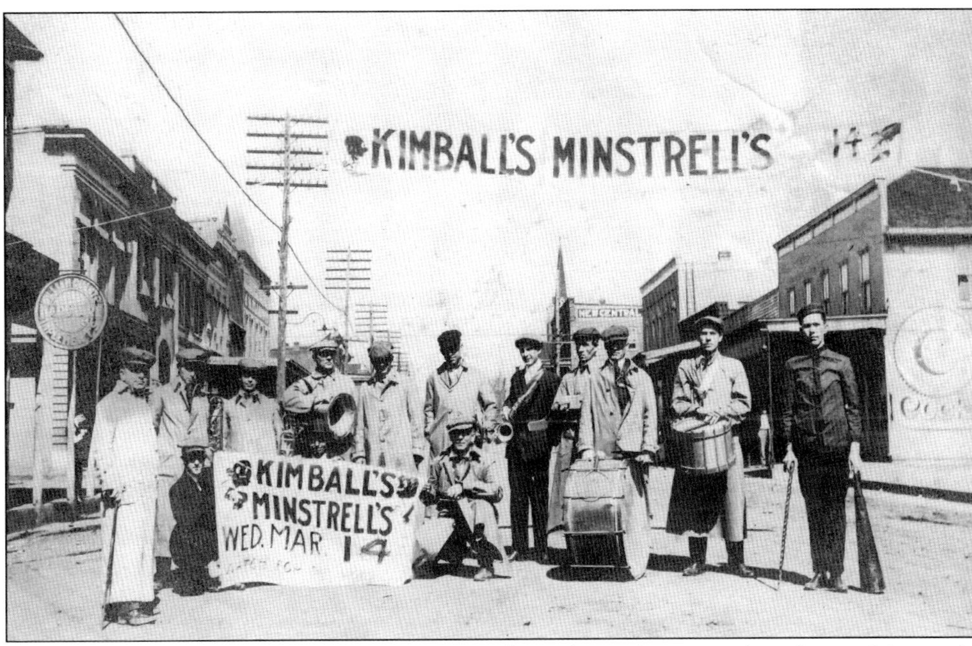

Standing on lower Ferry Street, Kimball's Minstrell's are here advertising their show in Metropolis on March 14, 1917. The building directly behind the drummer's head is the New Central Hotel, previously known as the Hotel Ward, and before that the State Hotel. Roy Rew and Earl Armstrong are holding the sign, and John Kimball stands on the far left.

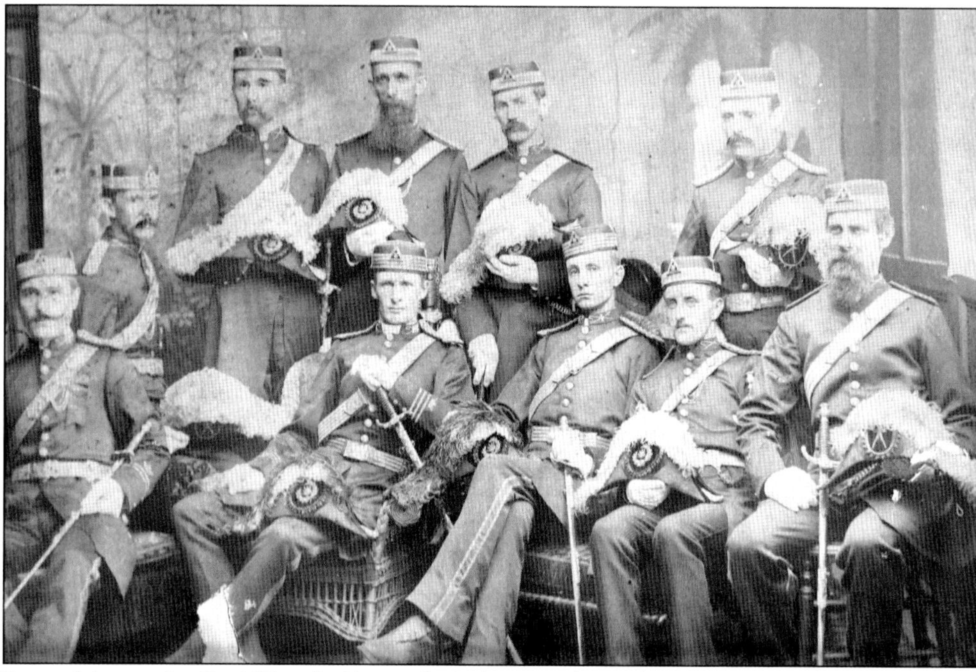

Formed during the Civil War, the Patriarchs Militant is the uniformed branch of the Independent Order of Odd Fellows. The only person identified here is David Smith (second from left), brother of Daisy Walsh. He married Grace McCartney but died early in the marriage. Grace then married widower Fletcher Trousdale.

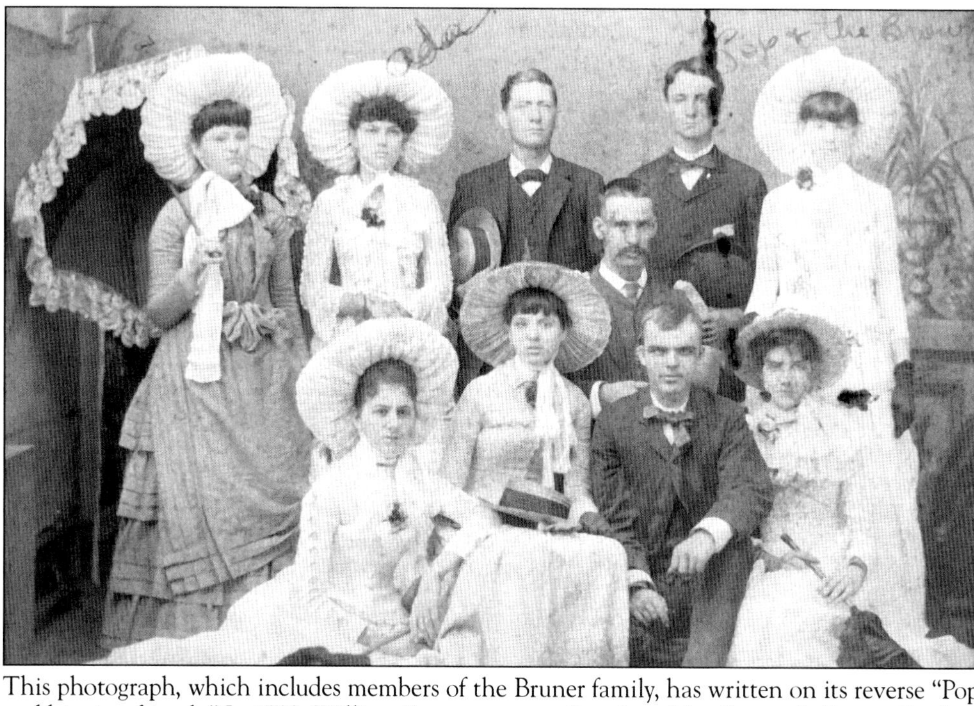

This photograph, which includes members of the Bruner family, has written on its reverse "Pop and his ritzy friends." In 1892, William Bruner was a cofounder of the Brown & Bruner Bank at the northeast corner of Third and Ferry Streets. (Photograph by Henderson's Studio.)

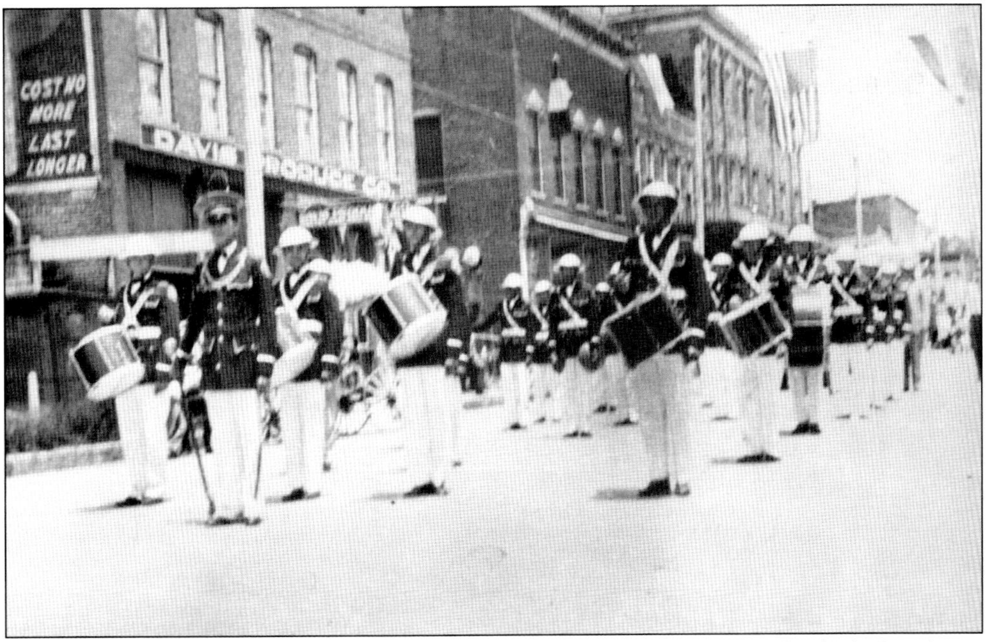

This band marches past the Davis Produce Company during the 1928 Fourth of July Parade.

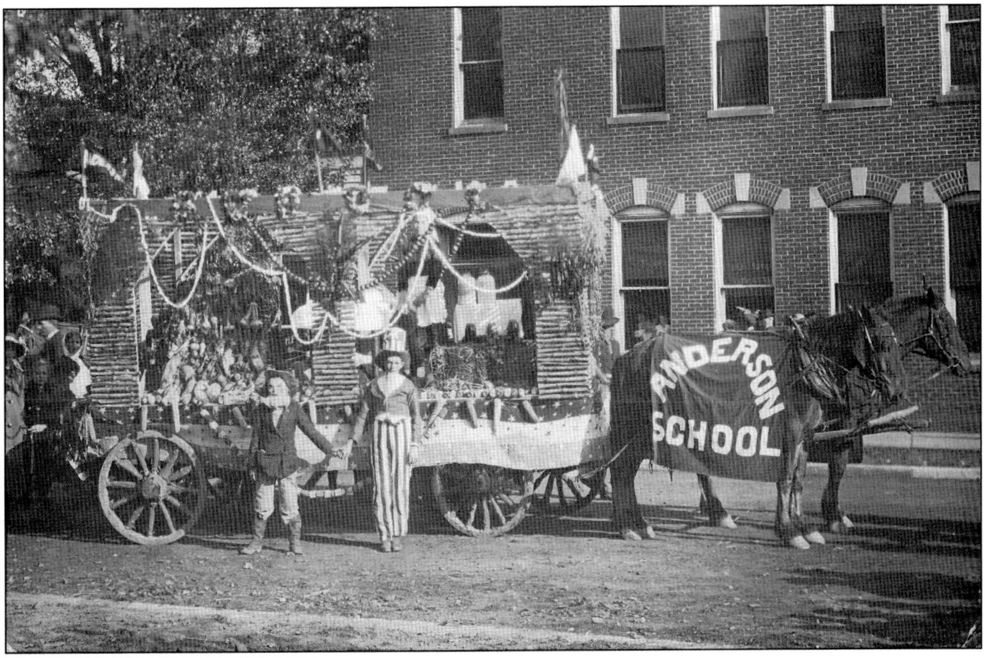

Anderson Elementary School's entry in the Massac County Farmers' Institute parade in 1912 or 1913 won honors. The event was similar to a county fair, where groups decorated wagons and everyone came into town to celebrate The photograph was taken on the Courthouse Square.

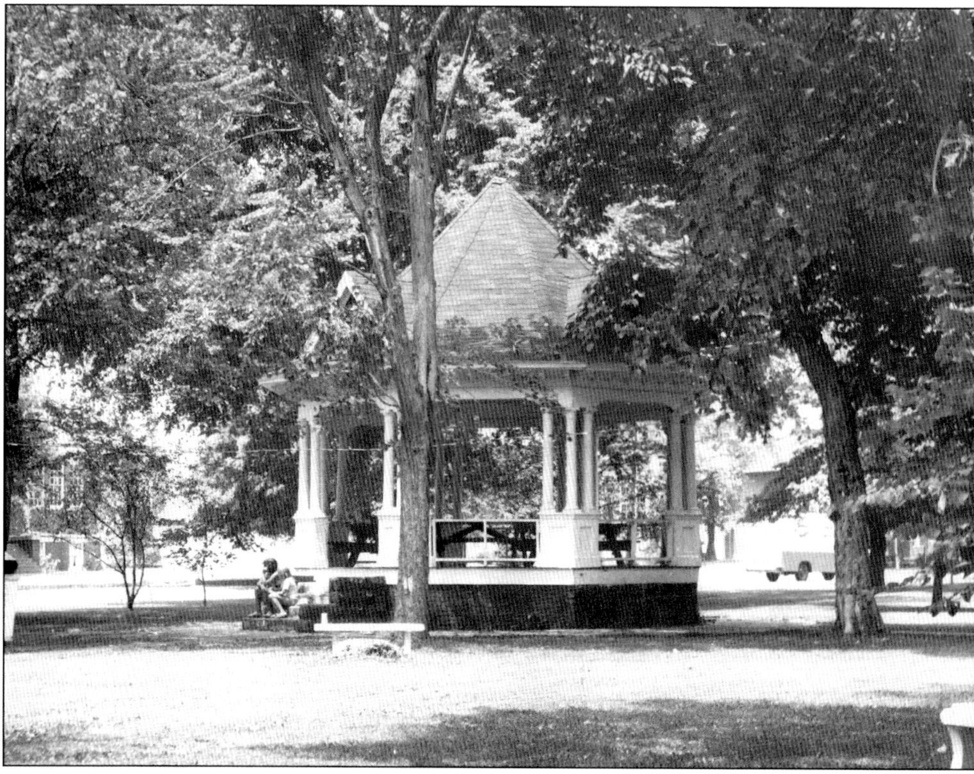

Pictured prior to its renovation, the bandstand at Washington Park was built around 1900. In the late 1980s, the base was reconstructed by a building trades class at Massac County High School. The work won the Governor's Hometown Award for preservation.

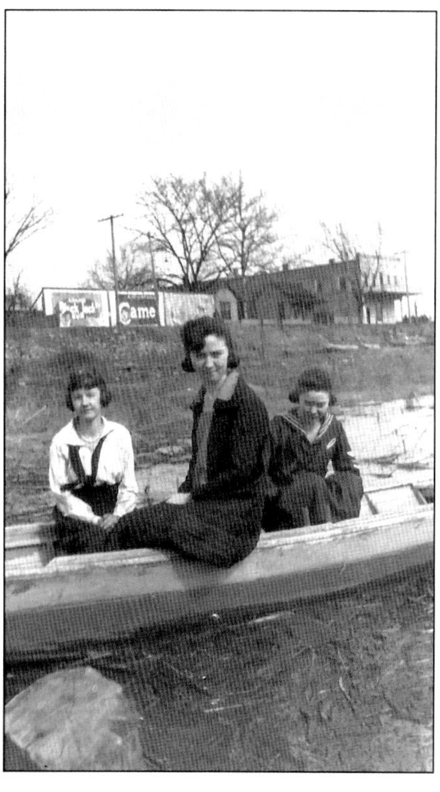

Beulah Clenendon (left), Ruby Dean (center), and her sister Ruth are pictured in a boat around 1918. The photograph was taken where Ferry Street meets the river. The old Covington Hotel is on the right in the background.

Centennial Parade participants and spectators line the streets of Metropolis on Sunday, June 4, 1939. This was the final event of the eight-day celebration of the 100th anniversary of the town's founding, and the next *Metropolis News* reported that attendance may have approached the somewhat unlikely figure of 40,000 people.

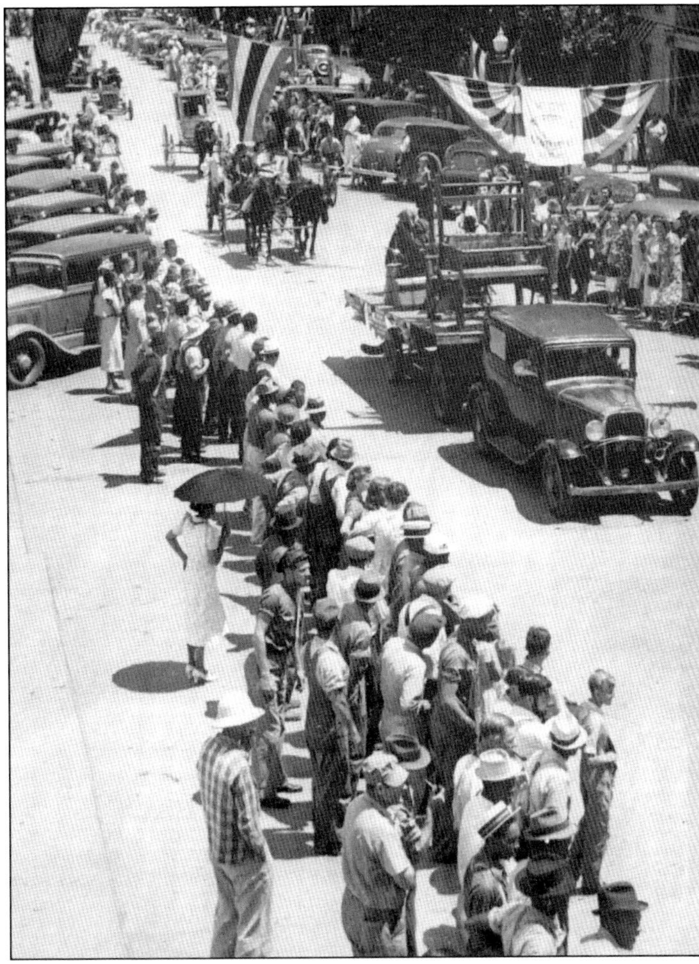

This re-creation shows how some settlers may have arrived in Metropolis and seems to prefigure reenactments of the Fort Massac encampments of the future. Metropolis has always been interested in its past. Somewhat ironically, the sign on top of the wagon states "complements (*sic*) of Standard Service Co.

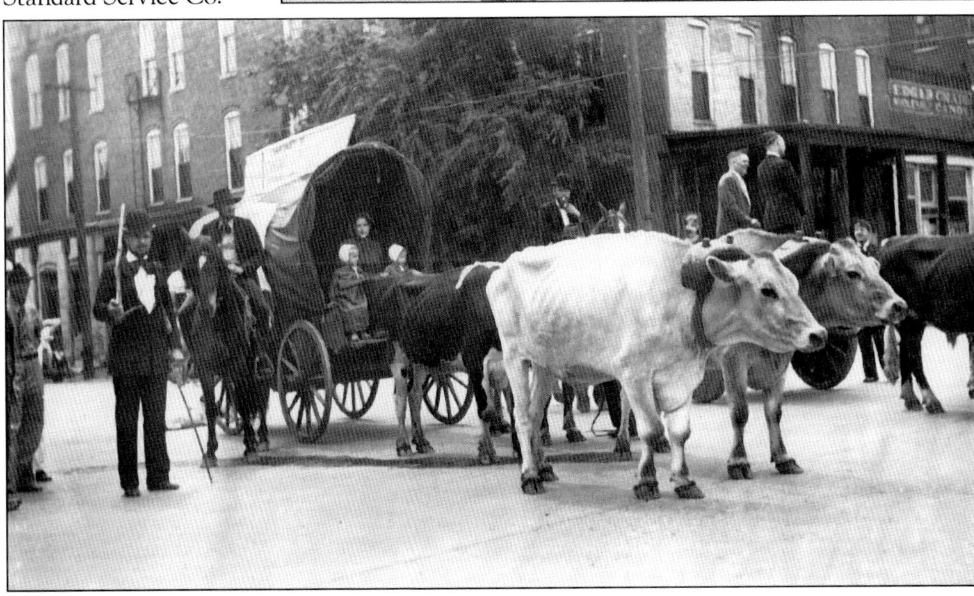

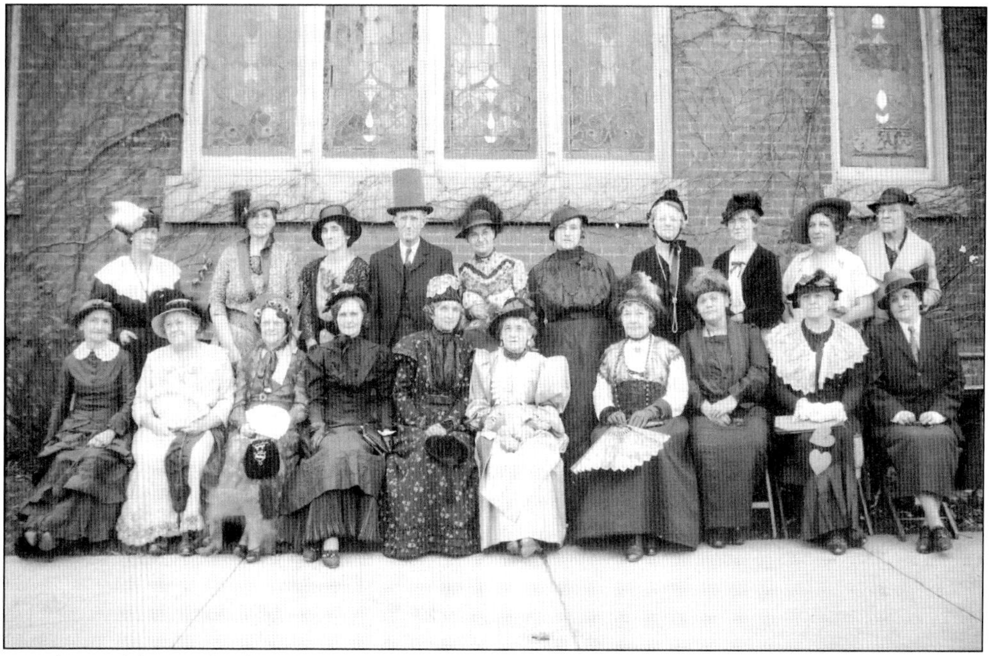

Members of the Methodist church's Daughters of Esther Sunday school class are all dressed up for Centennial Parade activities. The pastor, Otto Horsley, is in the top hat. Teacher Maggie Bruner is in the second row, on the far right.

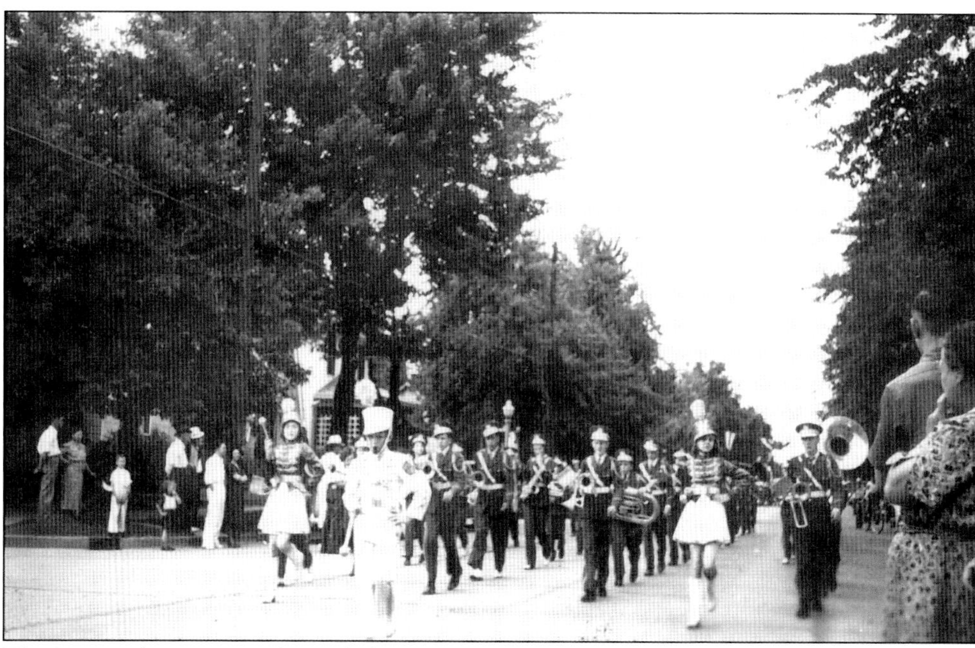

The Metropolis Centennial Parade hits a residential area on June 4, 1939.

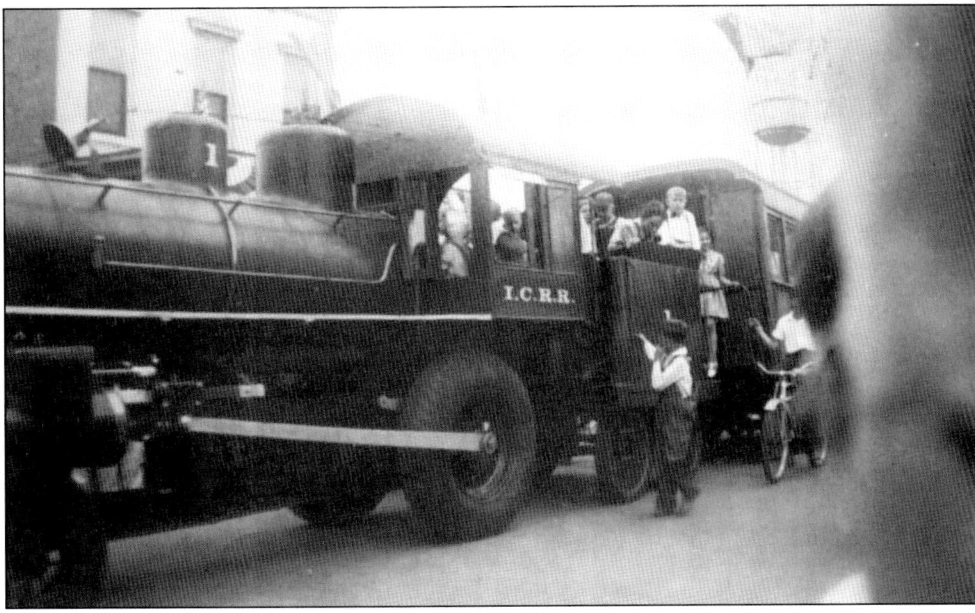

A trackless train, courtesy of the Illinois Central Railroad, takes part in the Metropolis Centennial Parade. The children running and biking alongside the train seem to be enjoying it.

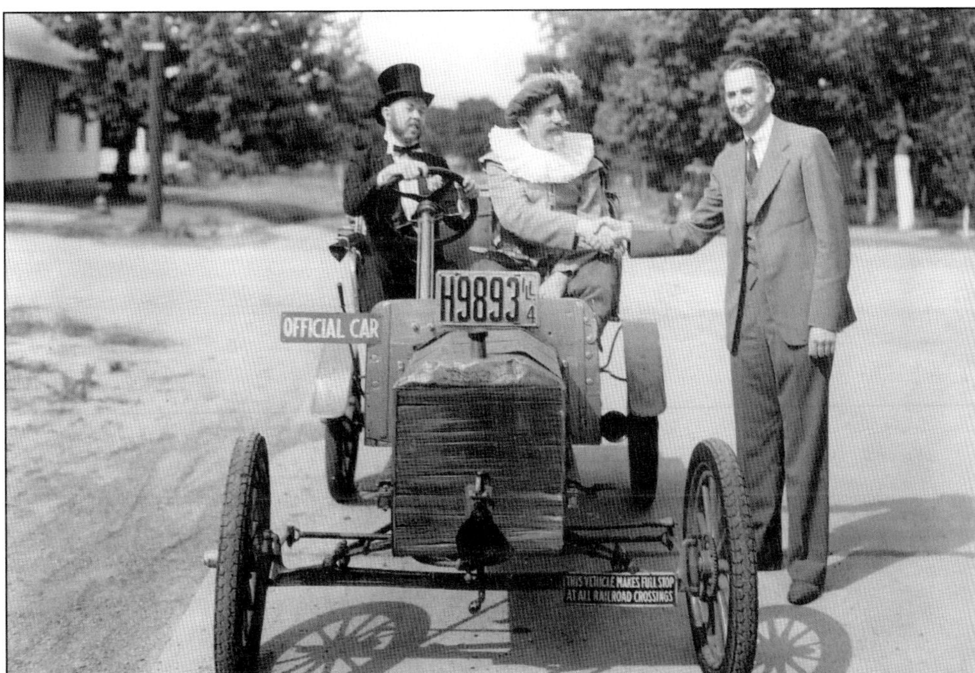

This vehicle, a 1904 Ford that had been restored by Russell Baker, owner of Baker's Paint Shop, was the official parade car for the 1939 Metropolis Centennial parade. The festively attired gentlemen in the car are Cecil "Dutch" Haverkamp (left) and J. Paul Neal. The man in the three-piece suit is unidentified

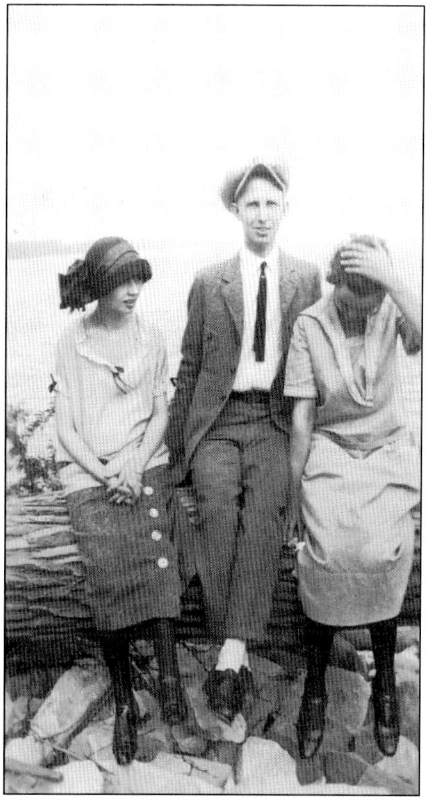

This unidentified trio appears to be at Fort Massac State Park, with the Ohio River as a backdrop.

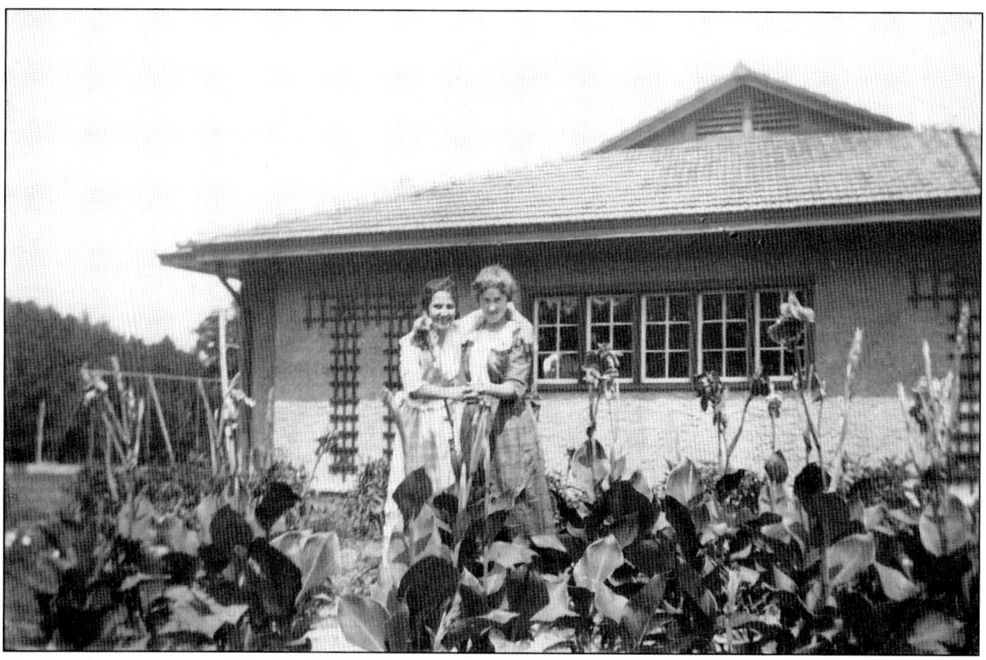

The landscaping around the Fort Massac Pavilion is shown in this photograph from 1924. The structure was built in 1912 and was famous for its beautiful flowerbeds. Sadly, the pavilion was demolished in the late 1960s to make way for the reconstruction of the fort and a visitors center.

Ten

Tourism and the Future

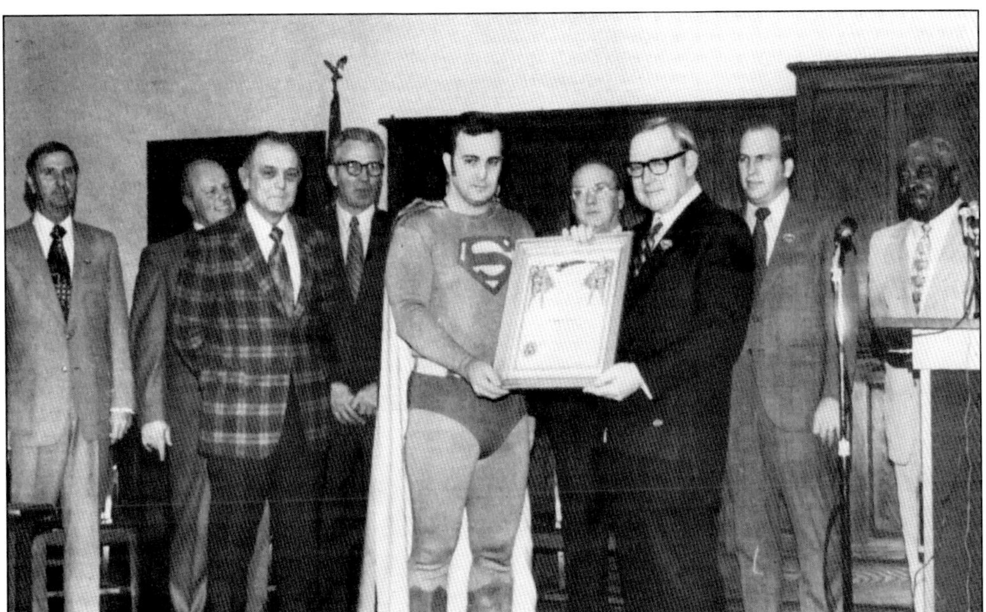

The first Superman Award was presented in February 1972 to Illinois governor Richard Ogilvie. Pictured at the ceremony are, from left to right, Harold Mescher, Bob Westerfield, Virgil Smith, Jack Hearn, Larry Davis (Superman), Jake Green, Governor Ogilvie, Bill Garland, and Garland McAfee. More often than not, the part of Superman at such events during the early 1970s was enacted by Rev. Charles Chandler of the First Baptist Church of Metropolis, who played the role from the initial "adoption ceremony" on January 21, 1972, through 1976.

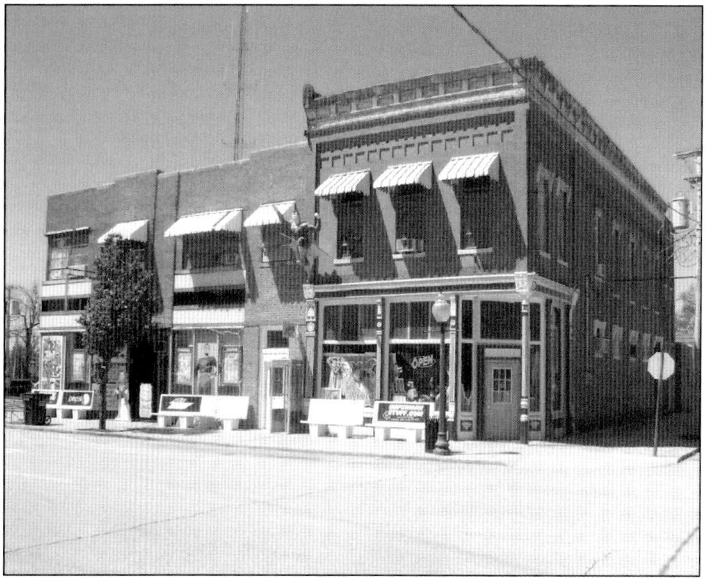

The Super Museum opened in 1993 and sits just north of Courthouse Square and the giant statue of Superman in Metropolis. The owner's collection is so large that less than one-third is on display at any one time. (Courtesy authors' collection.)

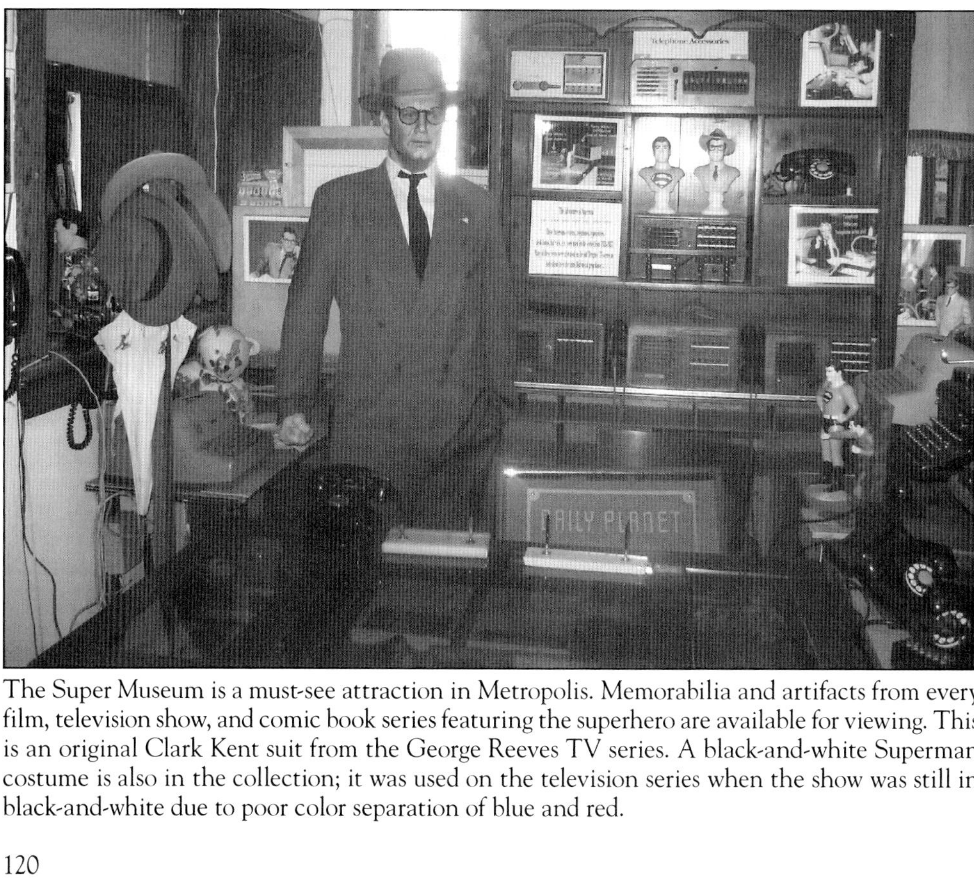

The Super Museum is a must-see attraction in Metropolis. Memorabilia and artifacts from every film, television show, and comic book series featuring the superhero are available for viewing. This is an original Clark Kent suit from the George Reeves TV series. A black-and-white Superman costume is also in the collection; it was used on the television series when the show was still in black-and-white due to poor color separation of blue and red.

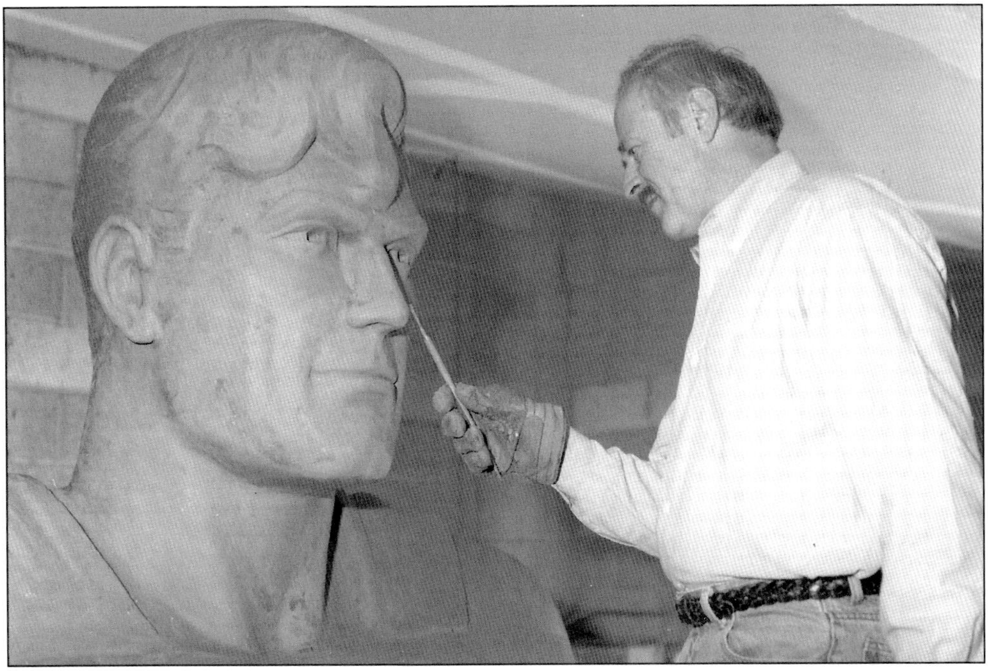

Gary Smith is seen sculpting the face for the *Superman* statue in the early 1990s. The final statue is cast bronze, and this clay sculpture was used by Kevin Maag to make the casting at Metal Arts Foundry in Utah. The same artist sculpted the *Noel Neill* statue, and the same foundry cast it.

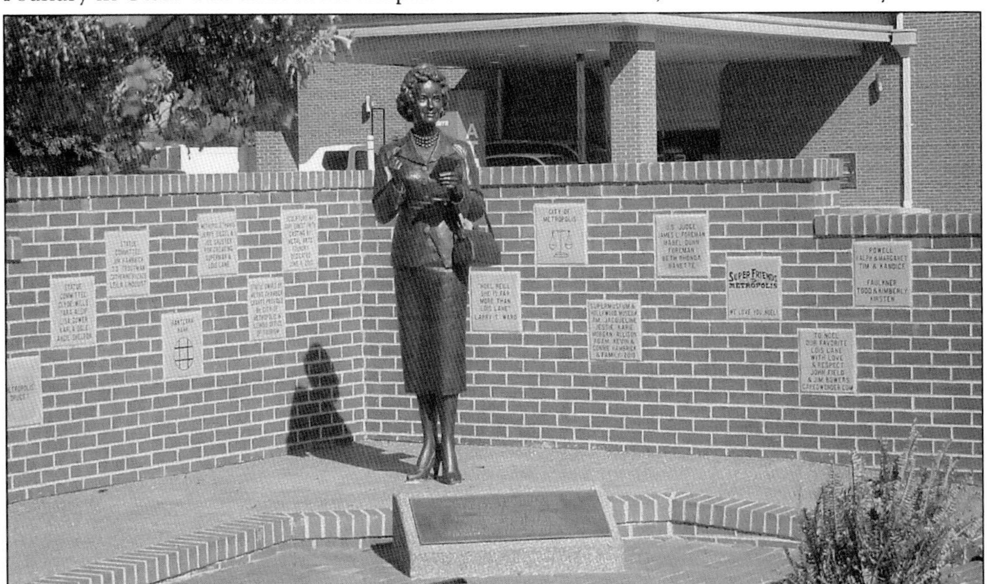

Noel Neill, the actress who played Lois Lane for the bulk of the 1950s *Adventures of Superman* TV series, has been a frequent visitor to the Superman Celebration over the years and has developed such a strong relationship to the town that she was dubbed the "First Lady of Metropolis." When it was decided a statue of Lois Lane should reside down the street from that of Superman, she was used as the model, and the statue was dedicated to her in 2010 in honor of her 90th birthday, with the actress in attendance. (Courtesy authors' collection.)

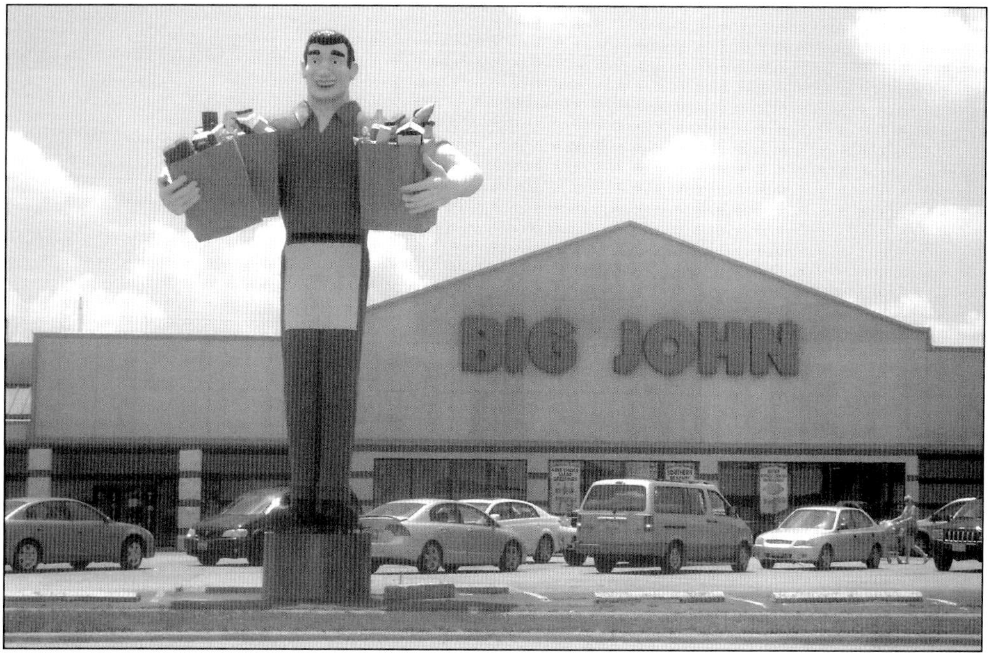

Not to be missed by lovers of roadside Americana, the statue in front of the Big John supermarket stands nearly twice the height of the *Superman* statue but lacks the man from Krypton's masculine pose and long-term durability, being made of fiberglass rather than bronze. One of the last of a fairly widespread independent chain of groceries headquartered in Illinois, *Big John* can be seen on the left as one drives toward the *Superman* statue. (Courtesy authors' collection.)

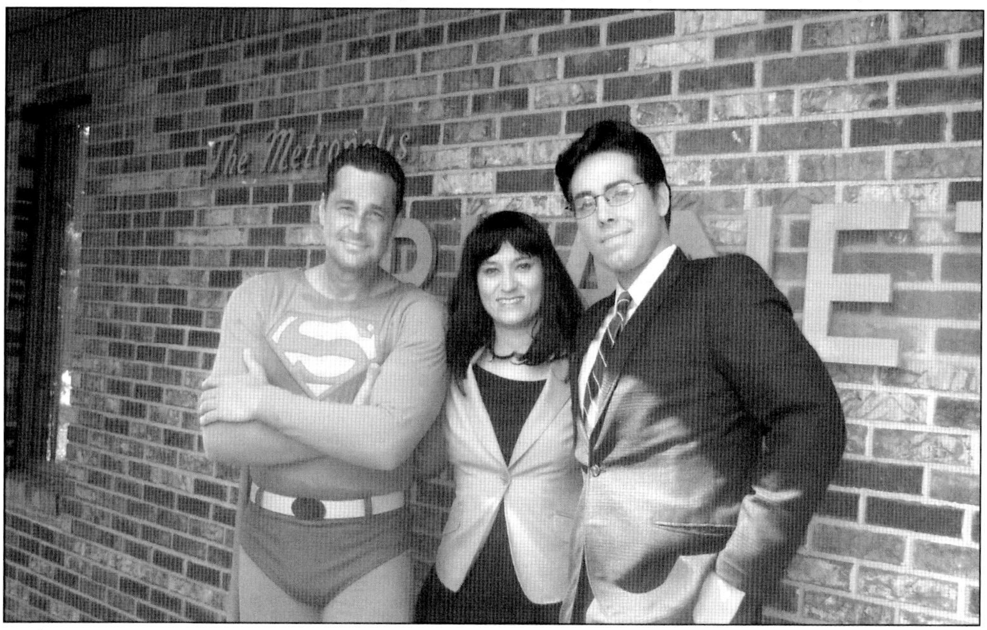

At last, Lois Lane's suspicions can be put to rest, as Clark Kent and Superman finally meet in front of the Metropolis Planet office. The weekly newspaper changed its name from the *Metropolis News* in 1972. As many as 30,000 people, a large number of them in costume, attend the Superman Celebration each year. (Courtesy authors' collection.)

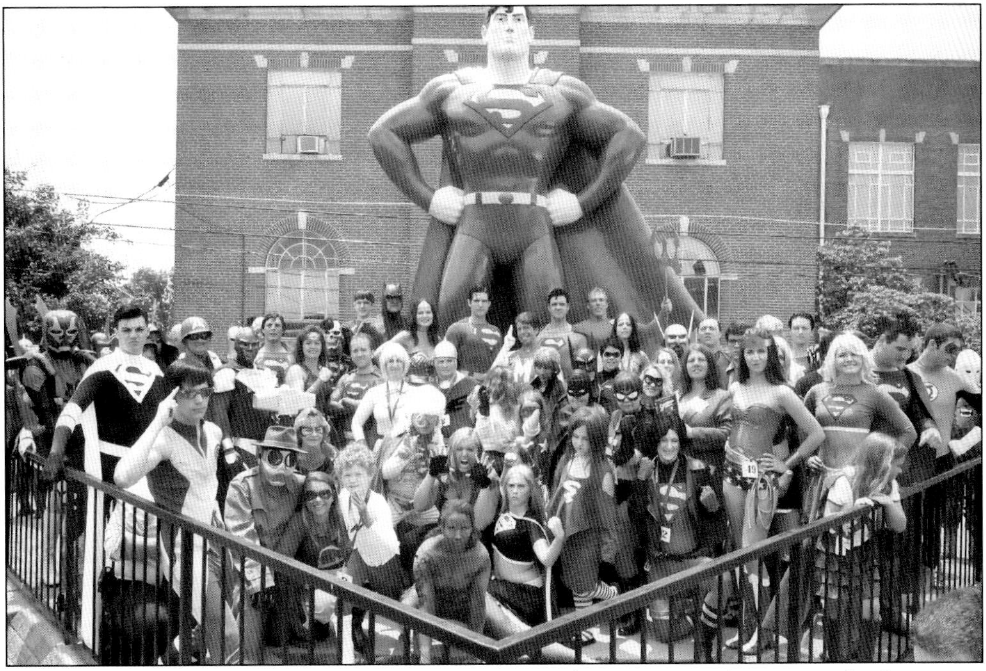

Superman and friends are not the only interesting people a person might meet at the Superman Celebration. The annual costume contest draws characters from every corner of the comic-book world, past and present. (*Metropolis Planet* photograph by Michele Longworth.)

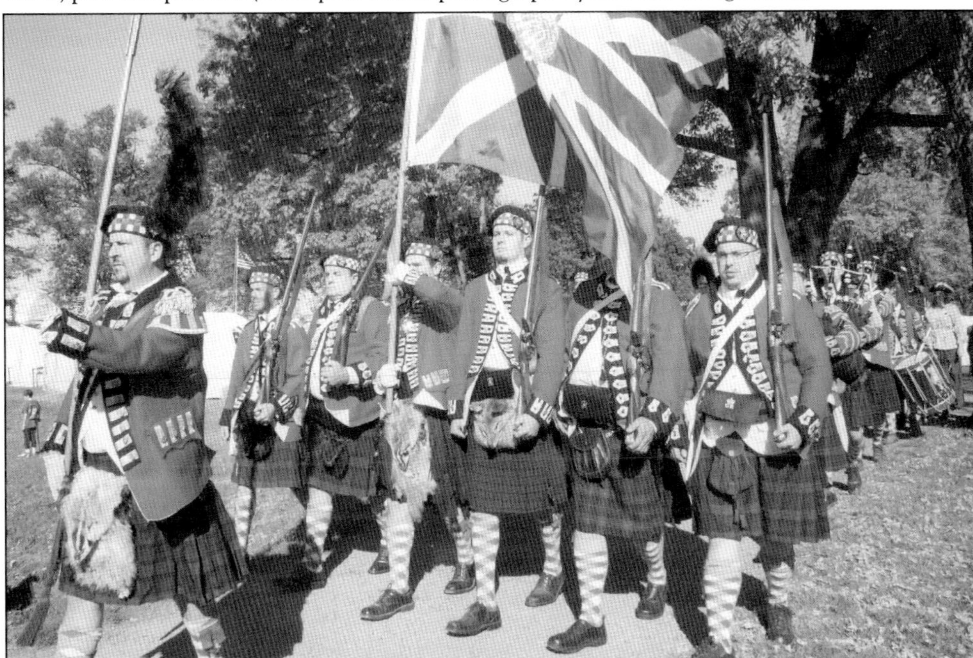

The encampment at Fort Massac includes many reenactment groups, among them American, French, and British regiments, fife-and-drum bands, Indians, and unaffiliated frontiersmen. The event began in 1974 as a function of the Illinois Department of Natural Resources (formerly Conservation), which oversees Fort Massac State Park. (*Metropolis Planet* photograph by Michele Longworth.)

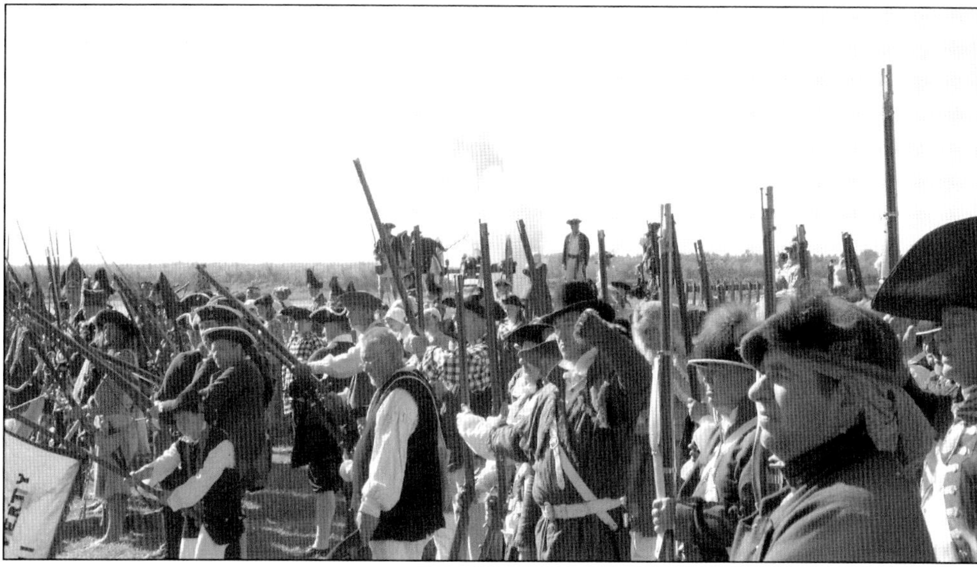

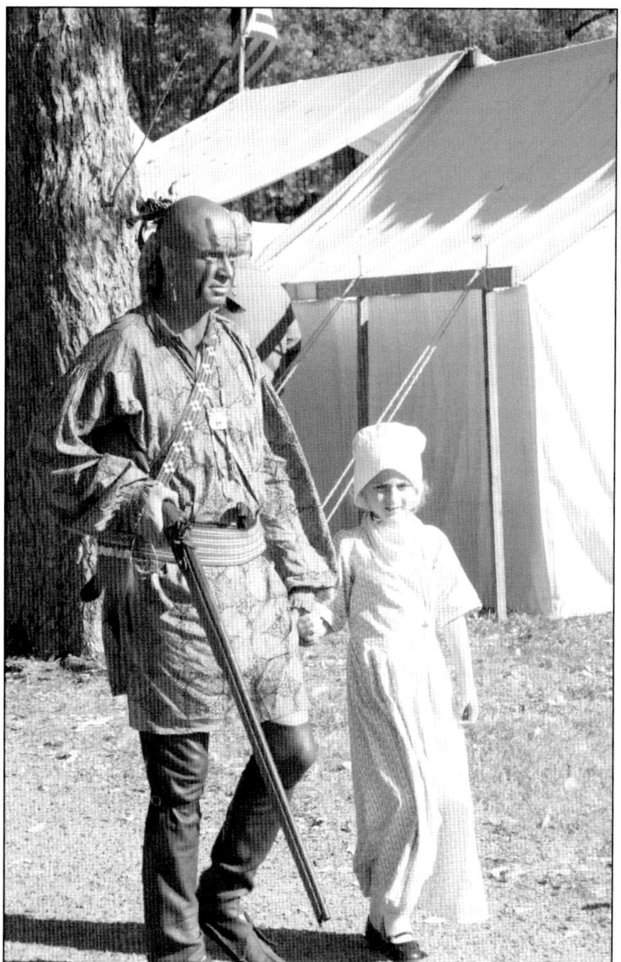

Battle reenactments, complete with cannon-fire, are one of the more popular pastimes during encampment weekend, but for those less interested in the history of warfare, the park's 1,400-plus acres offer plenty of other recreational opportunities, including hiking, picnicking, and boating. (*Metropolis Planet* photograph by Michele Longworth.)

All kinds of different cultures come together at the Fort Massac encampment—sometimes even within the same family. The celebration of the lives and times of past Americans attracts more than 80,000 people a year. (*Metropolis Planet* photograph by Michele Longworth.)

The focal point of Metropolis's burgeoning tourism industry is the *Superman* statue in front of the courthouse, on what is now officially called Superman Square. Initially, a seven-foot-tall fiberglass version was erected for about $1,000. Unfortunately, it provided an easy target for vandals eager to see how "invulnerable" *Superman* really was, prompting concerned citizens and fans to raise over $100,000 for a new one. While not literally a man of steel, it is an imposing 15-feet bronze that watches over the city's economic well-being, drawing people from all over the world. (Courtesy authors' collection)

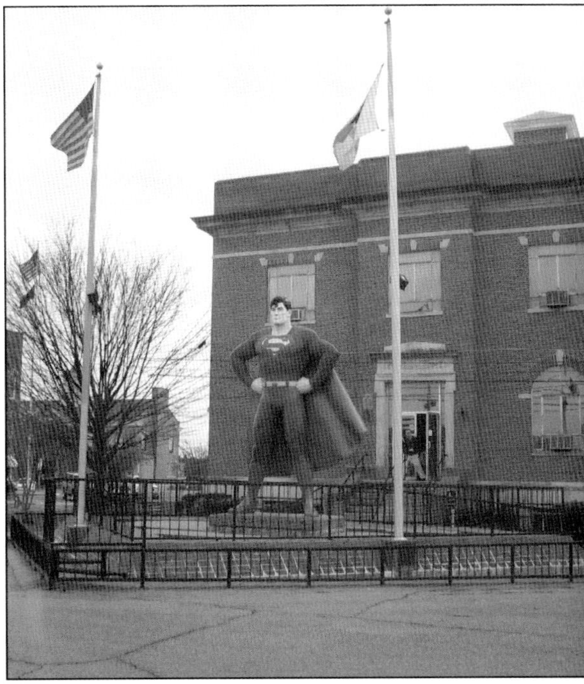

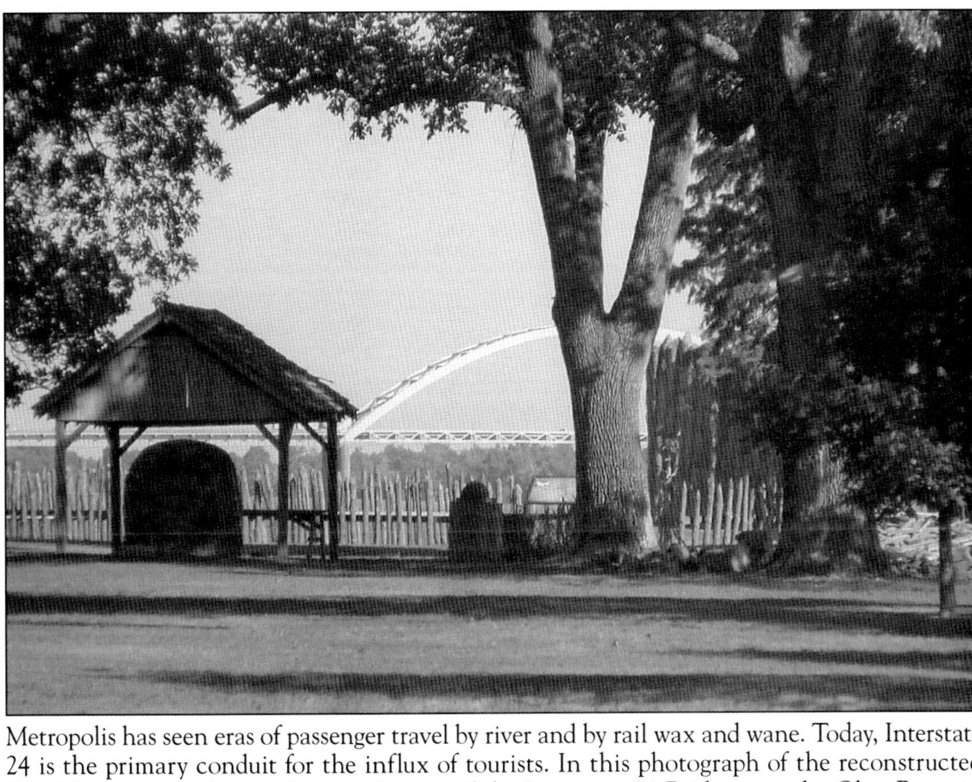

Metropolis has seen eras of passenger travel by river and by rail wax and wane. Today, Interstate 24 is the primary conduit for the influx of tourists. In this photograph of the reconstructed Fort Massac, with the northern arch span of the Interstate 24 Bridge over the Ohio River in the background, a glimpse of the city's past and future are visible in a single shot. (Courtesy authors' collection.)

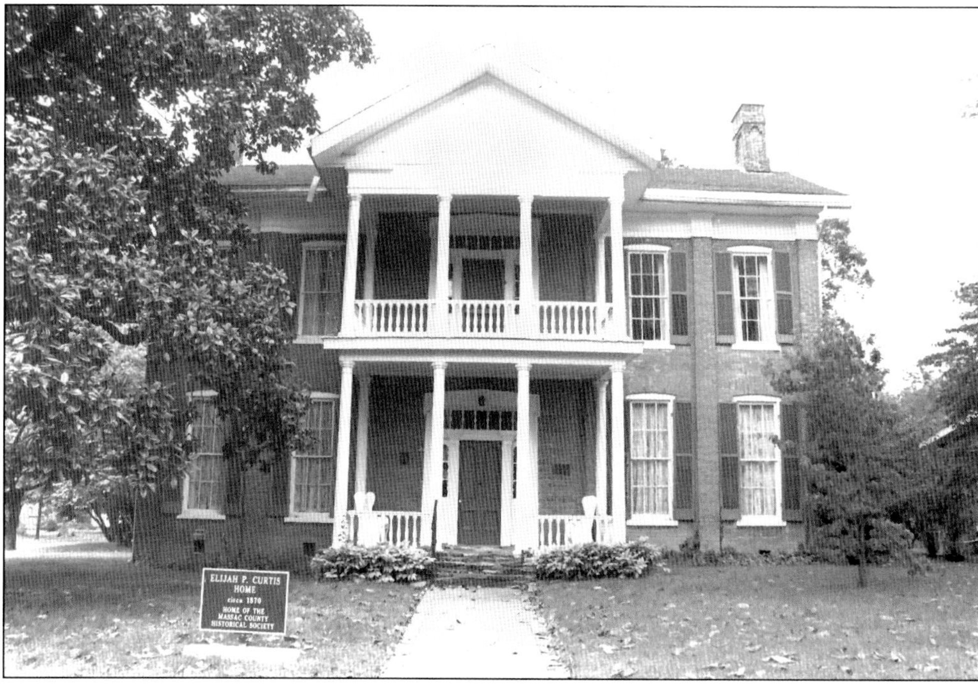

The Elijah P. Curtis House was built around 1870 and purchased by the Massac County Historical Society in 1977 for use as a headquarters and museum. After meticulous restoration by the society, the house was placed in the National Register of Historic Places in 1978. The museum is open on weekends or by appointment and is free to visitors, though donations are always appreciated. (*Metropolis Planet.*)

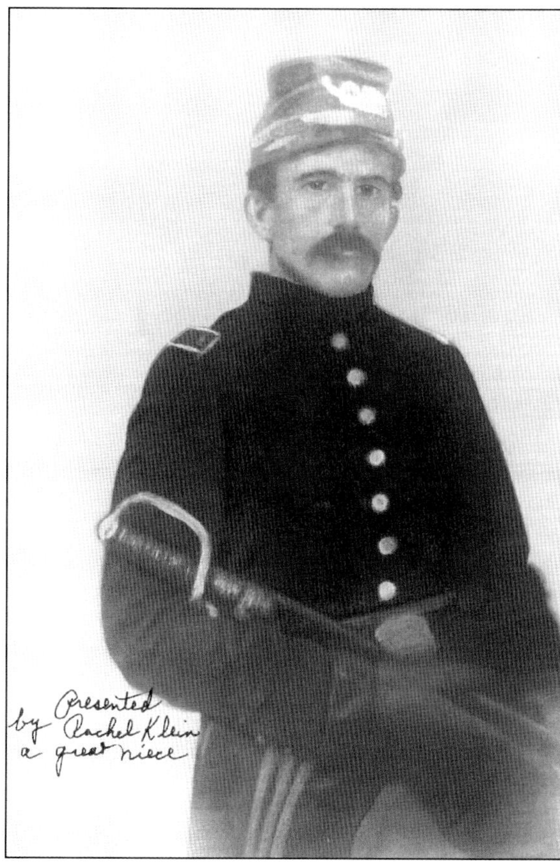

This reproduction of a tintype provided to the society by his grandniece, Rachel Klein, shows Elijah Patterson Curtis in his Civil War uniform. He joined the 29th Infantry Illinois Volunteers at the onset of the war. By the time he returned to Metropolis, he had attained the rank of lieutenant colonel but refused to be addressed by any rank higher than major, the title he reached in active service. Curtis had the house on Market Street built for his young wife, Isabella Hellen Gebhart. He later served as circuit clerk of Massac County for 26 years.

About the Massac County Historical Society

The late George May, former president of the Massac County Historical Society, once said the following about history: "History begins at home . . . local history is a part of our cultural heritage, which must be transmitted to our children. It is a civic imperative." The Massac County Historical Society began its development in 1976, with the first meeting being held on July 21, 1976, at the Metropolis Public Library. During the next few months, interested citizens gathered to discuss the need for a society to study the county's history and enact programs for preserving it. The meetings grew too large for the library and so were moved to the First Christian Church. Within that year, discussions were held on a permanent location for meetings and a museum and archive.

The c. 1870 home of Elijah Curtis at 405 Market Street came on the market, and the society voted to raise money to purchase the property. The funds were raised within three months, and the group had its home.

An effort was then made to obtain materials and furnishings for the headquarters while work was being done to update the infrastructure of the building. In June 1978, less than two years after the group's formation, an open house was conducted to show off the house. In July, the structure was placed in the National Register of Historic Places. The society received an award from the state historical society for being able to accomplish so much in so short a time period.

Each December, the society hosts a Christmas open house and uses its headquarters as a meeting spot for the festivities, while a tour of well-preserved homes is also conducted to highlight the history of the area. Each fall, the society participates in the annual Fort Massac Encampment, with volunteers in period clothing conducting fundraising activities. The group acted to facilitate the restoration of the bandstand in Washington Park by the high school's building trades class. The Massac County history book project allowed the society to publish histories of the various towns and settlements in the county and was well received.

The society members are continuing to try to keep green the memory of their ancestors through various projects. One was helping us to complete this book by sharing their archives with us. Thank you, and all the best for the future of your group.